THE
LASTING
HARM

THE LASTING HARM

WITNESSING THE TRIAL OF GHISLAINE MAXWELL

LUCIA OSBORNE-CROWLEY

4th ESTATE • *London*

4th Estate
An imprint of HarperCollins*Publishers*
1 London Bridge Street
London SE1 9GF

www.4thestate.co.uk

HarperCollins*Publishers*
Macken House, 39/40 Mayor Street Upper
Dublin 1, D01 C9W8, Ireland

First published in Great Britain in 2024 by 4th Estate

1

A catalogue record for this book is
available from the British Library

ISBN 978-0-00-859118-2 (hardback)
ISBN 978-0-00-859119-9 (trade paperback)

Set in Sabon LT Std
Printed and bound in the UK using 100%
renewable electricity at CPI Group (UK) Ltd

'My Dead Friends'

I have begun,
when I'm weary and can't decide an answer to
a bewildering question

to ask my dead friends for their opinion
and the answer is often immediate and clear.

Should I take the job? Move to the city?
Should I try to conceive a child in my middle age?

They stand in unison shaking their heads and smiling –
whatever leads to joy, they always answer,

to more life and less worry. I look into the vase where
Billy's ashes were – it's green in there, a green vase,

and I ask Billy if I should return the difficult phone call,
and he says, yes. Billy's already gone through the
frightening door,

whatever he says I'll do.

Marie Howe

The FBI declined to comment on the allegations made against them in this book.

West Palm Beach, Florida, 9 September 2022

The Floridian heat overwhelms me as I step out of Miami International Airport and begin to make my way to the airport hotel. The air is heavy and full of moisture, the hot wind carrying an ominous feeling, a sense of dread. My flight out of Heathrow was delayed by several hours due to the queen's death and so I have missed my train to West Palm Beach, and instead am staying in a hotel for the night and finishing my journey in the morning. Already, this trip feels doomed.

I am here because, a few weeks ago, I sent an email to a lawyer named Jack Scarola about his client, who is known only by her first name – Carolyn. Carolyn, who is now 36, was sexually abused by Jeffrey Epstein and Ghislaine Maxwell, beginning when she was just 14 years old. Carolyn testified at Maxwell's trial using only her first name to protect herself and her family from the disastrous consequences that too often come with speaking out. Carolyn has also never spoken at length to a journalist before.

When I emailed Scarola asking to interview Carolyn, I did not expect that she would say yes. But I nonetheless sat down and wrote, as I always do, a long email about all the ways I ensure that my journalism is trauma-informed and that my interview style is safe, sensitive, and always puts victims' needs and comfort first. I also, as I always do, disclosed that I myself am a survivor of child sexual abuse and have dedicated my investigative reporting skills to trying to contribute to a better understanding of the scourge of sexual abuse and its long shadow.

To my great surprise, Carolyn responded to Scarola almost immediately.

'Please tell this journalist I would love to speak to her for her book and to call me ASAP.' Before long, Carolyn and I had spoken on the phone and arranged for me to fly to West Palm Beach to see her.

In the airport hotel that night, I reflect on how surreal it feels to be meeting with Carolyn after thinking about her so regularly for almost a year, ever since hearing her testimony on the stand at Ghislaine Maxwell's federal sex trafficking trial in December of 2021. Her story affected me so deeply, and I feel honoured that she is willing to share more of her story with me; that she is willing to trust me with the intimate details of the worst things that have ever happened to her.

Carolyn's story was arguably the most important testimony in the Maxwell trial, for several reasons. First, because the charges associated with Carolyn's story carried by far the longest sentence – the two charges that relied on her evidence carried a total sentence of 40 years, whereas the charges associated with the other victims' stories carried between 5 and 15 years.

That's because Carolyn was trafficked by Jeffrey Epstein and Ghislaine Maxwell between 2001 and 2004, making her ordeal the latest of the four, with the other three victims being abused in the 1990s. When Maxwell and Epstein abused Jane, Kate and Annie – the other victims who testified at the trial – no substantive federal law existed criminalising sex trafficking. By the time Epstein and Maxwell abused Carolyn – unbeknown to them – a federal sex trafficking act had been passed that significantly toughened sentences for the offence. So it was that by the time Maxwell was charged for her crimes, 20 years later, the crimes she committed against Carolyn would be the only ones that could attract a substantive sex trafficking charge.

But there's a more important reason why Carolyn's story was crucial to bringing Ghislaine Maxwell to justice: because it laid bare, in an excruciatingly honest way, just how severe the lifelong effects of trauma really are; because Carolyn hid nothing from the jury about her life. Her testimony was raw, honest, unfiltered and completely heartbreaking.

Carolyn's story perfectly captures the way that trauma in childhood completely alters the course of our lives; the way it leaves us vulnerable to addiction, self-loathing and more trauma; the way it traps us in a cycle of violence and shame; the way it refuses to let us go.

So here I am, almost a year after verdict day, sitting on a Greyhound bus from Miami to West Palm Beach, to meet Carolyn in the flesh. To meet the person who contributed to changing the course of history.

As the bus makes its journey south down the Floridian coast, I get out my notebook from the trial and I review Carolyn's testimony, to make sure I am familiar with her story for our interview.

Carolyn has requested that I book a hotel room for our interview so that we can have some privacy. That afternoon, we meet at the hotel. I recognise her immediately, of course, from the witness stand, but what I didn't expect is that she would recognise me, too.

'Oh, I remember you from the trial!' she says excitedly, and hugs me. 'You were the person I chose to look at every time my husband had to leave the courtroom to go to the bathroom.'

We hug for a long time, and I thank her for being willing to speak to me.

The following day, we sit down in Carolyn's hotel room to begin our interview. Carolyn is open, warm and kind. When she asks me why I am interested in the Maxwell trial, I answer honestly.

'I was sexually abused and groomed as a child,' I say. 'And I'm still living with the effects of it. I want the world to understand it better.'

Carolyn's face changes and becomes even kinder and more open than it had been before.

'I'm so sorry that happened to you,' she says, very seriously. 'I'm so, so sorry. It's so unfair.'

Our eyes are locked together now, and she walks across the hotel room and hugs me. She is limping, because she has a terrible leg injury, but her hug is fierce and certain.

'I'm so sorry,' she says again. 'You didn't deserve that.'

'Neither did you,' I say, holding her tightly and wondering, not for the first or last time while reporting for this book, how people who have lived through so much still have so much empathy to offer.

'What kind of consequences have you had to face from your abuse?' Carolyn asks me in a quiet voice. 'Have you ever struggled with drugs?'

'Yes,' I say truthfully. 'I have had many periods in my life of struggling with opioid addiction. I have a chronic pain condition, so I always have easy access to painkillers.'

'Ah, yes,' she says knowingly. 'I've been there.'

Later that afternoon, her injured leg begins hurting. 'I have Tylenol if you want some,' I offer.

'Oh, thank you so much,' she says. My handbag rattles as I dig around for the bottle. 'Are you sure it's just Tylenol you've got in there?' she asks. 'You've got me looking out for you now.'

'Just Tylenol, I promise,' I say, and we smile broadly at each other, the warmth of shared understanding passing between us.

'Everything I said on that stand was true,' she says. 'You can put it all in your book.'

'Thank you,' I say.

Before we start our interview in earnest, Carolyn says she needs to tell me something.

'Someone turned up at my home this morning,' she says. 'He said he was a private investigator. He said something about someone writing a book. I think they know that you're here.'

'W-what did you tell him?' I ask, trying to hide the rattle in my throat.

'My husband told him to get off our property.'

I would meet Carolyn's husband, John, the following day. Like her, he strikes me immediately as genuine, open and warm. His smile is cheeky and infectious. He confirms to me the next day that a man in his sixties turned up at their house asking questions about a journalist writing a book.

Soon after we begin talking, Carolyn tells me she needs to take a nap as the effects of her daily methadone dose are kicking in. Carolyn has been in recovery from opioid addiction for many years – and she is very proud of how far she has come. As you'll hear later, Carolyn started taking opioids in order to cope with being regularly assaulted by Jeffrey Epstein. As someone who is chronically ill and requires a lot of naps, I understand this. I help her get into bed. We agree to meet later that night, for dinner, at the Italian restaurant across the street from the hotel.

I walk across to the restaurant and decide to write up my notes from the day until Carolyn is ready for dinner. I smile at my server, Manny – I have already been to the restaurant several times since I arrived in West Palm Beach two days ago – and take my usual seat. I pull out my notebook and start writing down my initial observations about Carolyn. I write down the exact exchange we had about our trauma, about the Tylenol, the look we shared.

I don't think I am conscious of this in the moment, but the connection I've shared with Carolyn has pulled at me; has left me with an impulse for some justice of my own. I pull out my phone and start googling my old gymnastics mentor – an older man who was involved with our gymnastics club – from my hometown. He still uses his Facebook profile – under a pseudonym – to write to gymnasts he used to train, including myself. On every one of my birthdays, he sends me a message saying that he loves me. When I still used Facebook actively, I would hear from him every time I changed my profile photo.

'You were always so beautiful,' he would say. 'You turned out so well.'

I scour his page and find image after image of him surrounded by gymnasts aged between 9 and 14 or 15. Many of the photos include girls I know – girls I grew up with. Almost all the photos are taken in the gym I used to call home.

Seeing these photos makes me doubt my memories of him: the way he used to talk to me about sex, tell me what would happen to my body when it got aroused, the way he used to rub his erections on my feet through his trousers while giving me a foot massage. *How could he have done all of those things*, I wonder, *while parading around in endless photos with underage gymnasts on Facebook?* It's like he is hiding in plain sight.

To reassure myself that my memories are real, I revisit a message I once received from my closest friend at the gym. This girl was older than me, and acted as a mentor as my gymnastics career became more and more serious. Like me, she was chosen to be in the small group of girls selected for his morning training squad – the most promising young gymnasts were invited to train between 5am and when we started school each day, as well as our regular after-school training sessions from 4pm to 7.30pm.

The girl (let's call her Lucinda) and I were inseparable for years. We told each other everything – almost.

One day in 2015, she messaged me on Facebook.

'I'm sorry,' she said, 'I just need to know: did anything bad ever happen to you at the gym?'

The message sparked something electric in me; I knew immediately what she meant. The next message came through: 'I'm sorry I didn't protect you.'

This girl was a mentor to me, and we had always been so close. She was five years older than me, so she was halfway between a peer and a coach. I knew how the guilt would eat away at her; I couldn't stand to be the cause of that. So I lied.

I wrote a long message back, and as I read it now, one phrase stands out: 'You don't have to worry, nothing ever happened to me.'

Later that year, Lucinda went to the police to report that she had been raped by the same man who abused me. Another girl came forward, too. She said she was never raped but she was groped by him repeatedly, and she reported exactly the same conversations about sex and arousal, the same massages, that I remembered from my own experiences.

The police ended up dropping the investigation because the statute of limitations on the rape charges had expired. The statute of limitations is a legal mechanism which mandates that you only have a certain amount of time after a crime or civil wrong is committed to bring a lawsuit. The basis for the principle is that justice should be swift and alleged perpetrators should know within a certain timeframe whether they are being charged. This is problematic when it comes to cases of ongoing child sexual abuse – but more on that later. I cannot stand that my abuser still has daily access to underage girls.

In Florida, I stare at the message, which proves, in black and white, that I lied to my friend when she asked me about our mentor's abuse. I lied because I didn't want her to feel bad for not protecting me. I lied because it wasn't her fault. Because I hadn't yet fully acknowledged to myself that I had been abused. That he had abused me.

Almost every day, my mentor used to say to me: 'You know I love you, right? You know I love you like a daughter?' I still dream about those words; they play like a refrain in my head. They intrude when I am awake, too. When my defences are down, they reappear like ticker tape running on repeat across my mind.

All I wanted was his approval. All I wanted was to impress him. So when I was about nine and he started talking to me about what happens to a girl's body when she gets aroused, when he started asking if I had begun thinking about sex yet, it felt new and thrilling, as if we were entering new territory together. I instinctively knew there was something secret about it, and I remember him telling me to keep it between us. I knew it was something that other people wouldn't approve of, but it was ours, and that was all that mattered to me.

Over the next few years, we grew closer and closer, and the conversations about sex became more frequent. As my gymnastics career took off – I started winning national titles; I competed at my first World Championships and things got more serious; I trained more and more often – my mentor started talking about all the ways my body needed to change if I was going to be the best.

He said my point needed to be better, so he asked me to sit down with my legs straight out in front of me while he sat with his full weight on my toes, bending them to artificially improve my point and my arches. I distinctly remember when I started noticing that he had an erection while he was doing this.

I had bad ankles as a gymnast; they constantly needed strapping and protecting. Every day, he would pull my feet into his crotch and massage them there while we chatted. I remember feeling queasy when I realised I could feel his erection, but I also didn't really understand what an erection was, so I said nothing.

I was getting more and more successful, training more, reaching ever more dizzying athletic heights. I was invited to go away with my mentor to a rural country town where he was the benefactor of a big gymnastics club.

I had a great time. But I remember coming home from one competition and he said how well I had done, and how he was going to give me a long massage to say congratulations. We were staying in a granny flat outside the house of a friend of his who lived in the rural town where we had competed (I ask myself now: *did that friend know?*) and the abuse escalated. It is a confusing memory. I did not understand what was happening. I never said a word to anyone.

Back in the Italian restaurant in West Palm Beach, I try to make sense of the memories, try to reassure myself that they are real, even though, at one time, I myself had denied them.

I realise as I look through my mentor's Facebook photos that I do not even know his real name. There is one surname that I was given when I was a child, but when I google it alongside 'Gymnastics' and the name of my home town, nothing comes up. I trawl through the internet and find nothing. Who was he?

Eventually, I read through hundreds of pages of annual reports from a gymnastics governing body and I find someone with his first name but a different surname, who is regularly given awards for services to the sport.

I google that name, and before long I find a photo of him, the man I'm looking for. The photo is from 2019, when he was interviewed by a local newspaper about one of his high-achieving gymnasts.

―――――

This is why I'm writing this book; why I set my alarm for 1.30am each morning for almost five weeks to ensure I was one of the first four reporters in the press line at the Maxwell trial; why I have put myself and my family at risk for this story, and why investigating it has consumed me for years.

My own experience of trauma had started early, and there was much more to come. While the abuse from my gymnastics mentor was still happening, and I was on track to compete at my second World Championships, I went on a night out with my friends. We were 15, we were underage, we were drinking – I would not have fared well under the kind of extreme cross-examination you will read about in this story.

A group of men distracted my friends while one man grabbed me by the hand, out of nowhere. I remember two things: first, the startling feeling of being touched when you aren't expecting it; second, the way his grip tightened and tightened and tightened until I couldn't feel my fingers. By the time the pins and needles kicked in, I knew he was a threat.

But as you'll learn from the brave survivors in this book, being sexually abused as a child encodes survival responses in you that you cannot control. Mine, I have learned over years of therapy and a stint in a trauma psych ward, is usually 'freeze', also known as submission. So when the man led me into a nearby McDonald's and up several flights of stairs to a disused bathroom, still with that terrifying grip, I followed him. I was frozen inside.

Once he locked the door to the bathroom, he pushed me onto my knees so hard I would have bruises for weeks and forced me to give him a blow job. Then he pulled out a Swiss army knife and raped me, over and over. I was sure that when he was done, he was going to kill me.

I noticed a glass bottle next to the toilet seat and I smashed it, hard, across the porcelain toilet bowl. My attacker was drunk and, I think, on drugs, so he was slow to react and to orient himself to the sound. It was enough time for me to unlock the door and run.

I got a taxi home and washed the blood off my thighs. I took time off training so no one would see the bruises. Two weeks later, my mentor – the one you know about already – was examining me and said: 'How did you get this cracked rib?'

The injuries from that rape ended my gymnastics career, and I have hardly been able to set foot in a gym since. I've developed chronic abdominal pain from the internal injuries caused by my assault, and have been diagnosed with endometriosis and

Crohn's disease, both of which have been linked to early experiences of sexual trauma.

I did not tell anyone about my rape, for the same reason I did not tell anyone about my gymnastics mentor: because I lived in a world that had taught me that I had done something wrong. Because I believed it was my fault. It took me ten years to work up the courage to speak about what happened to me, a refrain you'll hear again and again from the courageous voices in this book. So, here's something I can tell you for certain: if you have kept a secret out of shame and fear of punishment, this does not mean that it didn't happen. If anything, this is evidence that it did.

These complex traumas left me with some of the same symptoms as the survivors you'll hear from in this book: substance addiction, much like Carolyn's; eating disorders; addiction to abusive relationships and chronic self-harm. These symptoms, as you will see, would be weaponised against Epstein's survivors on cross-examination at trial, in an attempt to undermine their credibility, their morality, their memories. But I've written three books about the impact of sexual trauma, and I can tell you that some combination of these symptoms will show up in almost every single trauma survivor. So even though our society stigmatises and shames them – as Maxwell's defence team did – the evidence is clear: the presence of these difficulties in someone's life is not proof that the trauma they are describing didn't happen. It is proof that it did.

I understand – and sympathise with – a feeling you might have that you already know the Jeffrey Epstein story. But I am not here to tell you a story about Jeffrey Epstein, or even Ghislaine Maxwell. I am here to tell you the stories of these women, many of whom have never spoken at length before, and about the real impact of sexual trauma on their lives. I don't want to tell you about billionaires or private jets or Prince Andrew; I want to tell you about the actual people – both the 14-, 15-, 16-year-old versions of them that I've learned about through two years of interviews, and the 36-, 49-, 50-year-old versions of them that I know now. I want you to hear the voices of those who were abused, and then ignored, and then silenced – not only by Epstein and Maxwell, but, as you'll see in this book, by the police who were meant to protect them, by the FBI who knew of Epstein's crimes for almost 30 years before doing a single thing to stop him, *by their own lawyers*, and by the courts and the justice system who retraumatised them again and again and again and again.

Testifying at trial does not allow you to tell your story – and as you'll come to see, this particular trial certainly did not give Epstein's victims that chance. These are real people, with real lives, with real pain and real memories and real symptoms that haunt them every single day, even 30 years later. Because that's how sexual trauma works; it bleeds and metastasises until it shows up in every area of your life. I don't want the story of the Maxwell trial to end with what you read in the newspapers when it was happening, because those stories did not tell you who these women really are, or how hard they've fought to stay alive.

I'm telling this story because it hasn't been told before and because it deserves to be told. Like me – but to a far greater extent – these victims have been denied justice for 30 years and counting. Although I am legally trained, I am not a criminal prosecutor, so I cannot do anything about this in the courts. All I can do is attempt to do these courageous women justice on the page.

To be clear: a degree of justice was delivered in this trial, and for that, I know all the survivors are grateful. But as you'll see in this book, this story – and this investigation – is far from over, and one trial and one verdict does not even scratch the surface of what these women deserve. This is why I set my alarm in the middle of the night to stand in line in the mid-winter New

York snow to make sure I got a seat in the courtroom. This is why I've dedicated years of my life – and I cannot tell you how much blood, sweat and tears (mostly tears) – to this investigation. Because the Maxwell trial was the first hint of justice in 30 years, and even before it began I had done enough reporting to know that it wouldn't tell the full story. So I had to be there every day, sitting a foot away from Ghislaine, so I can tell you my first-hand experience of that trial – and so I can tell you what it was missing.

I have been accused many times of being a biased journalist because of my history of abuse. To that I say: yes, I am biased. Everybody is, whether we own it or not. I did not choose to be sexually abused beginning at nine years old, or raped at 15, and the only way I could approach a story with complete neutrality would be by writing about subjects that don't touch on any of my life experiences. But all journalists have had a great deal of life experiences, and so this is a tall order.

But here's the more important thing: the journalists I met at the Maxwell trial – mostly men in their forties – who did not have any experience of sexual trauma are also biased. These issues have never affected their lives and so they inherently subscribe to a patriarchal, societal and defensive narrative that believes that 'real victims' come forward immediately, have injuries, leave their abusers and never look back, go to the police, tell their parents, their friends. I know these journalists have these biases, because they said as much to my face during the trial. As you will see from the expert evidence presented at trial, none of those things are true of sexual abuse survivors.

The people who have not experienced what I experienced are the ones deemed 'objective'. In fact, they are operating with a deeply entrenched bias that is completely refuted by scientific and medical evidence. We are all biased; none of us is objective. I am owning my bias and my experience. It's the ones who truly believe themselves to be free of bias that you should look out for – trust me, I've met them, and I've heard the way they speak about the women you'll get to know in this book.

Women like Carolyn, who, as I become lost in my online search for the ghost of my gymnastics mentor in that Florida restaurant, is ten minutes late for dinner. I push away the memories and force myself back into the restaurant. I call her mobile, and then her room at the hotel, but there is no answer. I wait another 15 minutes, and I call both her numbers again. Nothing. She never shows up.

In truth, it had occurred to me that this might happen. Carolyn has five young children and, on many occasions over the years we've known each other, has asked to borrow money to make rent or pay her electricity bills. She and her husband struggle every day to keep food on the table. Neither of them is able to work full-time because they are dealing with substance abuse issues, so they subsist on the meagre amount of money that the Jeffrey Epstein Victims' Compensation Program pays them, which is only $2,500 a month. It doesn't surprise me that when Carolyn has an opportunity to spend a night away from her kids, away from the chaos of their home life, and rest in a hotel room to herself, she ends up sleeping through our meeting.

I send her a message saying that she should take the opportunity to sleep and put my phone down as I notice a man in his sixties approaching my table.

He nods at my blue notebook, open to the last page I have been scrawling on, and says: 'When you finish that book, I want a signed copy.'

I smile nervously.

'How did you know I was writing a book?'

'I've seen you here a few times, writing furiously in that notebook of yours.'

I shift uncomfortably in my seat, feeling watched. I laugh, trying to placate him.

'What's the book about?' he asks, taking a seat next to me and signalling to the server that he'd like another drink, and ordering one for me.

'It's about Jeffrey Epstein,' I say, sounding more confident than I feel.

'Ah, I thought so,' he says, and something on the back of my neck prickles.

'I know one of his pilots,' he continues. 'Would you like to go and meet him?'

Cautiously, I say yes and write down the name he gives me. I feel, in this moment, that playing along is the best strategy. I wonder to myself whether this man sitting next to me is the private investigator who visited Carolyn earlier that day, and I kick myself for not getting more of a physical description from her.

I ask him a few questions about the pilot, to try to figure out who this man sitting next to me really is, but he keeps changing the subject – he is offering me drugs, then showing me a pile of cash in his wallet, which he says adds up to $5,000. He asks me to tell him more about the book, and I offer vague descriptions – mostly I lie, not knowing what to say or how best to remain in control of my fear; I say it is a rehashing of what is already known about the Palm Beach aspects of the Epstein story – but he wants more. He says again how wealthy he is, how he likes to give his money away to people like me in exchange for favours – such as not writing books.

By this time, he has moved his chair so close to mine that his thighs are touching mine. There is a slit in my long skirt up my left thigh and he starts thumbing it, staring at me, saying, 'This slit is too tempting for people like me.' And then he has his hands all over me, under my skirt now, large, rough, strong fingers digging into the tops of my thighs and my groin.

I excuse myself and move towards the bathroom, catching Manny's eye on the way through. He comes over to me.

'Manny,' I say, 'I need help. I can't get away from this man. I don't know him; he's making me uncomfortable.'

'Okay, got it,' Manny says and walks off decisively.

I go into the bathroom and as I come out, the manager – a woman – is waiting for me outside the stall.

'My colleague said you are having trouble with that man?'

'Yes.'

'Don't worry, I'll take care of it. You stay inside the restaurant, and I'll ask him to leave.'

I nod, and she ushers over another server to take me discreetly back into the main restaurant. All the doors are shut – it's closing time – and I can see through the window that the man is arguing with the server who is asking him to leave.

Once the man has exited, the manager turns to me. 'Let's just wait a bit, to make sure he's not outside waiting for you.'

We watch his truck, sitting outside with the window down. Manny gets me a glass of water in a pint glass, full of ice. We all wait, but the man doesn't leave. We wait for 30 minutes, and he is still there.

'Okay,' the manager says, 'this seems dangerous. I'm going to take you out the staff exit and put you in an Uber.'

Once I am safely back at the hotel, I do not sleep all night. When I tell Carolyn and John the next day, they confirm that the man from the restaurant was the same man who turned up at their house.

Carolyn says: 'Someone knows you're here.'

We return to the same restaurant for Carolyn's rescheduled interview and, half jokingly, check underneath the table for recording devices. As Carolyn laughs about this, I see, suddenly, 20 years' worth of running from this, 20 years' worth of fear and isolation, and all of that has enabled her to be so brave, to sit in this restaurant, even in the face of intimidation. And in that moment, I decide that if she isn't scared, then I won't be scared to tell her story.

PART ONE

The Trial

CHAPTER 1

New York City, 2021

It is 3.04am and I am freezing cold, walking fast down Pearl Street in Lower Manhattan as light rain hits my winter hat. My fingers shake from cold as I take my gloves off to open Google Maps and try to find somewhere open to sell me a coffee. I find a 24-hour store a few minutes' walk away, and as I open the door and step into the warmth my whole body relaxes. I buy a scalding-hot coffee and three bottles of Tylenol for my chronic pain. Today is going to be a long day in court. The man who pours my coffee will become a close friend over the coming five weeks.

I know from my newsroom colleagues that us journalists need to arrive extremely early for high-profile trials if we want to secure one of the seats in the press gallery in the actual courtroom where the trial takes place. With these kinds of trials, the courts set up a series of 'overflow rooms', where reporters can watch video feeds of the trial from a separate, empty courtroom. But I am not in the least bit interested in that – I am going to be in the room if it kills me. Which is why I am here at just past 3am, hunting for number 500 Pearl Street – the building listed on all the official court documents for this trial.

I find the building and sit down on the cold cement floor outside, furiously rubbing my hands together to get warm. I pull on my headphones and start listening to my audiobook, hoping to pass the time. It is six hours until the courthouse will open.

About 30 minutes later, I am approached by a security guard. 'Everything okay, miss?'

I am crouching against the cold and he is standing over me, tall and muscly, so I am immediately intimidated.

I press stop on my audiobook and say, 'O-oh, yes, sorry, I am a journalist, just lining up for a trial.'

'Ah,' he says, and I realise that I needn't be intimidated. His tone is very kind and warm. 'I thought that might be the case, and I was worried you'd get cold. It's freezing out here!'

I laugh, and nod. 'I am very, very cold. But not much can be done about that!'

'Well, actually, that's why I'm here,' he says. 'I've been watching you from my office up on the twenty-first floor.' He motions towards a tall building behind him – the Metropolitan Correctional Center. 'And I can see you've been here for a while, and it's still hours before the court will open, so I wanted to let you know, if you take a few steps to your left – see this grate here? That's exhaust from the subway, which passes right underneath us. Every time a train goes past, you'll get a blast of warm air.'

I stand and smile at him and step across onto the grate.

'Thank you so much,' I say.

'Give it a minute or two,' he says. 'You'll see what I mean.'

After a beat, he says, 'So, the Maxwell trial, right?'

'Yes,' I say.

'I'll tell you a secret,' he says, and I think – not for the last time during this trial – that so much of good journalism is simply showing up; being in the right place at the right time.

'This building behind me,' he says, motioning to the tall, imposing, 35-ish-storey building, 'this is where she's being held. The MCC. That's my building. So at some point this morning, they'll walk her to the courtroom along this path here.' He motions to a dark, cordoned-off path that runs between the building he has just indicated and the one I am standing outside of. 'So keep your eyes peeled,' he says.

He winks at me as he says this, and I begin to express a gush-ing *thank you* for his kindness, but my breath is interrupted by a strong gust of deliciously warm air from beneath me, accompanied by a loud *whooshing* sound.

'It happened!' I said. 'Thank you so much – for the warmth and the inside info,' I say, and he nods.

'Take care of yourself,' he says as he walks away.

I smile to myself as I watch him go, and scribble down notes from our conversation in my notebook so I don't forget it.

I hit play on my audiobook again and close my eyes against the cold. I wrap my gloved fingers around my coffee, searching for some of its warmth.

It is around 4am when the security guard appears again.

'Miss!' he says, appearing frantic.

I pull my headphones out of my ears and stand up as he approaches me. He appears puffed, as though he has run down those 21 flights of stairs from his office to where I am standing.

'They've changed the courtroom,' he says. 'She's not being tried at 500 Pearl Street anymore – she'll be in the Thurgood Marshall. I'll take you there.'

Amazed at this man's kindness, I thank him profusely and follow him through a gated-off pathway that deposits us in the middle of a square surrounded by tall, slate-grey courthouses.

'That one over there,' he says, pointing towards a building I would come to know impossibly well in the weeks that followed.

'Thank you so, so much,' I say, very sincerely. I shake his hand and rush off, because I can see the shapes of other bodies waiting outside the courthouse, and I realise that others knew about the change of venue before I did – a fact that threatened my spot in the main courtroom.

I arrive to find three reporters and a man – who I would come to know as Robert – sitting alongside a bright yellow sign that reads 'SAME OL LINE DUDES'. Intrigued, I approach him.

'Hello,' I say, 'I love your sign. What does "SAME OL LINE DUDES" mean?'

Robert looks up at me. 'I have a business where I sit in line for people. Punters pay me to come here and line up for them, for big sales, or big trials. I got a load of work during the El Chapo trial.'

'That is *fascinating*,' I say, and I mean it. 'So who is paying you to be here today?'

'A journalist,' he says. 'I'm not supposed to tell you who.'

'Of course,' I say, holding up my hand. 'How did you get into this line of work?'

'My life was feeling a bit meandering. I was working as a tour guide over on the High Line, and then the lockdowns happened and I was out of work. And I thought to myself: why don't I set up my own business? I've always felt like New York could use a service like this – you hear about people camping out overnight for concert tickets and the latest iPhone and sample sales, and I thought maybe I could turn that into a business plan.'

'What a great idea!' I say enthusiastically.

He smiles at me, and I can tell he knows I am being genuine. 'And how's it all going?' I ask.

'Really great, actually,' he says. 'It started off as just me, about 18 months ago, but we grew so quickly that I now have about 50 line sitters on my staff, and they're all working constantly.'

'Wow,' I say. 'Well done.'

'Thank you,' he says earnestly. 'What's your name? Are you a reporter?'

'I am,' I say. 'Lucia.' I reach out my hand to shake his, and as I do I hand him my business card and ask if he has one. He hands me a bright yellow card with 'SAME OL LINE DUDES' emblazoned across the top. Twelve months later, as I write this, I still have the card in my coat pocket from that first day.

'So,' I say, 'tell me all your best stories.'

His eyes light up. 'Well,' he says, rubbing his hands together. It is only as he does this that I clock his surroundings. He is sitting on a bright-yellow fold-out chair – the same yellow as the business card – and he has covered himself with a yellow blanket and sleeping bag. Over the six weeks that follow, I will learn just how many tricks Robert has up his sleeve to protect himself from the elements. There will be more sleeping bags, hand-warmers, foot-warmers and even a plastic tent that he erects outside of his chair when it is raining or snowing – which it will be, a lot, as November turns into December and winter deepens.

The next person in line arrives. She is my friend for life – but at 4.30am on 29 November, I do not know this yet.

She is small and glamorous, wearing heeled boots, very flattering tight jeans and a gorgeous coat. She has a shoulder-length brown bob with a red tinge to it, and enormous, kind brown eyes, whose every expression I will come to know.

She offers her hand to me and then to Robert.

'Hi,' she says. 'I'm Leslie.' She smiles her winning smile. 'What are you guys both doing here?'

I tell her that I am a journalist, and Robert explains SAME OL LINE DUDES. Leslie's eyes light up as she listens to him.

I turn to her. 'And what about you, Leslie?'

'I'm an actor and a writer,' she says. This, I will soon learn, is a huge understatement – Leslie is an incredibly well-known Broadway actor and television star, and is beginning a career in screenwriting as well. But she is impossibly modest, so it takes me some time to work this out.

'I'm interested in trials,' she explains. 'In what they tell us about our society and about ourselves. I love to watch people in the courtroom, to see what I can find out about them. I love the complex psychology of big trials like this – as an actor, those things fascinate me. I came to a few days of the El Chapo trial, and it made me realise that it would be great to really commit to coming to every day of one of these trials and trying to make something out of it. So I'm coming to this one, and I'm going to write about it.'

I tell her I'm writing a book about this trial, that my journalism career has always been focused on sexual abuse, trauma and recovery, but I realised when Maxwell was arrested in 2020 that this particular trial was going to ask, and perhaps even answer, really complex questions about grooming, abuse, power dynamics and trauma. I tell her that, like her, I just realised one day: I have to be there. I have to try to understand what this trial is going to reveal to us about how this kind of abuse works, and how it has hidden in plain sight for so long.

Leslie is smiling and nodding. 'Exactly,' she says.

We continue to talk as the queue grows, about El Chapo, about what we already know about Maxwell, about what it's like to make it on Broadway. In a quieter moment, Leslie nods towards the south side of the square we are standing in. The sun is coming up behind one of the other courthouse buildings.

'It's finally getting light out,' Leslie says, and we both pause for a moment and watch the golden light seep onto our tired eyelids.

We check the time: 6am.

It's about an hour later when a very tall man comes over to us from his spot at the very front of the line.

'Hi,' he says, in a quiet voice, and I immediately notice a British accent. 'I'm Dan – are you guys reporters?'

'I am,' I say, and I allow Leslie and Robert to introduce themselves.

Dan turns to me. 'We are starting an email thread with all the reporters who will be here every day, so we can share info and resources. I don't know about you, but we've all had a terrible time dealing with the press office here.'

My experiences of the court press office have been nothing short of impossible. Gratefully, I write down my name and email address.

As I am doing so, a woman makes a beeline for our group. I recognise her immediately. Though this is my first time seeing her in real life, I feel as if I already know her, having read all of her books and listened to her podcast.

Vicky Ward walks straight up to Robert – identifiable a mile off with his yellow sign. She is the journalist that he is standing in line for. She hands him a wad of cash and they shake hands.

Vicky Ward has been a part of this story for a very long time. As a young journalist at *Vanity Fair* in the early 2000s, with twins on the way, she was assigned to write a story about Jeffrey Epstein. It was supposed to be a piece about how the Long Island boy with unglamorous roots ended up a billionaire managing the asset portfolios of New York's elite. Epstein was an enigma then – as, in some ways, he still is – and Vicky's feature was intended to capitalise on a growing feeling among uptown New Yorkers that they had someone special in their midst.

But as she investigated the story, it morphed into something very different indeed. One of the people Vicky spoke to was a recent employee of Epstein's – Maria Farmer. During Vicky's conversations with Maria, she became the first journalist to ever be told about Jeffrey Epstein's sexual abuse of young girls.

Maria told Vicky, on the record, that both she and her little sister Annie had been sexually abused by Jeffrey Epstein. Vicky took the allegations to her editor, Graydon Carter, but Carter refused to include the allegations in the piece. In the 20 years since this happened, Vicky and Carter have tussled over what exactly happened – a tussle that culminated in Vicky releasing transcripts of her conversations with Carter at the time.

Vicky says that Carter, and her line editor, told her that the story would be better as a straightforward business story. Carter also told Vicky – on tape – that he believed Epstein's denial of the allegations, and so he didn't want to print them.

Carter says now that Vicky did not have the reporting to back up the allegations, an assertion she disputes. Vicky had Maria and Annie Farmer on the record, as well as their mother, and two other sources close to Epstein who were willing to corroborate the story. Carter also argues, now, of Vicky, that 'my staff – to a person – did not trust her'.

I am recounting this to you because it, like everything in this story, is much more complicated than it seems, and because it looms large in the story of what happened over the 30 years that this sex trafficking ring went unpunished. The story was published *without* the sexual abuse allegations, and with Vicky Ward's name on it. That has meant that she is a complicated figure for victims of Epstein. They see her as someone who failed to report the truth back in 2002. But it is clear to me that Vicky fought very, very hard for her story to be published, and that as a very junior journalist going up against a media figure like Graydon Carter, it is not all that surprising that she failed.

Vicky and I now know each other very well, but on this morning, she is still a stranger. I tell her immediately that I admire her work and I ask her for a photo, and she kindly agrees. It is the beginning of a close friendship, during which we will sit in the same room, often right next to each other, for six weeks, and we will discuss everything – everything that happened back in 2002 with the Farmers, and then with Carter, and everything that's happened since.

Finally, there is movement at the door to the courthouse. By this point, I feel sure that the cold and rain has seeped all the way into my bones. My teeth are chattering and my extremities shaking; Vicky and I are doing squats and lunges to try to warm up our muscles. But it looks like we are about to be allowed inside.

Vicky is the fifth person in line that day, I am the sixth and Leslie is the seventh. We learn that only four people will be allowed in to the main courtroom, and we have just missed out. This is a mistake that none of us will make again. After that first day, I manage to get into the main courtroom for every single day of the Ghislaine Maxwell trial.

After extensive security checks and after handing in our phones, laptops and even all of our chargers – this federal courthouse does not allow reporters or the public to have any electronic devices at all in the courtroom – we are siphoned off into the first two overflow rooms. Vicky and I are directed to courtroom 901, and Leslie is directed across the hall to courtroom 902.

We take our seats and absorb our surroundings. The empty courtroom has TV screens set up at the front of it, and on the screens we can see a live feed of the main room – which, we will soon come to learn, is courtroom 318, below us on the third floor. The live feed only takes up about a third of the TV screen and the image quality is terrible, so it's hard to see anything clearly. I make a decision to arrive at 2am the following morning, and every morning after that. This is too important.

We are complaining about the screens when we notice movement in the courtroom. Eight attorneys have filed in and are separating themselves between the prosecution table, on the right-hand side of the room, and the defence table, on the left. A few moments later, Ghislaine Maxwell enters the courtroom from a secure door behind the judge's bench. She is flanked by two federal marshals, but to our collective surprise they are both very small, very young women – about 25, I would guess – who, it transpires over the coming weeks, have a warm and friendly relationship with their charge.

For weeks after this, I will sit within two feet of Ghislaine Maxwell. I will get to know her mannerisms, her moods and her habits intimately. But for now, I am seeing her only on a screen and I do not get a fraction of a sense of who she really is. We can't even work out whether Ghislaine's jumper is white, cream or pink, because the image quality is so bad. I will often reflect on this day, in the weeks and months to come, and think about the fact that the dominant media narrative told about this trial will, and did, come from reporters watching it on this tiny screen. The only reporters in the actual courtroom consistently were me, Vicky Ward, and two others whom you will soon meet.

Two loud knocks ring out and Judge Alison Nathan enters the courtroom for the first time.

Nathan is short in stature but has a powerfully commanding presence. She has short, close-cropped black hair and thin black glasses. She walks to the bench assuredly, like she knows exactly what she is doing. She moves some folders around when she arrives at the bench and removes her black KN95 face mask in order to speak into her microphone.

These details are not easy for me to work out from watching the small screen, but I can still sense her presence, if not her minutia. Or perhaps I am filling these details in from the five weeks I will spend in the same room as her from the following day onwards; I can't be sure.

'Morning, everyone,' she says, not standing on ceremony, as though we are not commencing the trial of the century. This is how she will approach everything about this trial – without fanfare or pomp, as though purposefully paying no heed to the opulent wealth and, until now, impunity that has been afforded this particular defendant and her co-conspirators. She is utterly unfazed.

'I hope we are all well this morning,' she is saying now. 'Is all counsel ready?'

Alison Moe, a federal prosecutor who is leading the initial parts of the state's case against Ghislaine Maxwell, stands up and says: 'Yes, your honour,' with a dramatic nodding of her head. She puts me in mind of a schoolgirl who is consistently best in class.

Bobbi Sternheim, Ghislaine Maxwell's lead defence attorney, leans into her microphone, without standing all the way up, and says: 'Yes, judge.' Sternheim will be the only one of eight attorneys throughout this whole trial not to refer to Judge Nathan as 'your honour'.

It is during these idle moments on the morning of 29 November that another very important character enters this story.

I am writing notes about the brief interaction between the lawyers and Judge Nathan that we have just witnessed when a distinctive voice floats over the top of the hubbub and catches my attention. The voice is high-pitched and slightly nasal, with a particular American accent that I can't quite place. I know I recognise it, as though it belongs to a close friend – but which of my close friends would be here, in this room? And if not a close friend, why do I know this voice so well?

And then it hits me: the voice belongs to Julie K. Brown. And the reason I know the voice is because I have listened to the audio-book of Julie's masterpiece, *Perversion of Justice*, three times by the time I hear her voice floating towards me in courtroom 901. Julie narrates the preface to her book herself in the audiobook, so after three listens I have become very, very familiar with her particular cadence and intonation.

Julie is speaking with two women behind me as I realise this, and I stand up.

'So sorry to interrupt,' I say, thinking to myself that this particular part of my personality is so at odds with the rest of me. I am usually polite to a fault, always pretending I'm not really there, never drawing too much attention to myself. But when it comes to writers I admire, it seems like all of that social anxiety, all of those manners, seem to just fade away in the face of my much stronger desire to make connections with people whose work has changed me.

The three women in the conversation look at me expectantly.

'Are you Julie?' I ask, looking at the woman with the familiar voice.

'I am,' she says kindly.

'My apologies, I am just such a big fan of your reporting. I've read your book three times – your work on this case is second to none.'

'Oh, well, thank you so much,' Julie says, seeming genuinely happy and not bothered by my interruption.

Julie Brown is the reason we are all here. She is the reason, to my mind at least, that this trial is happening. She is living, breathing proof that fighting for justice and truth through investigative reporting is not always as pointless as it sometimes seems. That good, dedicated journalism really *can* change the world.

Julie started investigating Jeffrey Epstein in 2016. She was working as the *Miami Herald*'s top investigative reporter, and at the time her beat was focused on Florida prisons – famously one of the most dysfunctional state carceral systems in America. She decided she wanted to write a story about any modern-day sex trafficking that still took place in Florida in 2016. But when she googled 'sex trafficking' and 'Florida', she just kept coming across stories about Jeffrey Epstein.

Now, Epstein's name was *not* widely tarnished for being the orchestrator of a huge global underage sex trafficking ring back in 2016 – although it should have been, and it will turn out that it will be Julie who ultimately uncovers why this isn't the case. So back then, his name didn't immediately recall the kind of depravity we now associate with it. So it was curious to Julie that a Google search of 'sex trafficking' and 'Florida' kept pointing her back to a person she only knew at the time as a wealthy, enigmatic money manager from Wall Street.

Insatiably curious, she looked a little deeper. She found local news stories about Jeffrey's arrest in 2007 for solicitation – but what she hadn't known was that those solicitation charges had begun their lives in the criminal justice system as sex trafficking charges. Julie was familiar enough with the criminal justice system through her extensive reporting on it to know that state prosecutors will often plead down criminal charges as part of negotiations with defence attorneys. But pleading down a *sex trafficking* charge to a solicitation charge? That seemed extreme. Sex trafficking is taken extremely seriously by both federal and state law, and to say that the solicitation charge that Jeffrey ended up pleading guilty to was not taken at all seriously would be a major understatement. How did that happen?

Julie started looking at the other reporting that had been done on the Epstein story, but none of it felt complete to her. As a Palm Beach police officer would say to her later on in her investigation, reporters will often 'start working on the Epstein story only to end up being transferred to the paper's real estate department'.

In particular, no reporters had found out what Epstein's victims felt about the fact that he pleaded down to minor charges – and charges which cast them as adult sex workers when they were, in fact, children. *Why has no one spoken to the victims?* Julie asked herself.

This would become the mantra for Julie's reporting and, in turn, mine. The reason Julie broke this story open in a way that nobody else could, or did, was precisely because she was the first journalist to take these victims' stories seriously, to honour what they had lived through by believing them and doing the work required to corroborate what they had to say. The simple fact of Julie's commitment to allowing victims' voices to be heard changed everything.

Julie and I sit down together as I tell her how much her reporting on this case has meant to me, how much her singular focus on the forgotten voices of victims has shaped me as a journalist. She thanks me in earnest and asks me what I think about the trial.

Behind us, I hear someone speaking with a thick South African accent, and I turn around to see who it is.

It is Sarah Ransome, a victim of Jeffrey Epstein and Ghislaine Maxwell. I have never met her, but I recognise her from one of the documentaries about the sex trafficking ring.

What on earth is she doing in an overflow room, I think to myself, *surrounded by reporters?*

She's been thrown into a shark tank, I think, feeling shocked. I know that there is a federal law that protects the rights of victims to be in the courtroom to see the trial of their abusers – so why on earth has Sarah been placed here, with us?

I will learn later that Sarah was forced to wait in line, in the cold – again, exposed to a horde of hungry reporters demanding that she relive the worst moments of her life for them – only to be placed in an overflow room because she didn't arrive early enough.

A male reporter in his forties makes a joke about Ghislaine seeming close with her female guards.

'Don't worry, they're too old for her,' he says, laughing along with a gaggle of other reporters.

The joke makes my skin crawl, and I look over at Sarah, who has also heard the remark. I leave soon after.

As I stand at the sinks washing my hands, a woman walks in who immediately captures my attention. She is beautifully dressed in a gorgeous camel-coloured jumpsuit and fabulous boots, and has a friendly smile. I remember very clearly that the first words I ever spoke to Jessica Reed Kraus were, 'I love your outfit'. This is particularly striking given how intellectually demanding our relationship would later become, and I like this juxtaposition. We do not have to be women interested in either fashion or acute issues of criminal justice. We can be, and are, both.

———

By the afternoon, Judge Nathan tells the attorneys to prepare for opening statements. It is now that I begin to know these vital characters for the first time.

I want to start with Alison Moe, because you'll hear from her first. Alison is tiny – about five foot three – but she's not even the smallest person on the prosecution team. She wears a sensible court skirt-suit, all black with a crisp white shirt underneath. She wears sheer stockings and flat black shoes. Her hair is a beautiful mousy-brown with a blonde shine underneath it when caught in just the right light. It is straight and shoulder-length.

Over the next six weeks, the chatter in the press gallery will centre around how *young* the prosecutors look; these small young women with no experience, how silly they appear next to the all-star defence team. But right from the beginning I never really saw this in them; I saw a team who meant business, a team who believed in the power of the courts to set things right, a team who believed in justice and were willing to fight for it. A team who were young, yes, and hungry.

Alison's fierceness comes through not in her looks but in her cadence. Everything she says is careful and measured – not a single word out of place. In law school, and at my first law firm, I was always in awe of the lawyers who could do this. These lawyers are as careful with their words as writers are, but they do it in real time. When Alison Moe speaks, I get the impression she has never said anything she hasn't absolutely considered from every angle.

Alison is sitting on the far left of the prosecution table today, closest to the centre of the room, because she is giving the government's opening statement. This seat is known among lawyers as 'first chair' – whoever is leading the team for each day of trial sits there and becomes 'first chair' for the day.

To Alison's immediate right is Maurene Comey. Maurene is the opposite of Alison in stature – she is incredibly tall, just like her father, James Comey, the famed ex-chief of the FBI who oversaw the agency during the 2016 presidential election.

Maurene seems acutely aware of her immense height when she walks. She is always slightly bent over herself, as though apologising. But when she questions witnesses or addresses the court and the jury, there are no apologies. She is fierce and, like Alison, incredibly self-assured. I get the impression she has never said something she wouldn't stand behind and couldn't prove.

Also like Alison, she wears a dark skirt-suit each day of the trial with a pressed white shirt underneath and flat shoes. She wears no make-up, as though she wants to direct all her energy to the task at hand.

To the right of her is Lara Pomerantz, the tiniest of them all. She is maybe five foot one, at a push. When she stands next to Maurene, the taller prosecutor has to almost bend double to whisper prosecutorial secrets in her ear. Lara has long brown hair that reaches beyond her chest. It is straight and well kept, and she wears it loose for the majority of the trial.

Lara's small stature belies a fiery core. When she speaks to the court, her voice is steady and assured, and always feels like a warning: *Don't push me, I know exactly what I'm doing.*

On the other side of the room, the defence table. These are, without a doubt, some of the most talented attorneys I have ever seen at work. They are formidable when it comes to dextrous legal argument. What they actually believe, underneath it all, is a mystery to me.

My favourite is Bobbi Sternheim. She will become an obsession of mine over the next few weeks. How to capture her on the page?

Bobbi is less a person than a *presence*. She lights up a room when she walks in – not with a smile, necessarily, but with something else: intellectual heft, perhaps; a sense of purpose. She always wears starchy white shirts with a popped collar. Every day, the popped collar. (One day, Leslie musters up the courage to ask her about this in the elevator during the lunch break, and she says, 'It's a statement.')

Atop the popped collar, Bobbi wears a different-coloured blazer each day. But not a muted court blazer like the ones we come to expect from the prosecutors. Hers are velvet, tweed, linen. They are purple, green, maroon. They, too, are a statement. Alongside the blazers and popped collar, Bobbi wears fantastic ankle boots, with a slight heel on them and a pointed toe. Black with silver studs along the bottom. Half country and western, half runway.

I could spend my life trying to understand Bobbi Sternheim. She is a prominent left-wing activist and she and her progressive wife are very active in the LGBTQI+ legal community. And yet here she is defending Ghislaine Maxwell with a passion that, to me at least, reads as genuine.

Bobbi doesn't know me yet, on this first day, but soon enough she will recognise that I am one of only three or four reporters who is here every single day of the trial. When she registers this, she begins to say 'good morning' to me each day in this wonderfully warm manner; one that jars with the way I will come to see her treat, and speak about, victims during the course of the next few weeks.

Next to Bobbi is Christian Everdell – a small, unassuming man but one I will come to recognise as one of the smartest legal thinkers I've ever witnessed at work. Christian is an interesting addition to the defence team because he is, at heart, a prosecutor. He has only recently *switched sides*, as they say in the legal world. In fact, when Leslie was last in this very courthouse, for the El Chapo trial, Christian Everdell was at the prosecution table.

He is the only one of the defence team that does not profess to have a genuine emotional connection with Ghislaine Maxwell. Rather, you get the sense that he believes strongly in the idea that everyone deserves a defence, and that he likes to challenge his legal mind. The heated spats he will get into with Judge Nathan over the coming weeks will prove this.

Next to him is Jeffrey Pagliuca, who I will come to recognise anywhere on the streets of Lower Manhattan – and I will start to see him around an awful lot – by his distinctive backpack. In truth, it isn't distinctive at all; it stands out in its plainness. It is a standard sports backpack, like the one my dad used to carry cycling while I was growing up. The others have posh briefcases, but Jeffrey Pagliuca doesn't stand on ceremony, not for anyone.

Finally, on the defence table, we have Laura Menninger. Laura Menninger is the one I will come to see as Ghislaine Maxwell's *fixer* – her equivalent of Rudy Giuliani. She has been representing Maxwell for many years and you can tell from the way that she walks into this room that she is on a mission to clear her friend's good name. She is an attack dog, and the moments when she is unleashed on Maxwell's victims will be the hardest for me to sit through of this whole trial.

Judge Nathan swears in each individual juror, and when that is done, she addresses them as a group. With these words, the trial begins in earnest.

'The first step in the trial will be opening statements,' she says, deliberately and thoughtfully. 'The government will make an opening statement. After that, the lawyers for the defendant will make their own. Those statements are not evidence. They serve no purpose other than to give you an idea in advance of the evidence that the lawyers expect you to hear from the witnesses. Those statements permit the lawyers to tell you a little bit of what the case is all about, but the only evidence comes from the witnesses and the exhibits.

'Let me explain the jobs that you and I are to perform during the trial. I will decide which rules of law to apply to this case. I'll decide that by making legal rulings during the presentation of the evidence,' she continues.

'While I decide the law that applies to this case, you, ladies and gentlemen of the jury, are the triers of fact,' Judge Nathan is saying now, and as she does so, I am reminded of when I first learned this distinction in law school. While so many of us are familiar with the legal world, it wasn't until I started training as a lawyer myself that I understood this crucial element of the criminal justice system: that judges are there *only* to interpret the law and decide questions about the rules of evidence – what the jury should and shouldn't see. The jury's job is to completely ignore questions of law and make a determination about what actually happened – to decide the facts.

One of the most interesting things about being a legal journalist is that I get to see both sides – I get to see the lawyers arguing about what should and shouldn't be shown to the jury, and I get to see how that evidence is ultimately presented. The jury doesn't know what is being kept from them, but I do. These questions about the rules of evidence will loom large in this trial, and I will have a front-row seat.

'You'll weigh the evidence presented and decide whether the government has proved beyond a reasonable doubt that the defendant is guilty of the charges in the indictment,' Judge Nathan is saying. 'You must pay close attention to all of the evidence presented, and you must base your decision only on the evidence in the case and my instructions about the law.'

She pauses. 'There is no formula to evaluate testimony or exhibits,' she says carefully. 'For now, suffice it to say that you bring with you into this courtroom all the experience and background of your lives. Do not leave your common sense outside the courtroom. The same types of tests that you use in your everyday lives are the tests that you should apply in deciding how much weight, if any, to give to the evidence in this case.'

CHAPTER 2

New York City, 2021

It was the early 1990s, and Ghislaine Maxwell had recently met Jeffrey Epstein for the first time – most likely through her father, media mogul Robert Maxwell, but my own and other investigative reporters' efforts on this question have not been able to confirm the exact circumstances. Soon after, Ghislaine started an intimate relationship with Epstein and they were a couple for many years. When their relationship ended, they remained, in Ghislaine's own words – as we will hear at trial – the 'best of friends'.

From what was argued at trial and from what I know from the victims I have become close with, it seems that Ghislaine became Epstein's closest associate and second in command. She was involved in every detail of Epstein's life. During the ten years the defendant and Epstein committed these crimes together – the prosecution will argue – the defendant was the 'lady of the house'. She ran Epstein's various properties, hiring and firing employees. She imposed rules, instructing employees not to speak directly with Epstein or with other people visiting Epstein's homes. When she took charge of those homes, the rules for staff were strict. Employees were to see nothing, hear nothing, say nothing.

There was a culture of silence. That was by design, because behind closed doors, the defendant and Epstein were committing heinous crimes, the prosecution would argue. They were sexually abusing teenage girls.

Ghislaine and Jeffrey were partners in crime, the jury will be told. They had a playbook. First, they got access to young girls, then they gained their trust.

The thing I will learn, not only as I listen to opening arguments, but also from years of speaking with victims of Ghislaine and Jeffrey, is this: Ghislaine was unbelievably beguiling and knew how to use her charm incredibly effectively. She was rich and fabulous-looking and everyone wanted to be like her. She was well spoken and clever, and her Oxford accent made her magnetic. This is important, because here's what I've also learned about Jeffrey from the victims who, unfortunately, had to spend so much time around him. He was an introvert. He hated socialising. He was *not* a charmer. That's why he needed her.

As I sit there, listening to the opening arguments, imagining these moments back in the early 1990s, I realise that this trial might actually go some way to achieving what I had spent the last year hoping it would: explaining the process of grooming and its place in child sexual abuse; explaining that it begins with trust and salvation, so that when the abuse comes along the child is confused and immediately blames themselves.

Some of the girls had difficult home lives and came from families that were struggling to make ends meet. That's why they were chosen. Ghislaine and Jeffrey were wealthy, powerful and well connected, and they flaunted it. They made sure everybody knew that they held court with billionaires and presidents. They made young girls believe that their dreams could come true. They figured out what the girls wanted to be when they grew up and they promised to help – to pay for school fees, to pull strings so they could become actresses, models, professional musicians. They made these girls feel seen; they made them feel special.

I am, again, reassured, that this prosecution team understands grooming. *They made them feel special.* I know that feeling.

They were wealthy and influential people who used that cover to make the girls and their parents feel comfortable and safe. But what came next was anything but safe. The next stage involved getting the girls comfortable with sexual contact involving Epstein. To do this, the defendant discussed sexual topics with the girls and then she used the same excuse over and over to get the girls to touch Epstein – massage. You will learn that the cover of massage was the primary way the defendant and Epstein lured girls into sexual abuse.

The defendant massaged Epstein in front of the girls, then she encouraged the girls to massage Epstein.

I bring myself out of my imagined version of the past and hear Lara Pomerantz's next words clearly:

'And before I describe those so-called massages for you, let me just say, I know this is hard to hear, but these are the facts of the case. This is what happened to these children. These are the crimes the defendant and Epstein committed.'

I circle this statement several times in my notebook. This is something I've been very interested in lately: in our movement towards acknowledging the extent of sexual abuse, it seems to me that we have a way to go in terms of actually being willing to hear the detail of it. And that is a fatal mistake, because the devil is always in the detail.

But Pomerantz is fighting against this urge, and I notice the jury shift. I feel, and I think the jury does, too, the power of what she is saying: this will be painful for us to hear. But not nearly as painful as it was for these children to live through – so we must bear witness. We owe them that.

'Ghislaine helped Jeffrey find those girls back then. She helped him recruit girls for supposed massages. She manipulated the girls, groomed them for abuse, helped the girls feel comfortable as friendliness escalated to abuse. Sometimes she was even in the room for the massages herself, and sometimes she touched the girls' bodies. And even when she was not in the room, make no mistake, she knew exactly what Epstein was going to do to those children when she sent them to him inside the massage rooms of the houses she ran for over a decade. When the defendant sent a 14-year-old girl into a massage room with an adult man, she knew exactly what was going to happen.

'She was *essential* to this scheme. As an adult woman, she was able to provide a cover of respectability for Epstein that lulled these girls and their families into a false sense of security. She was in on it from the start. The defendant and Epstein lured their victims with the promise of a brighter future, only to sexually exploit them and forever change their lives.'

I didn't know this on 29 November, as I was sitting in that room listening to the opening statements, but within a year I will have collected evidence to prove that the sex trafficking conspiracy that Lara Pomerantz is describing right now in fact went on for much longer than stated at this trial. I will be able to prove that Ghislaine was involved in the scheme as early as 1991, and will be able to trace her involvement right up to the abuse of Sarah Ransome, which ended in 2007.

Back in courtroom 318, Lara Pomerantz is continuing her opening argument.

'For example, you will learn about a 16-year-old girl who travelled to Epstein's ranch in New Mexico and found herself alone with the defendant and Epstein,' Pomerantz continues. 'Once the girl was isolated, the defendant took steps to normalise sexual contact under the ruse of massage, preparing her to be sexually abused by Epstein. The defendant told the girl she was going to give her a massage, and once she got the girl on the massage table, the defendant started touching the girl's breasts. The girl was 16 years old.

'You will also learn about a 17-year-old girl the defendant spotted in a parking lot and recruited out of the blue. You'll hear that the defendant made her driver pull over so that she could approach that 17-year-old girl to recruit her to give Epstein massages.

'And you will learn about the way the defendant and Epstein's sexual abuse evolved over the course of a decade. You will learn that in the 1990s, they used the cover of mentoring young girls, of promising them scholarships and opportunity, to introduce massage, inviting them on trips and transporting them across state lines, and you will learn that they used these so-called massages as a way to sexually abuse the victims.

'During that earlier phase, the defendant and Epstein had to find each girl individually themselves, but by the early 2000s, the defendant and Epstein found an easier way to maintain a continuous flow of girls to abuse. They were no longer finding girls through the cover of scholarships and opportunity. Instead, they devised a pyramid scheme of abuse, a scheme that no longer required the defendant to personally find young girls for Epstein.

'Under this pyramid scheme of abuse, the defendant could just call girls to schedule massage appointments and hand them cash afterwards, overseeing the operation and normalising the abuse by showing these young girls that she, an older, purportedly respectable woman, had no problem with the paid sex acts that were taking place during these so-called massages.

'For a decade, the defendant played an essential role in this scheme. She knew exactly what she was doing. She was dangerous. She was setting young girls up to be molested by a predator.'

For much more than a decade, I think to myself as I type up these notes in late 2022, knowing so much more now than I did when I first heard those words. The government's indictment at the trial you will read about in this book charges Ghislaine with a conspiracy beginning in 1994 and ending in 2004. But I now know that Ghislaine was likely involved in this scheme much earlier than 1994. In fact, Ghislaine was calling the landline phone of an Epstein survivor's Brooklyn apartment as early as the summer of 1992.

'That's what we expect the evidence will show: that the defendant enticed and groomed multiple young girls to engage in sex acts with Jeffrey Epstein; that the defendant and Epstein enticed some of those girls to travel to Epstein's homes in different states, which the defendant knew would result in sexual abuse.'

Lara Pomerantz's tiny frame walks away from the podium defiantly.

CHAPTER 3

New York City, 2021

Bobbi Sternheim and her impressive boots walk towards the podium, and I hear her speak for the first time.

'Ever since Eve was tempting Adam with the apple, women have been blamed for the bad behaviour of men, and those women have been villainised and punished,' she says. 'The charges against Ghislaine Maxwell are for things that Jeffrey Epstein did,' Sternheim says confidently. 'But she is not Jeffrey Epstein, she is not like Jeffrey Epstein, and she is not like any of the other men – powerful men, moguls, media giants – who abuse women.'

Months and months later, Judge Nathan will use almost these exact words to refute what Sternheim has said here. She will say: 'The defendant is not being prosecuted for the crimes of Jeffrey Epstein. She was tried for the crimes that *she* committed, the choices that *she* made.'

'Epstein is not on trial, but his name and his conduct, as you have already heard, will be mentioned throughout this trial,' Sternheim is saying now. 'He's the proverbial elephant in the room. He is not visible, but he is consuming this entire courtroom and the overflow courtrooms that other members of the public are viewing.

'You will hear plenty of testimony, some of which the government has already previewed, which revolves around Epstein's conduct, not Ghislaine's. But you are not here to judge whether

Epstein committed the crimes; you are not here to judge whether the government could prove beyond a reasonable doubt that Epstein committed the crimes – you are here to determine whether the government can prove beyond a reasonable doubt that Ghislaine Maxwell has committed the crimes charged. When all is said and done, the evidence will show that the government cannot, because Ghislaine did not.

'Now, together with my colleagues – Christian Everdell, Laura Menninger, and Jeffrey Pagliuca – I stand before you proud to represent Ghislaine Maxwell.'

Sternheim has her hand on her heart as she says this.

'This case is about memory, manipulation and money,' she says, and I see all the reporters write this down.

'As you will see, the accusations that you will hear from the mouths of four accusers – not like the hundreds that the government suggested you would hear from – you will hear from them and they will recount their memories, memories of a quarter-century ago, memories that have been corrupted by things that have happened throughout the years, manipulated by a narcissistic man and self-interested civil lawyers, and a desire for a big jackpot of money.'

I bristle. To hear this particular argument – that the victims are lying, making up stories in pursuit of a quick payday – rattles me.

'The government's proof, the government's story, relies on the claims of four accusers, four who will say that Ghislaine prepared them or – to use a term that you will hear in this trial through expert testimony – groomed them to engage in acts with Epstein.

'Now, we're talking about events that took place 15 to over 25 years ago, and as we all know, memories fade over time, and in this case, you will learn that not only have memories faded, but they have been contaminated by outside information, constant media reports and other influences.

'Jeffrey Epstein manipulated the world around him and the people around him. He compartmentalised his life, showing only what he wanted to show to the people around him.

'Ghislaine Maxwell is on trial because of her association with Jeffrey Epstein. She is a scapegoat for a man who behaved badly.'

That's a mild term for the repeated rape of children, I think to myself.

'Objection.' Lara Pomerantz stands up.

'As stated, sustained,' Judge Nathan says. Later, I will consult pre-trial transcripts and learn that Judge Nathan has banned the defence from explicitly trying to suggest that Ghislaine is only being prosecuted because Jeffrey died without ever being held accountable.

'She is a target, a bull's eye of anger for women who were or otherwise believed they were victimised by Epstein. Epstein's death left a gaping hole in the pursuit of justice for many of these women.'

'Objection!' Pomerantz is angry now.

'Sustained, as stated,' Judge Nathan says, giving Bobbi Sternheim a warning look.

'Ghislaine is on trial here, and you heard about the conduct of Jeffrey Epstein. She is filling that hole and filling an empty chair. She is a brand name, she is a lightning rod, she is a convenient stand-in for the man who—'

'Objection,' Pomerantz stands up and says.

'Let me speak to counsel, please,' Judge Nathan says. A tape player emits a fuzzy white-noise sound, so that the jury and the gallery cannot hear them speaking.

I find out later that this is what they said.

'Your honour, this is in violation of the pre-trial ruling made by the court,' Maurene Comey says, but she is cut off by Judge Nathan.

'They can argue that, for the witnesses, Maxwell is a scape-goat or a stand-in.'

'That is permissible, your honour,' Comey says. 'But the reference to an empty chair is clearly a reference to this case and the prosecution.'

Judge Nathan cuts her off again.

'I won't allow the line to be crossed into where I ruled on, which is that you can't talk about motivations of the prosecution. The government is not on trial. To the extent that you want to argue motivation of the witnesses to not tell the truth or credibility with respect to them, you may do that,' Judge Nathan says to Sternheim. 'But don't play with the line,' she warns.

Sternheim nods, and the attorneys return to their tables.

She continues. 'Four women will come into this courtroom and they will point a finger at Ghislaine Maxwell, but what they say and the evidence that you will see is not going to support these charges beyond a reasonable doubt.'

Writing this now, I think about the catchphrase that this defence team will ultimately use in their closing arguments, weeks later. Laura Menninger will say that these women saw an opportunity to point the finger at Ghislaine, and they collectively decided to say *her, too*.

Her, too, Menninger will say snarkily, playing on #MeToo, the movement of women speaking up about sexual harassment, the movement that arguably led us all to be gathered here, in this room. *She was there. She knew. Her, too. Her, too.*

'You've heard many negative things about Ghislaine Maxwell,' Sternheim is saying now. 'And the evidence is going to show many exceptional things about Ghislaine Maxwell – well educated, well travelled, a graduate of Oxford … She socialised with extraordinary people, she can pilot a helicopter, she speaks numerous languages, and she has worked her entire adult life. She is being pegged as the rich girl, the socialite. But privileged background, comfortable lifestyle, status – they may be things that easily check the wrong box, but they are not crimes and nor should they factor negatively into your consideration of the evidence because, as you may recall, during jury selection, you all agreed and you all said that you would not be biased by affluence or opulence, and your word is your bond.

'What you are going to see and what you are going to hear basically centre around four women. They are going to tell four different stories, they are four completely different people, and they are going to recount things that they claim happened to them decades and decades ago. They are not going to be able to pinpoint dates; they are going to tell stories that have changed over time and grown over time – stories that they have told for the first time after Epstein died. And Ghislaine has been inserted in those stories as they reframed [them] for a payday.'

Opening statements are meant to be rhetorical and argumentative. But they are also supposed to be based on the evidence that the lawyers making them are planning to rely on at trial. It strikes me that this accusation – that these women have entirely made up Ghislaine's involvement in order to get compensation – ought only to be made if it is actually supported by evidence – which, I will discover when we hear the defence's case-in-chief, it is not.

'Now, they will come in here and they will point their finger at Ghislaine Maxwell,' Bobbi Sternheim continues. 'There is nobody else to point the finger at in this trial. And I ask you to consider, when you hear their testimony, those core themes that I mentioned before: memory, manipulation and money.

'You are going to decide, when you hear these witnesses, if you find them reliable, credible, plausible. You are going to see, based on the evidence and, importantly, the lack of evidence, that they do not support the charges in this indictment, certainly not beyond a reasonable doubt. There will be no eyewitnesses to their accounts, even when they claim there were all these other people involved in the activities that the government has alleged. There will not be documentation, even that which still exists some 25 years later, that is going to corroborate their testimony.'

CHAPTER 4

New York City, 2021

'I want to tell you about a young girl named Jane.'

Lara Pomerantz has removed her face mask and opened her notebook. She has taken a breath and turned her body towards the jury box.

'It was 1994 and Jane was spending her summer at a camp for talented young kids. Jane turned 14 years old that year. She was sitting at a picnic table with friends when a man and a woman walked by. The man introduced himself as a donor who gave scholarships to students at this camp. The man and the woman spoke with Jane and, after discovering they all lived in Palm Beach, Florida, they asked Jane for her phone number.' Pomerantz is looking the jurors in the eye, and she is speaking deliberately, making every word count.

'What Jane didn't know then was that this meeting at summer camp was the beginning of a nightmare that would last for years, that this meeting would pull Jane into a relationship with the man and the woman, who were each more than double her age.

'What she didn't know then was that this man and woman were predators. What Jane didn't understand then, and what you will learn at this trial, was that this meeting was the beginning of that man and woman targeting Jane for sexual abuse that would last for years.

'Between 1994 and 2004, the defendant sexually exploited young girls,' Pomerantz says. 'She preyed on vulnerable young girls, manipulated them, and served them up to be sexually abused. The defendant was trafficking kids for sex. That is what this trial is all about,' she is saying now.

'The defendant took these girls on shopping trips, asked them about their lives, their schools, their families. She won their trust. She discussed sexual topics with them. She helped normalise abusive sexual conduct. She put them at ease and made them feel safe, all so that they could be molested by a middle-aged man.'

Pomerantz is setting out, in very clear terms, the government's answer to a question that the defence will ask them repeatedly throughout this trial: *Is this really about my client? Isn't she just a scapegoat? Don't you have bigger fish to fry?*

Aiming squarely at this anticipated criticism, and motioning at where Maxwell sat behind her, Pomerantz says: 'She knew exactly what was going to happen to those girls.

'The defendant walked the girls into a room where she knew that man would molest them' – Pomerantz pauses for effect here, needing the next part of the sentence to hit home – '*and there were times when she was in the room when it happened.*'

CHAPTER 5

Michigan, 1994

It was August in northern Michigan, but everything was autumnal. On the last Thursday of camp, Jane practised her vocal solo in front of a group of other middle-school girls to prepare for the next day's final performance – the heady, complicated last day of summer. The girls were huddled together inside a cottage built high with deep red-brown slats, brown pews and wooden floors that clunked as the girls walked, socks pulled high over knobbly knees and shifting uncertainly in ill-fitting shoes bought the day before camp in a hurry to feel pretty and new.

The singing teacher called on Jane to perform a scale and then her vocal solo at the front of the room. Breathing in and out and in again before she started, Jane landed every note. It was her third year at arts camp, and each year her singing teacher had said she was the best in class.

As Jane and four of her friends walked out of the tall oak door of the amphitheatre, two men passed them on their left side. Between the men was a limp banner that the girls realised they must be about to erect for the next day. In block letters, it read: *INTERLOCHEN ARTS CAMP GALA, SUMMER OF 1994.* The girls walked through bright, crunchy leaves away from the amphitheatre, past two of the red-oak residence lodges with white walkways, and towards the area with the cafeteria and gift shop. One of the girls suggested they all get ice cream, and they agreed, pleased with themselves after a hard day of rehearsal and eager to soak up the last drops of summer they had together.

Jane's friends teased her when she got plain chocolate, keen as they all were to differentiate themselves from one another that year, choosing pistachio or mint choc chip instead – grabbing with both hands that time in life where every small decision you make is a chance to tell everyone who you are.

A few moments later, while they were all sitting around a picnic table, a bell rang to tell the girls to go back to their cabins until dinner. But Jane lagged behind. She wanted to watch the sky a little, spend some time on her own. As her mind drifted away, she heard a bark. She looked down towards the noise and saw a small, delicate, marmalade-yellow terrier. No older than six months. Her eyes widened as the dog approached her.

Jane's eyes moved up the dog's lead towards its owner – a tall, slim woman wearing a thin white sundress and gigantic floppy hat. Amid the wooden slats and squeals and slightly ramshackle buildings dotted across the camp, Jane couldn't help but notice that the woman seemed out of place, as though transported here from a different world.

'Would you like to pet him?'

Jane looked up into the woman's eyes for the first time. They were pitch-dark and curious, framed by a short black bob like the ones Jane had seen in the old movies she used to watch with her father; the ones he used to love the soundtracks to.

At the same moment, as she tried to register the woman's face, she attempted to decode her butter-toned voice. It was inviting but also regal; lofty and far away. *English?* she thought to herself. *French? German?* Jane had never been to Europe – she didn't know yet that the following year, the year she turned 15, she would be flown to Italy to sing.

'Yes, please,' she said, remembering her manners. 'What's his name?'

'His name is Max.'

Jane wanted the woman to say more, partly because she was mesmerised by her and partly because she wanted to decipher the accent. She waited, but the woman just held her gaze and said nothing.

'Hi, Max,' Jane said shyly, grateful for a reason to break eye contact.

'What's your name?' the woman asked.

'Jane.'

'It's lovely to meet you, Jane.'

Those five words were enough – definitely English. *She sounds like the queen*, Jane thought.

A loud clattering sound diverted both of them, and they turned towards a large lodge nearby. It was the biggest lodge on the grounds – twice as wide as the others, two full-size bedrooms, or so the rumours went. An M-shaped oak façade with freshly painted white steps leading up to a big white door. Jane had noticed this cabin because it hadn't been there the summer before. But as far as Jane could tell, it had sat empty since they had arrived. She had asked her singing teacher about it, who had said it belonged to someone who would be arriving for the final performance on the last day of camp.

When the singing teacher had told Jane this, she'd wondered if the cabin's occupant might be a famous musician – they sometimes invited them to the final performance to assess the students. A composer maybe? But that thought had come with a sharp sting, made her miss her father, so she'd quickly brushed it aside. Jane's mother got angry when she spoke about her father, and sometimes it felt as though her mother was in her head, too, trying to banish the thoughts of him, saying, '*We don't talk about that*' – even to ourselves. Especially to ourselves.

Now, another clatter reverberated from the lodge and a man stumbled out, tripping over himself clumsily. He wiped his hands on his blue-jeans shorts and walked towards Jane, the woman and Max. He smiled so broadly, so kindly, that Jane found herself instinctively mimicking his grin. The man's sneakers crunched leaves as he approached, hands now spread across his chest, drumming his fingers on his plain white T-shirt, seeming so at home in the world, Jane thought.

'Jane,' the woman said, 'I'd like you to meet my friend Jeffrey.'

The pair held hands as the man approached. *She's his wife,* Jane realised, and then remembered to hold out her hand for him.

'It's a pleasure to meet you, Jane,' he said.

She smiled up at him. She guessed he was about 40, maybe older. He didn't seem like a musician, though. As if reading her mind, he started speaking then. 'I'm a benefactor here,' he said, sitting atop the picnic table. 'I give out scholarships. That's why I have a lodge here.' He gestured towards the cabin. A pause. Jane nodded but said nothing. She thought back to yesterday when she was looking around the new lodge and remembered the sign: *The Epstein Lodge.*

By the time Jane tells me this story, 28 years later, the sign will have been taken down and the lodge renamed; the camp will refuse to accept any donations from their one-time star benefactor or his estate.

Because she wasn't saying anything, he continued. 'Are you enjoying camp?' he asked, focusing closely on Jane.

'Yes,' she said. 'I come every year.'

'Oh, that's great,' Jeffrey said. 'I love to hear from students about whether they are enjoying themselves, which classes are their favourite, how we can improve – that kind of thing.'

Jane considered this, and again paused for a long while. 'I'm a singer,' was the only thing she could think to say in response.

'Ah.' Jeffrey became very animated. 'I would have guessed you were a dancer, but I'm so pleased you're a singer. I love music.'

Twenty-eight years later, at Ghislaine Maxwell's trial, witnesses would say this again and again: 'Jeffrey loved music.' They called him an 'audiophile' – a word that implied respectability and taste. One witness was tasked with setting up cinema-grade sound systems in the massage rooms in every one of his homes.

'Do you like your singing class?' he asked.

'Yes, they're great,' Jane said, relaxing slightly.

The woman spoke now, and Jane realised she had forgotten she was there.

'Where do you live, Jane?'

'I live in Palm Beach, Florida,' Jane replied.

'Oh!' Jeffrey became animated again. 'We live there, too. What a coincidence!'

They were both smiling at her now.

'What are your parents' names, Jane?'

A pause. A heartbeat. A flutter.

'My father just died. My mother's name is Janet.'

Jeffrey reached out a hand and touched her wrist lightly, saying, 'I'm so sorry, Jane.'

She looked away, self-conscious. 'Thank you,' she said in a small voice.

'What was your father's name?' he asked, and Jane told him. 'Ah, I think we might know him.' He turned to the woman: 'Do we know him?'

'I think we might.' She nods slowly. 'It's a small town,' she says, winking at Jane almost imperceptibly.

'That makes sense,' Jane said. 'He was in the music scene.'

The woman perks up now. 'Oh, was he?' she said.

'He was a composer.' The *was* still stings, and the woman can tell.

'When did he die?' she said gently.

'In the fall,' Jane said. 'End of October.'

'How did he die, Jane?' It was Jeffrey this time.

'Leukaemia.'

'How dreadful,' the woman says, and Jane notes the very British phrasing.

'And what does your mother do for work?' Jeffrey again.

'She doesn't work really.'

'That must be hard now, with your dad gone.'

Jane nodded but said nothing.

'Well, look,' Jeffrey said then. 'We'd love to hear you sing and maybe offer you a scholarship. Would you and your mother like to come around to our house for tea when you get home?'

Jane nodded and said, 'Yes, thank you.'

'Write her number down on this pad,' Jeffrey said, and Jane etched out the digits of the landline of the friend's house they were staying in until they got back on their feet.

Her father's studio had cut off his health insurance when he got ill without them knowing, and he deteriorated so suddenly and required so much hospital care that they were left with almost nothing. 'Jane?' Jeffrey was asking, and she realised she had drifted off again, thinking about her dad. Jane snapped her eyes up to lock with Jeffrey's and passed the pad back to him with the number written on it.

They began to leave, and as they were about to say their good-byes Jane realised she didn't know the woman's name. Again, as though reading her mind, the woman held out a long, fragile-looking hand polished pink and said, 'I'm Ghislaine.' Jane shook both of their hands and said thank you, and the couple and the dog walked back into the lodge together.

CHAPTER 6

New York City, 2021

'You consider yourself an actor?' Laura Menninger asks Jane on cross-examination.

'Yes,' Jane responds.

'An actor plays the role of a fictional character?'

'Yes.'

'An actor endeavours to effectively communicate the character they are playing to an audience?'

'Yes.'

It is only now that it dawns on me what Menninger is suggesting – that Jane is playing a fictional role for the jury, telling them a fictional abuse story.

'Using their voice, body, actions, right?'

'Yes.'

'An actor takes lines borrowed from a writer and uses those lines to convincingly portray someone else in front of an audience, correct?'

'Yes.'

Jane is visibly anxious as she fields this accusation from Ghislaine Maxwell's lawyer: the suggestion that because she is an actor who plays fictional roles for a living the jury should mistrust her, should discount the hours of testimony she has just given about the worst things that have ever happened to her.

I've spent a lot of time in court as a journalist, and cross-examination tactics shouldn't shock me. But this exchange leaves me breathless, angry. How dare they?

For hours, Laura Menninger stands and attacks Jane's credibility in any way she can. She presents Jane with a copy of her application for Interlochen Arts Camp in 1994, the year Jane was 14. She directs Jane's attention to the page on which the application asks if she would like to apply for financial aid, to which Jane had responded 'no'.

'You checked "no", correct?'

'Correct.'

Menninger then shows Jane her applications for Interlochen for the following two years, 1995 and 1996, and again asks her to turn to the financial aid page.

'You checked "no", correct?'

'Correct,' Jane says, and explains that her mother borrowed money from her aunt and uncle to send the children to camp. Jane is shifting uncomfortably, feeling the venom in Menninger's voice as she tries to land this gotcha moment, when she tries to convey to the jury that Jane has lied about the fact that she and her family were struggling financially after her father's death.

I look over at the jury to see if this has had the intended effect, has made them doubt Jane, has made them think to themselves: *If she lied about that, what else would she lie about?*

Most of the jurors seem unfazed; only two are frowning. But this is just the beginning of what will be a truly brutal five hours of exactly this: nit-picking questions intended to add up to a lack of credibility – death by a thousand paper cuts.

Menninger asks Jane to flip to another section of the Interlochen application, in which one of Jane's teachers has written her a glowing recommendation about her talent and commitment and love of the arts. But the letter also mentions Jane's brothers and says the three come from a 'stable and loving' family.

'That says "stable and loving family", correct?'

'Yes.'

Menninger pauses as she hopes the jury recalls Jane's own testimony about her mother, about their difficult relationship, thinking to themselves that this is an inconsistency in Jane's account of her own life.

Jane herself has told the jury that she grew up in a home in which it was absolutely not permissible to speak about domestic tensions to those outside of the family. In that context, it seems obvious that a teacher at Jane's school would not know the things she was afraid to speak about. Given even a tiny bit of thought, then, this line of attack falls apart. But no matter; that's not what cross-examination in our system is designed for.

'You testified yesterday on direct examination that you were sitting with friends at a picnic table, and a tall, thin woman approached you with a dog. And you chitchatted with her, and then a man came and joined her, right?'

'Right.'

'You recalled several details about that incident in 1994, right?'

'Yes.'

With a smirk on her face, Menninger goes in for the kill: 'But when you spoke to a reporter in 2018 you only mentioned Epstein being there that day, didn't you?'

'I don't recall,' Jane says.

Menninger sounds excited now, as she turns to the first time Jane spoke to the FBI about her abuse, in 2019.

'And what you told the government on that day with your attorneys there is that Ghislaine walked by with her dog, correct?'

'I don't recall my exact words,' Jane says.

I feel myself frowning and looking at the other reporters with whom I share the courtroom's long wooden bench. I know that Menninger is trying to draw attention to perceived inconsistencies in this story, but to me these memories seem remarkably consistent.

Jane is being asked to recall a 28-year-old scene and, crucially, one that at the time she did not know would herald the beginning of a new and traumatic era of her life. There is no reason why 14-year-old Jane would have known, on that summer day in

1994, that this memory would become important. To her teenage self, the memory was mundane. And yet, the key details of the memory remain the same in each telling: the setting, the couple, the dog. But Menninger is trying to make it seem as though a detail as small as whether Ghislaine walked past with the dog, or approached her with the dog, fractures the credibility of this memory.

As the judge adjourns the courtroom for the morning break, I am still thinking about this.

'Yikes,' a fellow reporter says to me. 'That's pretty damning, the thing about the dog. That really does make it seem like a lie.' I am baffled.

Later in the cross-examination, something happens that gets all of us in the press gallery talking. It seems – at first glance – that Laura Menninger has hit on some more serious inconsistencies in Jane's story.

'Yesterday you testified that for the first few months when you spent time with Jeffrey Epstein in Palm Beach, you were there by yourself,' Menninger said.

'By myself as in without my mother,' Jane replied.

'And then you clarified that your mother did not go back to his house with you for meetings because she was "not invited". That was your testimony yesterday, correct?' Menninger hit back.

'Correct,' Jane said.

'That is not what you told the government when you met with them in September of 2019, is it?' Menninger quipped.

'I don't know,' Jane says meekly.

'What you told the government in September of 2019, including Ms Moe, is: "In the beginning, I would be with my mother and brothers,"' Menninger presses her.

'I don't recall that,' Jane says.

'What you said to Ms Moe and the agents was, "In the beginning, I would be with my mother and brothers at Epstein's house," correct?' Menninger says again.

'I don't recall.'

The atmosphere in the courtroom is tense. It feels unnerving to hear Jane saying, 'I don't recall,' over and over again. But I wonder to myself: *Where is Menninger quoting this from?* No interview notes or transcripts from any of Jane's interviews with the FBI have been entered into evidence, and Menninger hasn't once moved to admit into evidence the document she is now reading from.

Casting my mind back to my advanced criminal law classes, I find the answer. Menninger is using these documents as 'impeachable material'. This rule allows lawyers to rely on documents that are not in evidence if they are being used for impeachment purposes – that is, to contradict a witness's testimony.

It transpires later that what Menninger is holding are handwritten notes from various conversations between Jane and FBI agents. These cannot be introduced into evidence because they are hearsay – unless the person who wrote them comes to court to verify them. But again, hearsay documents are allowed to be used to impeach witnesses in cross-examination.

The problem is that Jane doesn't find out until later that these are just scrawled, handwritten notes from her conversations with the FBI – they are not a transcript or an exact record. Also, Jane has never seen these interview notes before – she didn't write them. So she doesn't know how accurate they are, or who wrote them, or how long after the interview they were written. But during cross-examination, we don't yet know this.

The reporter next to me shuffles in his seat.

'This really isn't good,' he says. 'That's way too many inconsistencies.'

CHAPTER 7

West Palm Beach, 1994

One evening in late 1994, when Jane had recently begun eighth grade, she arrived home from school to find her mother waiting for her in the pool house they were staying in. She and her mother and two brothers shared two double beds between them in a friend's cabana, just until they could pay off her father's health insurance bill.

'Someone called today,' her mother said. 'Someone you met at camp.'

Camp was only four weeks previously, but life felt dull and slow that summer, so already it seemed far away; Jane just stared at her mother blankly.

'Someone from an office called – they said they were calling from the office of Jeffrey Epstein?'

'Ah, yes,' Jane said.

'They said he saw you in your final performance and wants us both to come over for tea,' her mother said, looking excited.

Thirty minutes later, a black town car pulled up outside the house that Jane and her family were staying at. The driver, who would identify himself decades later, at trial, as a man named Juan Alessi, picked up Jane and her mother and drove them to a mansion on El Brillo Way – known in Palm Beach as 'billionaire's way'. Alessi turned the car into a driveway in front of a vast white house with a tall white fence. He walked them through the front door into a towering lobby with sickly pink carpets and blue walls. Jane felt intimidated. Her mother was impressed.

As they walked through the house, Jane noticed that it was filled with photographs, sculptures and works of art. She noticed photographs of very well-known people. She noticed images of naked women all over the walls. And animals. Lots of paintings of creepy-looking animals.

They were walked through to an office area that opened onto a glistening pool. Jeffrey was on the phone, standing over a desk covered in paper and notebooks. When he hung up a few moments later he smiled that big, broad smile at Jane's mother, shook her hand and introduced himself. He led them out towards the pool, where a long table had been prepared, full of sandwiches and croissants and tea and fruit, and he told them to help themselves. The door to a nearby pool house opened and the woman who had introduced herself as 'Ghislaine' appeared, all legs and arms and eyes. She introduced herself to Jane's mother, and Jane could see that her mother was impressed by the accent, just as Jane had been.

The four sat around the table for about 30 minutes, Jane would later estimate at trial. They talked about Jane's interests, her singing, her school.

As the conversation petered out, Jeffrey turned to Jane's mother and said: 'Well, I am – I'm very impressed with your daughter and, you know, would love to see her sing next time.' Jane's mother smiled, thrilled, and said, 'Thank you, Mr Epstein.'

Juan Alessi then came around to take Jane and her mother back to the car to drive them home. This time, they went out through a side exit by the pool house – the room in which, a few weeks later, after three or four more of these visits for tea, Jeffrey Epstein would sexually abuse Jane for the first time.

Jane's mother chatted happily to Juan Alessi up ahead of Jane as they walked to the car, while Jane was inside her own head, contemplative. She heard Jeffrey whisper her name behind her. She turned around, and he placed a thick stack of hundred-dollar bills in her hand and closed her fist around them. She tried to shake her head, pushed her hand back towards him, but he held his hand up in front of her face as if to shush her. 'It's for your mother,' he said. 'I know she's been having a hard time with money since your father died. I just want to help.'

After that day, Jane started visiting Epstein's Palm Beach mansion once or twice a week. She would get a call from either Ghislaine Maxwell or one of Jeffrey Epstein's assistants to arrange for her to visit the house. Epstein's house manager Juan Alessi would then drive to Jane's house and collect her.

When recalling these months almost 30 years later, Jane would say, 'We would spend time at the house and sort of chitchat ... or eat in the kitchen or hang out by the pool, sometimes going to the movies. Casual stuff.'

Jane started hearing names she recognised from Jeffrey and Ghislaine. They mentioned Donald Trump and Bill Clinton. They would always give the full names of the people who were calling them, and Jane knew instinctively that the names were supposed to mean something to her. That these were names of important people, and that this made Jeffrey and Ghislaine important, too. She was intimidated and tried to keep up with all the names she heard.

One day, Jane went out to the pool and found Ghislaine sunbathing with a group of other women. All the women, including Ghislaine, were topless. Some were completely naked.

On another day during those first few months, Ghislaine took Jane aside.

'I want to hear about your life,' she said. 'How is school going?'

Jane saw Ghislaine as something like an older sister at this time, because she guessed that Ghislaine was a similar age to her oldest sibling, who was 27 in 1994. Ghislaine would tease her like an older sister, but also looked out for her.

'It's going well,' Jane replied, excited to have Ghislaine's full attention.

'Do you have any boyfriends?'

This question seemed strange to Jane, but she answered.

'No, not yet,' she said.

'And why is that?' Ghislaine asked.

'There's just no one I like,' Jane said.

'Well, remember when you do that once you fuck them, you can always fuck them again because they're grandfathered in,' Ghislaine said.

Jane giggled but felt something prickle under her skin, taken aback by the left turn this conversation had taken. She didn't know what 'grandfathered' meant. The phrase, which has its origins in racialised legal language, is slang for the idea that once a sexual relationship with another person is entered into, the sexual element of that relationship has been consented to indefinitely. Existing expectations remain in place even once a situation has changed.

Ghislaine and Jeffrey took Jane shopping for the first time. They bought her a cashmere sweater, some blouses, some trousers and a pair of loafers.

As the shopping trip was winding down, Jeffrey suggested they all go to Victoria's Secret.

Jane was nervous entering the store because, at 14, she didn't yet wear lingerie, and the outfits on the mannequins intimidated her. She worried that Jeffrey would want to buy her something very grown-up, but in the end, he didn't. He led her towards a rack of very plain, white cotton briefs. The kind you would wear 'you know, when you're ... younger', she would later recall him saying.

One afternoon after school, back in his Palm Beach mansion, Jeffrey told Jane he wanted to talk to her about her career.

'You really need to focus,' Jeffrey said, almost chiding her. 'You have to decide exactly what you want to be.'

Jane sat and listened, waiting for him to continue.

'You can't be a generalist in this business,' he said. 'You have to choose: do you want to be an opera singer? An actress? A model?'

'I … I'm not sure,' Jane said, but Jeffrey cut across her.

'Well, you know, I know everybody. I know all the agents. I know all the photographers. I know the owner of Victoria's Secret. So I can make things happen, but you just have to be ready for it. You have to be ready.'

Jane looked up at him with grateful eyes, was trying to figure out what to say next, when Jeffrey, out of nowhere, grabbed her hand.

'Follow me,' he said.

She got up shyly and Jeffrey led her into his pool house. When they walked through the glass doors, Jeffrey led her to a futon couch on the left-hand side of the room. He drew her close to him, pulled down his tracksuit pants and started masturbating. He finished, went to the bathroom, cleaned himself up and acted like nothing had happened.

Decades later, Jane would describe being 'frozen in fear' in this moment.

'I had never seen a penis before,' she told the jury.

When asked at trial whether she told anyone about what happened in the pool house that day, Jane said no.

'Why not?' the prosecutor asked.

'Because I was terrified and felt gross and I felt ashamed.'

'After the incident that you just described, did you continue spending time with Maxwell and Epstein in Palm Beach?' the prosecutor continued.

'Yes.'

It was not long after that day in the pool house when the strange, abrupt 'follow me' command was issued for the second time. This time, Jane was sitting in the living room of the Palm Beach house with both Jeffrey and Ghislaine, talking about school. In an almost synchronised move, the pair got up together and Jeffrey said, 'Follow me.' The two adults led her up the winding staircase towards Jeffrey's bedroom.

They ushered Jane towards Jeffrey's imposing king-sized bed

and started taking each other's clothes off. They were fondling each other and giggling, with Jane just standing there, looking on.

'Take your top off,' Jeffrey asked Jane. He and Ghislaine touched Jane. Then, just like in the pool house, Jeffrey started masturbating, and a few moments later, it was over.

'I just want to be clear about this,' prosecutors would ask Jane at trial. 'For the incident that you just described, when you were alone in a room with Epstein and Maxwell, how old were you when that happened for the first time?'

'Fourteen.'

A few weeks later, Ghislaine told Jane that she would have to learn how to massage Jeffrey. 'I'll teach you,' she said.

Ghislaine taught Jane that Jeffrey liked to be massaged hard – on his shoulders, his feet and his head. He also liked his masseuses to twist his nipples hard, Jane remembers. In Jeffrey's massage room, which was off the master bedroom, Ghislaine showed Jane how Jeffrey liked to touch her breasts while being massaged, and, eventually, she showed Jane how to touch Jeffrey's penis. Ghislaine behaved very casually during these incidents, Jane would recall later, like it was 'no big deal'.

'It made me feel confused because that did not feel normal to me; I'd never seen anything like this or felt any of this, and it was very embarrassing. You know, it's all these mixed emotions. When you're 14, you have no idea what's going on,' Jane would say, decades later.

One day, during a massage, Jeffrey began touching Jane's vagina. Later, he introduced sex toys into his massages with her. He pulled out vibrators of all different sizes, and used back massages on her so hard that she remembers being in pain.

During some of the massages, Ghislaine would also touch Jane's breasts. Eventually, these massages were taking place every single time Jane visited the Palm Beach mansion.

Soon after that, Jane experienced a group sexual massage for the first time. There were a group of other adults spending time at the Palm Beach house – chatting, eating – and again, very abruptly, Jeffrey said, 'Follow me,' and led the group to the massage room.

Once in the room, the adults all started taking their clothes off and touching each other. Jane was asked to strip down to her underwear.

These group sessions became more and more frequent in the year that Jane was 15. She would watch a rotating group of adults perform sex acts on each other and on Jeffrey.

Between 1994 and 1996 – the years when Jane was 14, 15 and 16 – these episodes of sexual abuse happened around once a fortnight.

———

The first time Jane flew to New York City on Jeffrey's private plane, she was 14 years old. Jeffrey told her that he wanted her to come with him to stay in his Manhattan mansion, and someone from his office called Jane's home phone number to arrange the trip.

The house seemed more like a building to Jane than someone's home. It had eight storeys, an elevator and two security doors. It was made of stone and old wood, Jane noticed the first time she visited. It felt dark and foreboding, with fabric wallpaper and red curtains. The house was full of statues and paintings that made Jane uncomfortable, much like the Palm Beach house, but everything here felt darker and more sinister. There were more paintings of naked women, of orgies, but Jane was used to that by now.

On that day, Jeffrey led Jane to what would become her bedroom in the house: a large guest bedroom on the eighth floor, right at the top, overlooking Manhattan. But that wasn't where Jane spent most of her time in that New York house. This house, just like Palm Beach, had a massage room close to Jeffrey's bedroom.

The massage room in the New York house felt dark and foreboding, Jane would say years later at trial. It included an expensive stereo system; Jeffrey was an *audiophile*.

Not long after Jane arrived in Manhattan that first time, the sexual abuse began again.

Jeffrey began putting his fingers inside Jane, asking her to straddle his face, and would use his vibrators on her. He asked her to pull on his nipples while he came.

When Jane was 15, Jeffrey and Ghislaine flew her to New Mexico for the first time. Again, someone from Jeffrey's office called her home to make the travel arrangements, and soon Jane was being driven to Epstein's private plane to make the journey to his mansion, Zorro Ranch.

As they drove towards the ranch from the airport hangar, a looming T-shaped wooden archway arose out of the dust, signalling the entrance to the estate. The sky was big and wide and imposing. Moments later, an enormous building structure came into view. Pale pink with white trimmings and a lavender entryway, the home – if you could call it that – looked like it could house countless bedrooms.

Jeffrey and Ghislaine led Jane to a large double bedroom, which, over the next few years, would become hers. She unpacked and sat on the bed, staring out of her large window onto the unfolding expanse of the property.

Then someone – Jane doesn't remember who – came to knock on her door.

'Jeffrey would like to see you.'

Jane's heart paused, sank into her stomach. She knew what this meant. She didn't want to go.

When she arrived timidly at Jeffrey's massage room, the script began to play out again, until she could return to her room.

At the end of the weekend, Jane was looking forward to flying home to Palm Beach and going back to school on Monday. But the private jet wasn't flying back for another few days, so

Ghislaine and Jeffrey told Jane that she would have to catch a regular commercial flight.

Jane arrived at the airport relieved to be leaving, but when she showed her ticket to the desk assistant, the woman asked her for ID. Jane didn't have any. She didn't have her learner's driving licence yet, because she was only 15.

'I'm sorry, but you can't get on the flight without showing some ID,' the woman said, kindly but firmly.

Jane felt panic rising in her throat, unsure of what to do, feeling alone and suddenly very vulnerable. She called Ghislaine, her voice pitched high, afraid.

'Don't worry,' Ghislaine said. 'I'll take care of it. Let me make a call.'

And before she knew it, Jane was on the flight, hurtling towards Palm Beach and home.

Jane missed her father, but she knew her mother well enough to know that she wasn't allowed to speak about that at home. In her house, emotional vulnerability was seen as shameful and not tolerated. Her brothers knew this, too, and so no one spoke about the gaping hole in their home where their father had once been. Her mother was always too preoccupied with appearances, Jane would say, decades later.

'Well, I grew up with a mother who didn't allow us to talk about our feelings because that was a sign of weakness. So grieving would be a part of that because she was very concerned with what we looked like, and how you should always sort of put a pretty face on,' she said. 'So we really didn't discuss those kinds of things at home and weren't allowed to discuss it with anyone else. So, being a kid and losing your dad and not being allowed to talk about it, not having anyone to talk to about it, it was really difficult.'

When Jane and her mother did speak during those years, it was often about how thrilled Jane's mother was with the attention she was receiving from Ghislaine and Jeffrey.

'My mother seemed very impressed and enamoured with ... the wealth, the affluence. She thought they seemed very generous, and they must think I'm special and that I should be grateful for the attention that I received.'

And the attention did make Jane feel special, at first. She didn't have anyone at home who was asking about how she was doing in school, about what she wanted to do with her life, about her friends. Jeffrey and Ghislaine were interested in her when nobody else was.

When asked, decades later at trial, why she didn't tell her mother about the abuse while it was happening, Jane said: 'Because I felt very ashamed. I felt very disgusted. I was confused; I didn't know if it was my fault, and my mother and I did not have that kind of a relationship ... I was raised in a household where you were sort of spoken to, and you [didn't] speak unless you're spoken to, and I [was] afraid that I would be in trouble.'

During those years, just after her father died and while she was being abused by Epstein, Jane started thinking about hurting herself. She felt hopeless, alone. Her mother was struggling with manic depression and was largely absent.

Even before meeting Epstein, Jane had felt isolated from her family and her peers in the wake of her father's death and its disastrous financial consequences for her now single-mother household. As you'll hear more about in this book, the prosecution will argue that Jeffrey was an expert at finding girls in this position. Girls who were already suffering or vulnerable, facing a chasm of unmet needs. Before the abuse started, in seventh grade, Jane's high-school guidance counsellor noticed that something might be wrong and requested a meeting with her.

'Have you had any grief counselling?' the woman asked the then 13-year-old Jane, referring to the recent death of her father.

'No,' Jane replied.

'And how are things at home?'

'I feel incredibly sad,' Jane said. 'My mom is so unavailable – she's not very supportive and I feel like I have no one to talk to.'

'Well,' the counsellor said kindly, 'now you have me. If you ever need a place to go, just come to my office and we'll talk.'

Jane left the session feeling less alone, but the feeling didn't last. Unfortunately, the counsellor called Jane's mother – who was furious.

Jane came home from school one day not long after that first session to find her mother fuming. The counsellor had called the house to say that she was worried about Jane, and explained that Jane had spoken in counselling about how she was feeling about her father's death.

'How dare you talk about our family and our private lives with other people!' her mother yelled. 'How *dare* you! It is an *embarrassment* to talk to other people about your feelings and about what's going on at home,' she went on, getting angrier and angrier, her voice reaching a scream.

In one swift movement, she stepped towards Jane's small frame and slapped her across the face.

It was also her mother who, years later, when Jane was 19 and had landed her first big modelling job, would ask her to send a copy of her first professional headshot to Jeffrey to thank him for everything he'd done to help her. On the back of the photo, Jane wrote: *Thanks for rocking my world.*

At 14, however, Jane was still being abused by Epstein almost every time she visited his house. Sometimes – the majority of the time – it would be just her and Jeffrey. Other times it would be her, Jeffrey and a group of other adult women. Sometimes it would be her, Jeffrey and Ghislaine.

But the memories blur together in her mind now, stretching and yawning into one another, making it almost impossible for her to distinguish between one day and the next, between one group session and another. That's what the brain does when something traumatic becomes routine; it finds it more and more difficult to find the edges of each memory, to split them up. Her teenaged brain did not know that she would be asked, nearly 30 years later, to do just that. *How many times? How many people? How often? How long?*

'It all started to seem the same after a while,' she said on the stand. 'You just become numb to it.'

When Jane was 17, Epstein offered to pay for her to attend the Professional Children's School in New York City – a top-end school for aspiring actors and models – as part of his offer to help her with her career. Jane accepted, and in 1999, she left Palm Beach for New York – where Jeffrey would also pay for her mother to live – to start her senior year of high school at the Professional Children's School.

But the abuse didn't stop. Ghislaine and Jeffrey, who both spent a lot of time in their respective New York mansions, continued to call on Jane throughout 1999. Jane was aware this whole time that Epstein was paying for her life in New York and felt she had no choice but to comply.

In October of 1999, Jane graduated high school and moved to Los Angeles to pursue her dream of becoming an actor. She achieved that dream, quickly getting a job on a major soap opera. But still the abuse didn't end. Jeffrey continued to demand that she travel on his private jet with him and continued to sexually abuse her.

It wasn't until the end of 2002 – eight years after the nightmare began – that Jane was able to cut off contact with Jeffrey Epstein.

She had met someone and fallen in love, and her new partner wasn't comfortable with how frequently she was speaking to Epstein. Their relationship developed quickly, and soon they were engaged. But her fiancé kept asking her, *Who is this person whose calls you feel you must drop everything to take?*

'He's my godfather,' she told him.

'Okay,' her fiancé said. 'Well, just text him and tell him you'll call him back.'

'It doesn't work that way,' Jane said.

Later in the argument, Jane's fiancé insisted that she not call him back at all.

Jane complied, but not because she felt safe cutting Jeffrey off – she knew there would be consequences. She did so because she was also afraid of what would happen if she didn't obey her fiancé, who, she said, had an abusive personality himself.

Jane did not go into this in her testimony, so I cannot give you any more details about the nature of this relationship. But it's worth noting, as Jane herself does – you'll soon hear her comment about a broken compass – that neurologically, abuse victims are more likely to be attracted to relationships that repeat the patterns of coercive control and abuse.

When Jane stopped calling Jeffrey back, the calls came thicker and faster than ever. He left voicemail after voicemail on Jane's phone.

'Jane, you need to call me back.'

'Jane, I'm coming to LA and I want to see you. Call me back.'

But Jane didn't answer, afraid of losing her new love if she did. The messages became more and more agitated.

'Jane, you are being very ungrateful. Don't ever forget everything I've done for you.'

'Jane, remember that your mother is still living in a New York City apartment that *I* pay for.'

But Jane never did call back. She never spoke to Jeffrey Epstein again. She escaped the relationship with her fiancé, too, and never married him. But trauma evolves; it bleeds. The nightmare doesn't end here.

During the trial, Jane's testimony would be corroborated by evidence that you'll need to keep in mind, so I'll explain it here: the flight logs. The prosecution called a man named David Rodgers to the stand, a pilot of Epstein's private planes for many years, in order to introduce into evidence Rodgers' personal flight logs. (According to the hearsay rule, you cannot admit a document into evidence unless the author of that document comes to court and testifies that they authored it and that it is true and accurate.)

Rodgers' flight logs are comprehensive and detailed. In particular, the prosecution argued, they placed Jane on Epstein's private plane in 1994 – when she was 16 years old. He told the court he remembered seeing her, and writing her name in the logbook, around four times altogether. In some of those flights, she is listed as being accompanied by Epstein or Maxwell or both, and these flight records line up with the dates that Jane recalls travelling with the pair. The flight logs also confirmed that Rodgers flew Epstein and/or Maxwell to the nearest airport to Interlochen Arts Camp.

Another pilot, Larry Visoski, walked into court wearing a pair of velvet shoes very similar to those owned by Jeffrey Epstein. Someone next to me in the press gallery notices. They were a gift from Jeffrey, she says, although I cannot verify this. If true, a very interesting choice of footwear – especially as the first witness for the prosecution. In the place that Epstein's shoes had the initials 'JE', Visoski's shoes had the initials 'LV', in the same font.

Visoski told the jury that he remembered many famous people on his flights with Jeffrey, including Bill Clinton. He also remembers Prince Andrew, who later famously settled a lawsuit brought by another victim, Virginia Giuffre for $12 million. Visoski also told the jury he remembers flying Donald Trump, Senator John Glenn and Senator George Mitchell.

CHAPTER 8

New York City, 2021

Laura Menninger's cross-examination of Jane is getting nastier and nastier.

Towards the end of it, she asks Jane a series of questions about the fact that she sent Epstein that photo of herself years after the abuse, saying, *Thanks for rocking my world*. This would also come up in Kate's testimony, another of Epstein's victims; the defence would try to use the fact that she stayed in contact with Jeffrey after her abuse to discredit her story and argue that she made it all up in hindsight for a paycheque.

When we bustle out of the courtroom, a male reporter who was in one of the overflow rooms mentions this to me.

'I just can't understand why you would stay in touch with an abuser,' he said. 'It doesn't look good – and it doesn't make sense.'

Once again, I am confronted with my own naivety about how the world really views the sexual abuse of vulnerable victims; how little the public actually understands grooming. I think again about my mentor, about the messages we exchanged years after his abuse had ended.

'It's not that simple', I say, 'when you are being abused by someone you trusted; someone you love. Someone you're attached to,' I say. 'Jeffrey looked after those girls, and so they ended up feeling confused about how the generosity and the abuse go hand in hand. That's how grooming works.'

'I don't buy it,' he says.

'I stayed in touch with my abuser via Facebook comments and messages up until about five years ago,' I say. 'Because I wanted to believe there were good parts, that he really did care about me.' After a pause, I say: 'I can show you the messages if you want. It doesn't mean it didn't happen.'

CHAPTER 9

New York City, 2021

It is 2 December 2021. I arrive at the press line at around 3am. I can see from my photos of that day that this was one of the most beautiful sunrises we got during the whole trial. An image I snapped at about 6am shows bright oranges and yellows bleeding into one another atop the Manhattan skyline. We call this 'the witching hour' – because, for some reason, the weather gets colder as the night clears and the sun rises.

'The government calls Dr Lisa Rocchio,' Alison Moe says from the prosecution table.

'Dr Lisa Rocchio may come forward,' Judge Nathan says.

In the press gallery, we collectively turn our heads as she walks past us. I am sitting on the far-right end of one of the benches, so she passes within a few inches of me.

Dr Rocchio walks confidently, as though she has done this before. She is dressed impeccably, in a fitted black skirt-suit, white blazer and black high heels. Her mousy brown hair is cut to her shoulders and styled in a neat long bob.

When she reaches the Perspex witness box, Dr Rocchio removes her black face mask.

As usual, Moe asks her to state and spell her name for the record, and then asks her to state her qualifications and professional background.

'I am a clinical and forensic psychologist,' Dr Rocchio says assuredly. 'I have 30 years' experience treating patients with traumatic stress,' she explains.

'And can you explain to the jury what traumatic stress is?' Moe asks kindly.

'Traumatic stress is the result of any event that overwhelms our ability to cope, so that includes exposure to actual or threatened death or sexual violence.'

As she speaks, Ghislaine's body moves. Since my very first hour sitting in a room with her, she has barely moved a muscle while sitting and listening to testimony. Throughout Jane's story, she did not flinch. But now she does.

Ghislaine moves her hand to her brow and buries her forehead in it. She is taking furious notes as Dr Rocchio is speaking.

'I also have 30 years' experience treating victims of child sexual assault,' the doctor is saying. 'Child sexual assault refers to any attempted or actual sexual contact with someone under the age of 18. It does not have to necessarily be physical contact,' she says.

I cast my eyes over to the jury box. Fairly still until this point, there is movement there now. Three jurors, including the woman I would later discover to be the foreperson, begin taking notes.

'My work also focuses on women who are chronically suicidal or self-injurious,' Dr Rocchio is saying, and the jurors continue taking notes. 'Most of these women have a history of childhood trauma.'

'Can you tell us what the term "delayed disclosure" means in the context of childhood sexual abuse?' Moe asks.

'Delayed disclosure is the term we use to refer to the fact that it is very, very uncommon for children to disclose their abuse until adulthood; it is not at all common to disclose right away,' she says. 'There are external and internal barriers that make it very unlikely that children will come forward until much later,' she adds. 'External factors include fear of getting into trouble, fear of judgement from others, fear that the perpetrator will get into trouble, and a general sense of loyalty to the perpetrator.

'Internal factors', she goes on, 'include intense feelings of self-blame, confusion and shame ... The younger someone is when the abuse happens, the more likely it is that they will delay coming forward ... It is *very common*' – Dr Rocchio pauses for emphasis here – 'to have a *significant* disclosure delay.'

Moe then asks something that stays with me for months.

'When a victim does decide to make a disclosure, how would you expect that to happen?' she asks.

'Victims are most likely to make the first disclosure to a peer, often their first romantic or physically intimate partners,' Dr Rocchio says. 'They are very unlikely to first report the abuse to law enforcement; in fact, law enforcement are the least likely group to be told about the abuse in the first instance.'

I look over at Ghislaine again, who has her notebook open and is writing something down.

'In your clinical practice,' Moe is asking now, 'how do victims usually speak about their abuse?'

'It's a slow process that builds over time.' Dr Rocchio is speaking slowly now, looking right at the jury, knowing that this point is absolutely crucial. 'Victims usually start by disclosing the general gist of the abuse but usually can only speak about it in detail over time ... Disclosure only happens when the victim starts to feel safe,' she explains. Every member of the jury is looking right at her. 'So, for example, the victim may begin to tell someone the story but then may quickly shut down if they are blamed by the person they've chosen to disclose to.'

'Can you explain which factors might contribute to long delays in disclosure?'

'Things like the closer the relationship between the perpetrator and victim, the longer the abuse has gone on—'

'Objection.' Bobbi Sternheim stands up. 'Asked and answered.'

'Sustained,' Judge Nathan says. 'Move on.'

'Can you tell us a bit more about how the relationship of trust factors into childhood sexual abuse?'

'Objection,' Sternheim says again.

'Overruled.'

'Trust is absolutely central,' Dr Rocchio says. 'The more they trusted the perpetrator, the more betrayal they feel, and the more they will struggle to understand what really happened.'

The jury stands up and shuffles out. Judge Nathan asks: 'Matters to take up?' Judge Nathan says these four words in exactly the same tone every time the jury leaves the room. It is an invitation for the lawyers to raise legal questions that the jury are not allowed to hear.

'Yes, your honour,' Alison Moe says, beginning an exchange that will define much of the trial. 'We believe that defence counsel plans to cross-examine Dr Rocchio on topics that were not brought up during direct examination, and we just wanted to register an objection to that.'

'What do they intend to raise?' Judge Nathan asks.

'We believe they intend to ask Dr Rocchio about topics such as suggestive memory, the effect of alcohol and drug addiction on memory and on disclosure, and whether there are potential other reasons for delayed disclosure.' What this means is that the prosecution suspects the defence of foul play in cross-examination – for example asking about whether drug use affects memory, which is outside her field of expertise and is merely being used as a tool to remind the jury that the victims are drug addicts.

'Well, it might be within the scope to ask about other reasons for delayed disclosure, but you have to have her explain her expert undisclosed opinions,' Judge Nathan says carefully, thinking as she speaks. What she means by this is that if she raises any concepts in cross-examination that have not already come up – as Moe is worried she will – then the defence will have to make sure she explains the as-yet-undiscussed concepts so that they don't get confused.

'We expect they will try and ask very leading questions during cross-examination,' Moe says.

'Well,' Laura Menninger says, 'these are very complicated topics.'

'I think we can handle it,' quips Judge Nathan.

At the defence table, Ghislaine shakes her head and rubs her brow as the courtroom adjourns for a break.

———————

In her black heels, Dr Rocchio re-enters the courtroom ten minutes later and Jeffrey Pagliuca shuffles to the lectern, de-masking as he arrives there.

'You are here as a blind expert – that means that you haven't performed an evaluation of the people involved in this case, have you?'

'No, I have not,' Dr Rocchio says.

'So you are not offering any opinions about what happened in this case, are you?'

'No.'

'You are not a neuropsychologist, are you?'

'No.'

'Is a person's memory a factor in delayed disclosure?' he asks pointedly.

'It can be,' she says.

'There are some things that can prevent you from being able to properly retrieve a memory, is that right?'

'Objection.' Alison Moe stands up.

'Sustained,' Judge Nathan says immediately, making clear that this question crosses the line they had discussed during the break.

'Are there other factors that might affect a person's ability to disclose abuse?'

'Objection.'

'Sustained.'

'Can alcohol and drug addiction affect a person's ability to remember or disclose abuse?'

'Objection.' Alison Moe is on her feet now.

'Sustained.'

'Are you familiar with the concept of confabulation?' Pagliuca asks, finally changing tack.

'Yes,' Dr Rocchio says hesitantly. 'I believe that's when the brain fills in gaps in a memory to get an entire picture.'

'So these memories might not be accurate?' Pagliuca tries again.

'Objection.'

'Sustained.'

'Are you familiar with the concept of the secondary gain that someone might receive as a result of disclosing abuse?'

'Object—'

Judge Nathan says 'sustained' before Moe has even finished the word.

'Are you familiar with the concept of *malingering*?' He lingers on the word.

'Objection.'

'Sustained.'

'Is it true that malingering refers to the fabrication of symptoms for financial gain?'

'Objection.'

'Sustained.' Judge Nathan is angry now.

———

As my three press colleagues and I leave the courtroom, I can only think about one thing – something Dr Rocchio said: *Victims are most likely to make the first disclosure to a peer, often their first romantic or physically intimate partners.* In the course of her hours-long testimony, only some of which I've recounted here, she made this point no less than three separate times.

I've seen enough trials – both as a lawyer and a court correspondent – to know that expert witnesses don't emphasise certain points in this way for no reason. And then the realisation crystallises in my mind: I think the prosecution has hunted down those high-school boyfriends, those once-teenage boys who were the first and only witnesses to the victims' disclosures, and plans to call them to testify.

I leave the courtroom hallway in my mind and travel back into a memory, one I haven't revisited for years. I am 16 years old, and I am in bed with my first proper boyfriend, let's call him J. I am full of that feeling of first love that can never be replicated; a desire to merge and subsume and become one completed soul.

He is trying to initiate sex for the first time and I keep freezing. Quite literally – I go still, I play dead. I am about ten months away from the night I was raped repeatedly at knife point by a stranger in the night, and in those ten months I have convinced myself that I have repressed the experience entirely. But now, in this teenage boy's bedroom in Western Sydney, it shows up all over my body.

I had told no one. But seconds later, in a moment I will never forget, he asked me the simplest and most powerful question he – perhaps anyone – had ever asked me, whispered so quietly it was barely audible: 'Did something bad happen to you?'

He was going to turn 20 that year. I knew, given our age difference, that falling in love with him would eventually mean sex. But I had also vowed to myself never, ever, ever to repeat voluntarily the most frightening thing that had ever happened to me. And then there I was, in his bed, facing the quandary I'd been running from ever since that terrible night.

My senses numbed. I remember floating above myself, looking down at this tiny, wretched, damaged girl, twisted in sheets and twisted in memories. But I was brought back into the room, into that bed, all of a sudden, just by the sound of his voice.

'Lucia, did something bad happen to you?' he repeated.

I found myself nodding my head 'yes', thinking about that night in McDonald's, about everything, and we stopped, and he held me. And I couldn't – not until ten years after that night – give him any more detail than one more tiny, almost-imperceptible nod. I couldn't give him the details because I believed it was my fault and that if I spoke the words out loud my disgust with myself would pour out of my throat like bile and poison him, too.

Even if he had known exactly what to say – *it wasn't your fault, you did nothing wrong* (and bear in mind this was a 20-year-old man living in 2008, so no one could have expected him to know exactly what to say) – I wouldn't have believed him. Not for a second. I think about that 16-year-old girl, how frightened and ashamed she was, and I know that no matter what he said, I would still have believed beyond any reasonable doubt that I had done something irredeemably wrong. But what matters is that he asked the right question at the right time, and I will never stop loving him for that. What matters is that he became my only contemporaneous witness.

I cried with gratitude for him as Dr Rocchio explained that most abuse victims only disclose to their first romantic partners, and never to parents or schools or police. Because the truth is that he was also the only person I ever almost told about my grooming and sexual abuse at the hands of my national team gymnastics mentor. I remember waking up crying before he drove me to training and just saying over and over again that I didn't want to go. When he asked, 'Why?' all I could say was, 'He hurts me.' Again, J didn't push me; he sensed that I had no clearer details to offer him. But, more than ten years later, when I finally reported my mentor's paedophilia, J was the first person to get in touch with me. *Thank you for trusting me with this all those years ago.*

J and I had an intense and tempestuous year-long relationship – one that involved deep hurt and pain inflicted on both sides, but profound joy, too.

Fifteen years later, we are still close friends. It took time – there is nothing so slow and seemingly endless as letting go of your first great love. But I did let it go, and now we have a genuine friendship that I will treasure forever. It seems right to me, somehow, that he was the only witness to the most formative event of my life. It seems right that, no matter how much anger and attachment (mine) or how much annoyance and desire for me to just let go (his) we feel, we always find our way back to each other.

We will never be those kids again. In most ways, the romantic part – the part that ended 14 years ago (with the exception of more than a few relapses in that time) – was destructive and bad for both of us. That's the truth. But I'll never stop being grateful that he asked me that question that night; that he stopped me floating away; that the soft cadence of his voice, which I'd come to trust and feel safe with, was able to bring me back into that bed with him. I'll never stop being grateful that he allowed me to give that silent nod.

The next morning, we woke up holding hands, the way otters do when they fall asleep in the ocean and don't want to be separated by the tides during the night. We'd had a night of tumultuous tides – memories, confessions, shame, love – and he wanted to keep me close while I was dreaming.

When we woke up, again he didn't push me for details. He didn't ask too many questions. In fact, he just asked one: 'Do you feel safe with me?' And I gave him that nod again, and whispered *yes*. And for all the hurt and pain we would later cause each other, for all the distance we would allow to grow between us, for all the fights and years-long silences, I meant it. And when I think about that 16-year-old girl that morning, having her hand held through the night, I know that I mean it still.

CHAPTER 10

Los Angeles, 2007

When Jane was 26, she met Matt. They fell in love, and their relationship would last six years, ending in 2013 when Jane was 33. In 2007, the couple moved in together. In that house, Matt became the first person Jane ever told about being abused by Jeffrey Epstein and Ghislaine Maxwell.

That's because, unbeknown to Epstein and Maxwell, one of the girls the pair abused during the Palm Beach years of the mid-2000s had gone to the local police. The victim's stepmother approached the police and said the child had been paid $300 in cash for a massage that turned into an assault at Epstein's Palm Beach mansion. The police began looking into it and collected testimony from more victims.

This was also one of the first times a victim went on the record with another important component of the Epstein/Maxwell sex trafficking ring: that when Maxwell liked a girl enough, she would pay her not only for massages and for sex with Epstein, but also to recruit other girls from her high school or local neighbourhood. Maxwell offered the girls an extra $200 or $300 to bring new girls for Epstein, telling the victims exactly what they should say to draw their friends into the spider's web.

The Palm Beach police's investigation began in 2005 – the same year that Donald Trump was recorded making the now-famous '*Access Hollywood* tape', in which he bragged about sexually assaulting women. He said: 'I don't even wait. And when you're

a star, they let you do it. You can do anything ... Grab 'em by
the pussy. You can do anything.'

As the police collected more and more evidence against
Epstein and Maxwell, the FBI became involved. By the end of
the 13-month investigation, authorities had testimony from five
alleged victims and 17 witnesses under oath, and a high-school
transcript, while other items found in Epstein's trash and home
allegedly showed that some of the girls involved were under
18, the youngest being 14. Authorities also conducted a secret
search of Epstein's house and found hidden cameras as well as
a trove of photos of underage girls either nude, partially nude
or performing sex acts. Police also found an Amazon receipt
for three books Epstein had purchased on sex slavery, titled *SM
101: A Realistic Introduction, SlaveCraft: Roadmaps for Erotic
Servitude – Principles, Skills and Tools* and *Training with Miss
Abernathy: A Workbook for Erotic Slaves and Their Owners.*

By the end of the investigation, police had identified 40 victims
and corroborated all of their stories. An investigation by the
Miami Herald said it had found closer to 80 victims.

It seemed like Epstein's luck was running out. In 2006, Palm
Beach police filed a probable cause affidavit, a document allowing the police to arrest someone without a warrant signed by a
judge, saying that Epstein should be charged with four counts of
unlawful sex with minors and one count of sexual abuse. But a
grand jury decided to drop the charge sheet to only one offence
– solicitation of prostitution.

The FBI released a 53-page indictment of Epstein in 2007.
He was given an extremely controversial 'sweetheart deal' in
which the police lowered the charges to solicitation only. He also
managed to secure an immunity deal for Ghislaine and other
co-conspirators, which was overturned many years later when it
became clear how unfair this deal was.

That's why, in 2007 when Jane met Matt, Jeffrey was never far
from her mind. The arrest of New York's most darling financier

made headlines for weeks. She saw his face again and again – on TV, online, in the news. And every time she saw that face next to a headline about his indictment for sexual abuse of underage girls, she got very emotional.

Matt started to notice that Jane's vulnerability seemed to come out whenever Epstein was mentioned around her. So one day, he decided to ask her about it. And very slowly, she started to tell him the outline of the story.

Jane told Matt about her home life, about what it was like growing up. She told him everything she would tell the Maxwell jury 15 years later: that when her father died after a long illness, the family had spent all their money on his treatment and had very little in the years after his passing. That Jane and her two brothers had to share a bed because they couldn't afford a bigger home.

When Matt asked how they got by during those years after her father died, she would mention a godfather. Someone who stepped in to help. Someone who paid the bills, helped pay the rent. But in those early conversations, in 2006 and 2007, that's as much as she told him.

But after Epstein was arrested, Matt remembers that Jane came to him and said: 'I have to tell you something … I need you to know that this is who that person is,' she said, motioning at coverage of Epstein's arrest. 'This is the godfather I told you about.'

A pause.

'Were you …' Matt trailed off. 'Were you one of the girls?'

'Yes.'

Jane had not spoken to any authorities at this point. She had told no one. Jane didn't go into any detail during that conversation about what happened in those massage rooms in Epstein's mansions during the eight years that she was entrapped by him. All she said was this: 'That money he gave me, that wasn't for free.'

Later during their relationship in around 2006 or 2007 Jane started mentioning the massages to Matt but didn't feel comfortable going into more detail. She told him that she had to 'do things' for Epstein during those massages.

'When did it start?' Matt asked her.

'When I first met him,' his girlfriend replied.

'How did you meet him?'

'At camp,' she said.

Matt gently asked Jane for more details when he felt she was able to share.

'Why would your mother let you spend time alone with a middle-aged man when you were 14?' he remembers asking.

Jane mentioned there was a woman there who made Jane feel more comfortable about the situation. That was, the prosecution would later argue at trial, the first time Jane told Matt about Ghislaine Maxwell.

Years later, Matt saw on the news that Maxwell had been arrested for her involvement in Jeffrey Epstein's sexual abuse of minors. He picked up the phone and called Jane.

'Is that the woman you told me about?'

'Yes.'

Matt asked her again about exactly what had happened in those massage rooms, but Jane became embarrassed and shut down. She was 'horrified', he would later say.

'Matt, the money wasn't fucking free,' she said again.

Later in their relationship, Matt was spending time with Jane and her mother, and things between the two women got heated. Matt remembers Jane saying that same phrase to her mother that day.

'That money wasn't free, Mom,' she said. 'How do you think I got the money? ... There's no way you didn't know,' Jane added, the final accusation hanging in the air between them.

At trial, when Jane was asked how her sexual abuse at the hands of Maxwell and Epstein affected her ability to have romantic relationships later in life, she said: 'How do you navi-gate the world with a broken compass?'

CHAPTER 11

New York City, 2021

'The government calls Matt to the stand,' Alison Moe says as we begin day six of the trial.

We all look around. *Matt?*

A tall man in a blue suit walks sheepishly into the courtroom. He is asked to state his name and occupation for the record.

He has been given permission to use a pseudonym to protect his privacy, so he only states that pseudonym – Matt – and explains that he is an insurance broker in North Carolina.

Again, the other reporters try to catch each other's eyes. *An insurance broker from North Carolina? What does he have to do with any of this?*

But I know the answer immediately. I can see it in his eyes – and I can see it in my own memories.

Alison Moe asks him if he has ever met the woman we are calling 'Jane' in this trial.

'Yes, I have, but we haven't spoken in many years.'

'And how do you know Jane?'

'She was my first girlfriend.'

As Matt testifies about the first night his relationship with Jane became sexual, about how uncomfortable she was, about how eventually she told him that she had a godfather figure who helped her mom pay the rent but also did terrible things to her, about how Matt was the only person she told for more than a decade, I think about all the high-school boyfriends and girlfriends the world over; all the people who have served as our first and only witnesses. I think about all those secret-keepers, all the adults who were once teenagers who became the only people we could trust with our greatest shame.

In my hotel later that night, I think again about the moment my first boyfriend and I tried to be physically intimate, about Dr Rocchio, about how it must feel for Matt, having not spoken to Jane for many years, to sit here in this courtroom with her, in front of a jury of strangers, and remember those disclosures and how the decision by a victim to share their experiences with their first love could end up being the difference between a conviction and an acquittal.

It turns out I would have this feeling many times. The court ended up hearing from three ex-partners of the victims in total, all corroborating the victims' testimony and also providing hard evidence to back up what we now understand as delayed disclosure: that disclosure of sexual abuse will almost always be made not to police or parents or teachers, but to their first intimate partners, and this disclosure will rarely be made all at once. Disclosures are made incrementally, beginning with vague acknowledgements that something happened, and slowly, over many years with different trusted people, finding the confidence to disclose the details.

CHAPTER 12

New York City, 2021

Carolyn, who is testifying at trial under her first name only to protect her identity, looks terrified as she walks past me on her way to the witness stand. Her back is hunched over, her eyes downcast, her gait lopsided and uncertain. I don't know this yet, as she walks past me, but she will be the most important witness in this trial.

Ghislaine Maxwell's defence team, it seemed to me, believed they would make quick work of Carolyn at trial. They believed that they would be able to paint her as amoral because of her drug addiction; as a willing participant in her own abuse because of the fact that she spent Epstein's money on drugs starting in her early teens; as unreliable because her poverty and addiction have led to arrests.

But something shifted when Carolyn took that stand. The problem for Maxwell's team was that they tried, throughout the whole trial, to construct a narrative in which the four victims who testified had carefully planned and executed a scheme to invent memories of abuse in order to profit financially from the Epstein Victims' Compensation Program. In this narrative, the girls 'made up a story' about Jeffrey Epstein and Ghislaine Maxwell in order to earn themselves 'a big payday', and global fame. In this narrative, the girls are calculating, conniving and vicious.

But Carolyn was not the witness they expected her to be.

'She's here by the grace of God,' Vicky Ward said to me in a whisper when Carolyn's testimony ended.

As Carolyn takes her seat in the box, she removes her mask and takes a big, desperate gulp of water.

'I grew up in New York and moved to Florida in 1999,' Carolyn begins. As a recovering addict, her speech is slurred. Several jurors lean forward in their seats, struggling, as I am, to make out some of her words. As I watch them, my heart breaks for Carolyn, because I know what's coming.

'Carolyn, have you ever been addicted to drugs?'

CHAPTER 13

West Palm Beach, 2000

Carolyn was only four years old when she was sexually molested for the first time. This molestation of her went on for years and defined some of the earliest periods of her life. And Carolyn's vulnerability didn't end there – her mother, a single parent, suffered every day with an addiction to crack cocaine and found it difficult to parent her. Carolyn had to drop out of school in seventh grade to work to try to help support the family. They struggled every week to make rent, to pay the bills. Everything was an uphill battle.

So Ghislaine Maxwell and Jeffrey Epstein knew they'd found the perfect victim when they met Carolyn. As you'll see from the stories in this book, this sexual abuse operation was founded on the idea of preying upon vulnerable girls who had crucial things missing in their lives: parents, affection, love, money. Things that every child needs. Things that Jeffrey and Ghislaine could offer them, knowing that they would be enough to draw these girls into their clutches.

But Carolyn was the most vulnerable of all the girls that Jeffrey and Ghislaine targeted. She had access to the least support and suffered the highest structural disadvantage (her poverty, her unstable home life, her mother's drug addiction, the fact that she dropped out of school so young) – and the result was that even after she escaped from them, she was never able to fully recover from the long-term effects of complex trauma.

Carolyn began using drugs more frequently soon after the

sexual abuse by Jeffrey Epstein began. She took opioids to cope with her fear and her shame, to 'block out' the abuse, she would tell a New York jury more than 20 years later, as I looked on from the press gallery.

Very soon after the abuse started, she became reliant on the money she received from Jeffrey and Ghislaine, both to help her mother make rent and to support the drug habit she relied on to cope with the abuse. Her opioid habit became more and more expensive, which meant that she had to accept more and more invitations from Ghislaine and Jeffrey to come over and be sexually abused, and so the cycle continued apace.

Carolyn became addicted to cocaine, dramatically increasing the cost of her substance abuse problems – the cost of her survival – and so she felt trapped, as though she had to keep going back, week after week, to the hell that awaited her at number 358 El Brillo Way, Jeffrey Epstein's now-famous Palm Beach mansion.

Two years after the abuse began, when Carolyn was 16, she found she was pregnant. She and her teenage boyfriend, Shawn, escaped from Jeffrey and Ghislaine for a period and had their son, but soon after he arrived, they realised that they simply could not afford all the things he needed – nappies, baby clothes, health insurance – and Carolyn felt she had no choice but to return to Epstein, Maxwell and the money they paid her.

By the time Carolyn finally did escape, when she was 18 years old, she had a drug habit that would stay with her for decades. At 36, Carolyn still takes methadone every day to try to recover from her drug addiction and stay sober.

On the witness stand, I could see so clearly how hard Carolyn has had to fight to stay alive. It was so clear to me that she has kicked and screamed her way through so much, and that she still struggles every day with the lasting effects of her trauma. She is a living, breathing testament to just how devastating this kind of trauma truly is, particularly when you do not have access to the safety nets that enable people to recover: a family network, enough money for treatment, job prospects.

Carolyn was sexually abused from the age of four. She had heard her cousin Jessica, who was even younger than her, screaming in another room. When she went to investigate, she found a man touching Jessica. As the older cousin, Carolyn felt a duty to protect Jessica. She offered herself to this perpetrator instead. Carolyn told me who this perpetrator was, but I am not allowed to print it here because he is still alive. When Carolyn tells me this story in early 2023, after my visit to Palm Beach in 2022, we speak via text or video call almost every day for the following nine months, it makes perfect sense based on what I know about her. She'd do anything for the people she loves. Anything.

'I couldn't let her feel that,' Carolyn tells me.

Years later, Jeffrey would ask Carolyn about her upbringing – about her parents and grandparents. She thought he was taking an interest in her, expressing care, but now she realises he was grooming her, getting her to feel comfortable.

When she and her family moved to Florida in her early teens, West Palm Beach seemed bright and hot compared to New York City, and she immediately liked it. She enrolled in the local middle school and started to make friends. She lived in a mobile home with her mother and brother, and things at home were terribly difficult. Carolyn's mother was a drug addict and had been for as long as Carolyn could remember. The family had precious little money, and when Carolyn was offered a chance to earn her own money to help with rent, she took it.

When Carolyn was 13, she started dating a boy she knew called Shawn, who lived across the street. Shawn was 18, and at first she lied to him about her age and told him she was 17. But a few months later, when she had her fourteenth birthday, she told him the truth.

That same year, Shawn introduced Carolyn to his friends, Virginia and Tony. They were both 18 – the same age as Shawn.

The two couples used to smoke pot together at Virginia's house. Carolyn didn't know it then, but meeting Virginia Roberts – who would later become Virginia Giuffre, taking the name of an Australian man she met in Thailand while escaping Jeffrey Epstein – would change the course of her entire life.

One day, the four friends were sitting around at Virginia's house, smoking weed and chatting.

'Carolyn,' Virginia said, 'do you want to make some money?'

Carolyn didn't hesitate.

'Yes,' she said. That day, Virginia didn't give any more details about her proposal. Later, she would explain that Carolyn could make money giving a very rich man a massage.

It was late spring, heading into summer, when Virginia drove Carolyn to 358 El Brillo Way for the first time. They pulled up in front of the white mansion, and Carolyn gasped at the sheer size of it.

Virginia ushered Carolyn inside through a huge, gaping white door and into a vast reception room, where she was greeted by a woman with short, black hair and an accent that she didn't recognise.

The woman put out her hand to shake Carolyn's and gave her name, but for all the years they would know each other, Carolyn would never be able to pronounce the name she heard that day. The accent and the foreign sounds overwhelmed her, and soon she would decide to call the woman only by her last name, which fell more easily off her tongue: Maxwell.

'This is my friend, Carolyn,' Virginia said as Carolyn and Maxwell shook hands.

'Excellent,' Ghislaine said in her Queen's English. Turning to Virginia, she said: 'You can take her upstairs and show her what to do.'

Virginia led Carolyn up the winding staircase towards the master bedroom, where she was then led into an adjoining room.

The first thing she noticed was the bright, polka-dot couch on one side.

Virginia drew Carolyn's attention to the middle of the small room, where a large, professional-looking green massage table was standing.

'This is the table,' Virginia said, then, motioning to a wall of shelves slightly hidden by the imposing table, she added, 'and here are all the massage oils you will need.'

Without saying anything else, Virginia started taking off her clothes and asked Carolyn to do the same.

Carolyn stammered, confused. 'I want to keep my bra and underwear on,' she said. Virginia nodded, and Carolyn complied.

'If you're nervous, have these,' Virginia said, handing Carolyn a Xanax and a beer to calm down. This became a pattern – Virginia would often give Carolyn Xanax before 'massages' with Jeffrey, to ease her anxiety.

A few moments later, a middle-aged man walked in. That was the first time Carolyn laid eyes on Jeffrey Epstein.

Wordlessly, the man removed a towel from around his waist, leaving him completely naked, and climbed atop the massage table, facing down.

Virginia showed Carolyn how to massage the man's legs using oils from the shelf, and then moved up towards his back. Then the man turned over.

It would be at this point in the story, when Carolyn is forced to relive this day in court, that she would break down for the first time, her voice cracking, tears filling her eyes.

Lying on his back, his penis erect, the man terrified Carolyn and she stepped away, sitting down on the polka-dot couch she had noticed when she had first walked in.

As she sat there, frozen with fear, she watched Virginia have sex with Jeffrey Epstein. It would be the first of many times she would witness this.

When the encounter was over, the two girls walked down-stairs together. There was cash left for both of them – $300 each, in neat piles of $100 bills.

Carolyn would cry again, decades later in court, when asked by Maurene Comey, 'And did you ever go back?'

Carolyn would say in the smallest, tear-choked voice: 'Yes.'

Before she left that day, Ghislaine asked Carolyn for her phone number, and Carolyn gave it. Carolyn did not yet have a cell phone, so she gave Ghislaine her home phone number. After that day, Ghislaine would call the number frequently to schedule massage appointments, during which Carolyn would come to the house and be sexually abused by Jeffrey Epstein. The phone call would go to Carolyn's mother, Dorothy, who would sometimes schedule the appointments on Carolyn's behalf.

Virginia asked Carolyn whether she had a history of suffering sexual abuse. She disclosed to Carolyn one day that she, too, had been sexually abused as a child – but now Carolyn doesn't believe this to be true; she thinks it was a tactic to gain her trust.

When I speak to Carolyn in 2023, she remembers that she once turned up to one of her appointments with Jeffrey stoned, and accidentally mentioned her age – something Jeffrey and Ghislaine had specifically instructed her never to do.

When she mentioned being 14, Carolyn remembers Jeffrey immediately cutting her off and saying, 'Let's disregard that.'

Every time Carolyn went for these appointments, either Shawn would drive her or Ghislaine would call and say that a car was on the way to pick her up. When Maurene Comey would ask her why she didn't drive herself, she would say flatly: 'Because I was too young to drive.'

When Shawn would drive her to appointments, he wouldn't come inside and usually didn't interact with Epstein or Maxwell.

But he knew that Carolyn would always get back into the car with the fistful of crisp hundred-dollar bills. Carolyn never told him explicitly what happened.

He met Epstein once, Carolyn recalled on the stand, and they had a brief conversation about cars.

When Carolyn says this, I think about Dr Lisa Rocchio, her words ringing in my head. *The first disclosure will normally be to a peer, often to their first romantic partners.* My head spins with the weight of this; all the high-school boyfriends the world over who occupy this role.

As Carolyn started to spend more and more time at El Brillo Way – eventually several times a week, every week, for years – Ghislaine started to ask her about school, about her life, about her family, what she wanted to do with her life. She started by asking how her day was, but then the questions were about her home life, her mother.

'My mother is an alcoholic and a drug addict,' Carolyn told Ghislaine one day.

Then, not long after, Carolyn told Ghislaine about the times she was sexually molested as a small child, about how she was raped for the first time at age four. Ghislaine listened intently, storing the information away.

Later, during massages, Jeffrey would start asking Carolyn similar questions. He asked her about her mother, her family. After a few of these conversations, Carolyn told Jeffrey about her childhood abuse, too.

As Carolyn's visits became more frequent, Ghislaine started mentioning to her whenever she and Jeffrey were flying to New York, or to their Caribbean island, for the weekend. One day, she asked Carolyn to join them.

'I can't,' Carolyn said. 'I'm too young – my mom would never let me travel on my own. I don't even have a passport.' This testimony would become crucial to the New York jury in 2021, who would have to decide whether to convict Maxwell on the most serious charge on her indictment – attempting to traffic Carolyn across state lines for the purpose of sexual abuse.

Another day, early on, Ghislaine asked Carolyn if she'd ever used sex toys. Carolyn shook her head.

A few weeks later, Carolyn was waiting in the massage room for Epstein to enter and for the massage to begin. But when the door opened, in came not Jeffrey, but Ghislaine.

'What is your bra and hip size?' Ghislaine asked, stepping into Carolyn's space. Then Ghislaine lifted her dainty hands and started touching Carolyn's body – first her hips, then her breasts and bottom. Carolyn was wearing underwear at the beginning of this encounter, but by the time it ended she was fully nude. It was just before Carolyn turned 15.

'You have a great body for Jeffrey,' Ghislaine said.

When Carolyn would recount this in court, I would think of Jeffrey Pagliuca trying to plant the idea in the jurors' minds that perhaps Ghislaine was a victim of Epstein's grooming, too. I would think of the fact that Pagliuca was trying to get the jurors to ask themselves: *But what if she didn't know?*

One day, Ghislaine asked Carolyn to write down her home address. Not long after, she received a FedEx package from Jeffrey. Inside, she found expensive lingerie that Jeffrey would later ask her to wear during massages. Later, Ghislaine would also arrange to buy Carolyn two tickets to an Incubus concert. This, too, would become important to establishing how much Ghislaine knew.

Sometimes, other adult women would join Carolyn and Jeffrey in the massage room. At least twice, Jeffrey pushed a button in the massage room and moments later other women would enter the room.

One day, the women came in nude, and Jeffrey had sex with one of them while at the same time performing oral sex on Carolyn. Once, Jeffrey tried to penetrate Carolyn with his penis – the only time he tried this – and she immediately said no. Jeffrey had sex with one of the other women in the room instead.

At some point during her visits to Jeffrey's house, Carolyn began suspecting that his mansion was being monitored by law enforcement. She noticed that a house across the street always had camera lenses and telescopes trained on the mansion as the young girls would come and go. She believed it was the FBI, and that they knew what he was up to with underage girls.

'Why would they keep letting me – a 14-year-old girl – go over there? Why didn't they do anything?' she says to me now via video call.

When Carolyn brought this up with federal prosecutors ahead of the Maxwell trial, however, she was instructed that she was *not allowed* to mention these observations on the witness stand.

When I ask Carolyn why she thinks they told her not to say this on the stand, her answer is immediate: 'They are trying to protect the FBI.'

Carolyn also believes that the FBI stole from her home a physical photo of her, while underage, posing with Epstein, Maxwell and Donald Trump.

The photo was in a folder that went missing after the FBI's first visit to Carolyn's house to ask her about potential victimisation by Jeffrey Epstein. When I asked Carolyn, she could not recall exactly which year this was. Carolyn's husband, who was also present for the interview, confirmed to me that he saw the photo before the FBI came and that it went missing afterwards. The photo was also on Carolyn's Myspace page, she explains – but when Trump became president, she was locked out of her Myspace account and has been ever since.

On one occasion, Carolyn was forced to have sex with an older, pudgier man that she hadn't seen before. It was at the Palm Beach mansion. There was another woman in the room when it happened. When we speak on a call in 2022, Carolyn can't remember the man's name, only that his surname began with a W.

So I get off my call with Carolyn and I open up Jeffrey Epstein's 'little black book' – the address book he used to keep track of all his contacts. The black book has been posted online. It was described at trial by a witness called Juan Alessi, who worked for Epstein at his Palm Beach mansion for many years. Here's how he described it:

'The book – the books, they were type of hard binding, either blue or black. I can't remember which one was blue, which one was black, but they were thick, I would say two inches thick, and the size of a large telephone.'

Maurene Comey asks: 'What was inside?'

'Inside was a list by alphabetical order of all the people, friends and families and business with Mr. Epstein and Ms. Maxwell.'

I figure I will go through every entry under 'W' and send Carolyn pictures of each of the men.

This is no easy task – Jeffrey's address book has 1,970 names in it. But I google and screenshot photos of all the men in the book whose surnames began with W, and I send Carolyn hundreds of photos of different men. As is best journalistic practice, I don't include any names with the photos – I don't want to tarnish her memory of the men she met based on the name associated with him.

She looks through each photo – which takes some time, because there are so many – but when her reply comes it is declarative and instant.

'That's him,' she says.

To double check, I send through another photo of the same man, in a different context, different outfit.

'That's definitely him,' she says.

The man in the photo is a well-known businessman.

———

The day Carolyn was trafficked to this man, she remembers him lying face down on the massage table; she was straddling him, giving him a back massage. But then, all of a sudden, he flipped over really quickly, pulled her underwear aside and shoved himself inside her. She screamed at him to stop but he wouldn't.

Then he said, 'Well, you're getting paid for this, you bitch,' Carolyn remembers. She jumped off him, grabbed her clothes and ran into one of the spare rooms in the Palm Beach mansion that the girls used to stay in. She picked up the landline telephone, which had an autodial for Ghislaine's phone.

'He just tried to rape me,' Carolyn said when Ghislaine picked up.

'Honey,' Carolyn remembers Ghislaine saying, 'it's not rape. You were willing.'

On another day in the nightmare of that Palm Beach mansion, Carolyn was forced to have sex with a man she was introduced to only as 'a billionaire'. She didn't know his name until later; by that point, she didn't much care to know who these men were.

Carolyn did try to escape Jeffrey and Ghislaine. They would call and she would say, 'No, I'm not doing any more appointments.' But whenever she tried to say no, the price they offered just went up and up and up.

Carolyn was a teenager with a drug problem, she explains to me in more detail in late 2022. She couldn't say no to $600. When we meet, Carolyn is ten years clean – a fact that she attributes to meeting her husband, John, in a rehab facility 12 years before, when she was still struggling with active addiction. Falling in love with John, and building a life with him afterwards, she says, is the reason she finally decided to get clean.

———

The next year, when Carolyn was 16, Carolyn discovered she was pregnant. By the time she was really showing, Jeffrey became obsessed with her pregnant belly, Carolyn tells me. He used to rub her stomach while he masturbated or force her to let him come on her pregnant belly.

'Pregnant women are so hot,' he used to say to her.

Not long after this, Carolyn decided she needed to escape Jeffrey Epstein and Ghislaine Maxwell. Like so many other victims in this book, the escape wouldn't last.

Carolyn and Shawn stole her mom's car and drove to Georgia She had her first child in Georgia on 12 March 2004.

Soon after their son was born, Carolyn and Shawn realised they were quickly running out of money and couldn't afford to raise him. So Carolyn did the only thing she could think of: she drove back to Palm Beach Island and began working again for Jeffrey Epstein.

Carolyn was often forced to have naked photos of her taken, for Jeffrey's enjoyment. Carolyn tells me in 2023 that she used to make a concerted effort to look miserable in the photos, to make the point that they were non-consensual.

'I didn't want Jeffrey to enjoy those photos,' she tells me now.

Not long after that, however, she found that Jeffrey had decided she was now too old for his tastes. So he started asking her to bring younger friends to the house, perhaps friends she knew from before she had dropped out of school, in the grades below her.

In another trial moment I will never forget – a moment that shows Carolyn's pure honesty, and the reason the jury believed her wholly – she laughs as she recalls saying in response: 'Why would I want to be friends with girls younger than me? I was in high school. That would be so uncool.'

CHAPTER 14

New York City, 2021

As Carolyn recounts this part of her story on the witness stand – the pregnancy, Epstein's reaction to it, the requests for young friends – Ghislaine Maxwell visibly shifts uncomfortably in her seat.

'Carolyn, did you continue taking drugs after you stopped seeing Maxwell and Epstein?' Maurene Comey asks her, gently, as she sits in the witness box.

'Yes.'

'Have you ever been arrested?'

'Yes.'

'Can you tell the jury about that?'

'In 2011, I was arrested for having drugs on me. I handed the drugs to the officer because I thought I could avoid getting arrested, but he arrested me anyway.'

'And have you been arrested any other times?'

'Yes,' Carolyn says. 'In 2013 I was arrested for having stolen property. Shawn had an Xbox that he said was our son's, and he pawned it, but it turned out it was stolen.' After a pause, Carolyn says: 'I spent 52 days in jail.'

All I can think about, in this moment, is the fact that Carolyn is the only person in this entire sex trafficking ring who has ever spent time in prison after being convicted of a crime.

'Are you on drug treatment at the moment, Carolyn?' Comey is asking now.

'Yes,' Carolyn says. 'I take methadone every day so that I don't take pain pills, and I take Xanax for anxiety ... I get panicked about my daughters being taken away from me and trafficked. I take a medication for schizophrenia and another medication to stay focused.'

'Can you tell us more about your fear that your daughters will be taken away?'

'I hear voices in my head telling me that someone will take my kids away.'

'Carolyn, do the drugs you take affect your memory?'

'No.'

'Do they stop you from being able to tell the difference between the truth and a lie?'

'No.'

'Have you ever spoken to Shawn about what happened with Jeffrey Epstein?'

'Yes.'

'Did you speak to the FBI about Jeffrey Epstein in 2007?'

'Yes.'

'During that FBI interview, you mentioned that the person you call "Maxwell" was there during your first visit to El Brillo Way, right?'

'Yes.'

'Did you give any other details about Maxwell during that interview?'

'No,' Carolyn says firmly, 'because I wasn't asked about her. I was only asked about Jeffrey.'

'Did you later file a lawsuit against Jeffrey Epstein and Sarah Kellen?'

(Again, Sarah Kellen has never been charged with or convicted of any criminal offences.)

'Yes, I sued Sarah because she was older and she knew what was going on, and because she took the pictures,' Carolyn said assuredly.

'Did you have lawyers helping you?'

'Yes.'

'Did you have conversations with your lawyers about who to sue?'

'Yes.'

'Did you give a deposition in 2009 in connection with your lawsuit?'

'Yes.'

'In that deposition, did you lie about whether you had worked for an escort service?'

'Yes.'

'And why did you lie about that?'

'Because I was embarrassed.'

'Is it true that you settled that lawsuit for around $250,000?'

'Yes.'

'And did you later apply for compensation as part of the Jeffrey Epstein Victims' Compensation Fund?'

'Yes.'

'And did the compensation fund award you $1.5 million?'

'Yes.'

'And has that money been wired to you already?'

'Yes.'

'As part of that award, were you asked to sign a waiver agreeing that you would not sue Ghislaine Maxwell?'

'Yes.'

'Do you have any financial stake in the outcome of this trial?'

'No.'

Carolyn is defiant, her face set. She is looking at a man in the public gallery – who I now know is her husband, John – because looking at him gives her strength. Her back is straight. She looks and sounds confident. Her defiance seems to course through me somehow, too.

It is 12.30pm exactly when Jeffrey Pagliuca stands up to begin his cross-examination of Carolyn, and I already feel chills running down my spine.

'Carolyn, you had an acquaintance named Virginia Roberts that was a friend of yours in 2002, approximately – correct?'

'Yes.'

'You and Virginia Roberts hung out at [her] apartment and smoked marijuana, for example?'

'Yeah.'

'Drank alcohol, correct?'

I know from my extensive reading that the expert witness the defence plans to call to the stand – psychologist Elizabeth Loftus – has previously testified that drug and alcohol use can interfere with memories.

'We didn't drink any alcohol,' Carolyn says.

'Did other drugs?'

'No.'

'Now, as I understand it, you were at a party when Virginia Roberts approached you first about making $300; is that correct?'

'Absolutely not.'

'Do you remember speaking to the FBI in 2007?'

The FBI notes again – the ones that the jury were never allowed to see. It seems that the FBI interviewed some of the victims in 2007, but only took handwritten notes and did not record the interviews. The victims never got to see these notes to verify that they reflected what was said in the interview. They were not admitted as evidence at trial because they are 'hearsay' (any document is hearsay unless the person who authored it testifies to its truth on the stand) and these FBI officers were not willing to testify. So the notes were never shown to the jury or admitted into evidence. However, there is something called the 'impeachment rule' in cross-examination: you are allowed to use otherwise inadmissible evidence during cross-examination if the lawyer is using it to impeach the witness or accuse them of being inconsistent.

'Yes.'

'And that was the first time that you talked to any law enforcement about Mr Epstein, correct?'

'Yes.'

'Where it says that "Virginia approached Carolyn at a party and asked her if she would like to make $300" – do you see that?'

'Yes, I see that.'

'Is that what you told the FBI in 2007?'

'No.'

'The FBI got it wrong?'

'We weren't at a party. We were at Virginia's house when she approached me.'

Now Pagliuca is asking more questions about that first encounter – and I can tell already what these questions are designed to do: to make Virginia appear to be the perpetrator, rather than Maxwell. A classic defence trick: give the jury someone else to blame and you have your reasonable doubt.

'You recall that Virginia Roberts was 18 when you first met her; is that correct?'

'Yes.'

The unspoken coda intended to hang in the jurors' minds: *So she was an adult at the time.*

'We were at her house for the first time, not a party, and it was only me, Shawn, Tony and Virginia, and she dressed me provocatively and that's when we went to Mr Epstein's home.' By this, Carolyn means that the first time Virginia raised the notion of working for Jeffrey was not at a party, but rather at Virginia's house just with Shawn, Virginia and Tony. This is a detail that the defence will try again and again to trip Carolyn up with – because there were two important occasions, one during which the idea was raised but not acted upon, and one where they actually decided to go to Jeffrey's house for the first time – but it ultimately will not work and Carolyn remains steadfast in her recollection throughout a brutal and confusing cross-examination.

'Okay. She knew where to go, right?'

'Yes, she did.'

'And she drove the two of you there, is that right?'

'Yes.'

'And it took about 30 minutes or so to get there, is that fair?'

'I have no idea, sir.'

'She parked the car, right?'

'Obviously.'

This is precisely the sharp, unexpected wit that I will learn over the following 12 months is totally, delightfully characteristic of Carolyn. The whole press gallery laughs, and Carolyn does, too. Later, in West Palm Beach in 2022, we would recall this memory together and laugh again. 'What a dumb question,' she said. 'What else would you do with a car when you arrive other than park it?'

We break for lunch, and the jury stands up and shuffles out. Judge Nathan looks to both attorneys' tables and says: 'Matters to take up?'

'I believe there are things that warrant more extensive examination,' Pagliuca says.

'Like what?' Nathan asks.

'Well, the witness is trying to minimise her ongoing drug use,' he says smugly.

When the discussion is over and Judge Nathan excuses us for lunch, Ghislaine turns around to her sister Isabelle. She pulls her mask down to her chin and this is the first time I have seen all of her teeth. She smiles widely.

For the first time, she turns to face us in the press gallery. Her eyes are so dark they are almost black. She looks at me for a very long time, and it almost feels as though a conversation passes between us. She picks up her biro and starts drawing.

Jane, the court artist, picks up her own pen and turns her gaze to Ghislaine. We sit like this for what feels like several minutes, Ghislaine staring right into my eyes, sketching us, while Jane sketches Ghislaine back.

———

At 2.15pm, Pagliuca's cross-examination of Carolyn continues.

'So, we were talking about 2002, when you went to Mr Epstein's house with Virginia Roberts. And I think where we stopped was, you were – you went into the house and you were taken upstairs by Ms Roberts. Do you recall that?'

'Yes.'

'Now, the only person that you saw when you entered the house, you identified as being an older lady with an unknown accent. Is that correct?'

'No,' Carolyn's voice is steady. 'I said she had shoulder-length black hair with an accent.'

'Okay. And you testified in your deposition that you told the FBI the truth in 2007, correct?'

'Yes.'

'What you told them, the only thing you told them, is that you saw an older lady with short, black hair and an unknown accent, correct?'

'Yes.'

'Now, at that point in your life, you knew what a British accent was, correct?'

'Yes.'

'And you didn't tell them a British accent, you said an unknown accent, correct?'

'I didn't say an unknown accent; I said with an accent.'

'Are you denying telling the FBI in 2007 that you said an unknown accent?'

Leslie and I roll our eyes at each other. On the one hand, reasonable doubt is reasonable doubt – they have to take it wherever they can find it. But the chances that this woman, who Carolyn described all the way back in 2007, with short, dark hair and an accent, could be some other woman with those same attributes seem slim.

This part of Carolyn's cross-examination is key. The defence would later use its closing arguments to tell the jury that all four victims *only* inserted Maxwell into their stories after Jeffrey's death in 2019, because they thought they would get more money from the compensation fund if they could be of use to the government in Maxwell's criminal case. But here, Pagliuca himself is pointing to an instance 12 years before Epstein's death when Carolyn identified Maxwell.

Maurene Comey will drive this point home later, in her own closing arguments, when she will say that, in order for the defence's theory to be true, Carolyn would have had to build a time machine and use it to go all the way back to 2007 and tell the FBI about a woman with short, dark hair and an accent.

'And then your boyfriend, Shawn, drove you, correct?' Pagliuca asks now.

My head spins again. I wonder if the government will, in fact, call Shawn to testify. If they do, he will be a powerful corroborating witness because he was 18 when this was happening, and he was often driving Carolyn to the mansion. But the fact that he was of age means he was also an accomplice, aiding and abetting the commission of a federal crime.

Pagliuca is still asking Carolyn about the first time she went to the Palm Beach mansion, about who greeted her, when she first met Jeffrey.

'A lot of it runs together because I had gone there so many times,' she says. 'So I'm a little confused on the timing.'

'And at this second time, there is no one else there that you have told the FBI about, other than Sarah and Mr Epstein, correct?'

'Yes. Maxwell was not brought up.'

'Now, in this entire first discussion with the FBI in 2007, it's true that you never said the name Ghislaine Maxwell once, correct?'

'Yes, because it's not who we were talking about.'

'So is it your testimony that the FBI limited your ability to talk in some fashion?'

'She was not the subject of the discussion.' Carolyn's voice is getting stronger and stronger, and I can almost feel the jurors move towards her.

Pagliuca then asks Carolyn to pull up a binder to take another look at the FBI notes. But he doesn't use her pseudonym, Carolyn, he uses her real last name.

The press gallery collectively draw breath, Judge Nathan physically tenses up and the government demands a sidebar, which the judge immediately grants.

The attorneys argue without the jury present about this issue that keeps rearing its head relating to the FBI notes that are not in evidence, and other lawsuits – for example, the ones Carolyn brought against Kellen and Epstein for which Kellen was never charged or convicted. It is important to note that while Kellen was named in a civil lawsuit, she has never been charged with any criminal activity.

'Other matters to take up?' Judge Nathan asks when the debate concludes.

Maurene Comey again takes issue with Pagliuca's line of questioning about the lawsuits filed by Carolyn, arguing that he shouldn't be able to rely on those lawsuits or admit them into evidence because they are not, properly construed, so-called 'impeachment material' – anything that proves a witness has been inconsistent.

Comey is arguing that the lawsuits are *not* inconsistent with Carolyn's testimony, because they don't directly contradict anything Carolyn has said about Maxwell.

'Your honour, it's impeachment by omission,' Pagliuca says.

Comey is fired up. 'No, your honour, the theory of impeachment by omission only works if there is an expectation to disclose, but you wouldn't expect a complainant to reference a non-defendant in her lawsuit. He is just trying to create a sideshow about this irrelevant 2009 lawsuit to which Ms Maxwell was not a defendant.'

Comey isn't finished. 'This document', she says, referring to the lawsuit itself, which the defence is trying to admit into evidence, 'was not written by this witness. It was written by a group of lawyers trying to satisfy a cause of action about two specific defendants ... This is a legal complaint; it necessarily does not include absolutely everything.'

This is Comey at her best. She is so confident making these legal arguments, and her manner is impeccable. It works. After having allowed some of the lawsuit to be admitted into evidence, Judge Nathan changes her mind.

'I've been re-persuaded to sustain the objections about the lawsuits,' she says.

The defence is trying to get the lawsuits against Epstein and Kellen into the record because it is what the criminal justice system calls 'impeachment evidence' – that is, if it shows any inconsistencies with the witness's prior testimony, it can be used on cross-examination without being admitted into evidence. Pagliuca is arguing that the entire lawsuit against Kellen and Epstein should be allowed because it is 'impeachment by omission' – i.e., you would have expected Carolyn to mention Ghislaine in these lawsuits.

But Maurene Comey has argued fiercely that it should not be expected that a claimant would bring up a third party, who is not being sued, in the lawsuit. Judge Nathan agrees.

Getting to the crux of the defence's argument, Pagliuca says: 'It is important in the context of this case where there's this changed memory over time.'

Judge Nathan disagrees again. We are back in open court.

Pagliuca is asking about Carolyn's escape to Georgia with Shawn when, without warning, he uses her full name again.

The entire courtroom stands still as everyone realises what Pagliuca has done. He has said Carolyn's last name – has read it into the record. Again. No one moves except Maurene Comey, who is on her feet quick as a flash.

'Objection.'

The chills slick up and down my spine and my blood runs hot with rage. I turn to catch Leslie's eye behind me; her expression is aghast. Silently, a whole conversation passes between us.

I can't believe he did that.

Do you think it was an accident?

God, I hope so.

Judge Nathan chides Pagliuca and directs everyone in the courtroom to disregard what they have heard. She directs Pagliuca to ask the question again.

'Did you ever have sexual intercourse with Mr Epstein?' Pagliuca asks.

'No.'

Pagliuca starts talking, but Carolyn cuts in.

'Can I finish my answer?'

Judge Nathan kindly says, 'You may.'

'You asked me the question, "Did you ever have sexual intercourse with Mr Epstein?" And I replied no. I replied no because I was not a willing participant. He had intercourse with me and I stopped it. I didn't ask to have sex with him.'

'Do you know what I mean by sexual intercourse or do I need to go through the various acts?' Pagliuca asks.

'Oh, I am pretty sure I know what sexual intercourse is, being that I have children,' Carolyn says snidely, and the whole room laughs. Again, writing this now, I reflect on her amazing wit, her courage. In that moment, I realise that she is not scared of Pagliuca at all.

'It's true, isn't it, Carolyn, that your story has changed signif-icantly since 2007, 2008 and 2009, correct?' Pagliuca does not explain what instances he means in 2007, 2008 and 2009, so it's not exactly clear – perhaps purposefully so.

'No.'

'And isn't it true – well, first of all, you had no contact with the government between 2007 and 2019, correct?'

No stunned silence this time, but a full-on collective gasp as the entire room inhales simultaneously. He has done it again.

My head spins round to catch Leslie's eye and again we silently share a conversation that we repeat out loud later.

That can't be an accident, right?

And now, Pagliuca moves on to the next part of Maxwell's defence: the 'they lied for money' piece. He asks Carolyn to confirm that she was in touch with her lawyer just one month after the opening of the Epstein Victims' Compensation Program, and she responds that this is correct. She confirms that she was awarded around $1.5 million from the fund.

Here, Pagliuca notes that her submission to the compensation fund *did* mention Maxwell, while her lawsuits in the 2000s did not – again trying to advance an argument that Maxwell had been inserted into the story at a later stage in order to get a payout (which, in this instance, does not logically follow – the fund concerned Epstein's conduct alone; she would not have been given more or less depending on whether she did, or did not, mention Maxwell – but this matters little to the defence, I imagine; it's all about building a narrative in which four women saw an opportunity to insert Maxwell into their memories for their own benefit).

When he pushes her again and again on the money, she says, 'No money will ever fix what's happened to me.'

'Move to strike the answer, your honour,' Pagliuca says angrily, meaning that the jury should disregard the last thing the witness said.

'Sustained.'

On redirect examination,which is when the prosecution gets a chance to question the witness *after* cross-examination, to clear up anything they feel needs to be clarified, Maurene Comey disposes swiftly with the weaknesses in the defence's impeachment evidence.

'Carolyn, did you write your civil complaint?' Comey asks, referring to the lawsuit against Epstein and Kellen.

'No.'

'Did you write your application to the Epstein Victims' Compensation Fund yourself?'

'No.'

'Carolyn, when you were shown a report of an FBI interview, had you ever seen that report before today?' Comey is making reference to the fact that these FBI notes were handwritten and never shown to the interviewee or checked for accuracy, and were never admitted into evidence.

'No.'

'Did you write it yourself?'

'No.'

'Did anyone ever ask you if it was accurate?'

'No.'

'Did anyone tell you what to say here today on the stand?'

'No.'

'Carolyn, are you trying to get money out of testifying here today?'

'No. Money will not ever fix what that woman has done to me.'

'Carolyn, why are you here today?'

'Because what she did was wrong, and she takes vulnerable young girls and—'

Pagliuca leaps to his feet. 'Your honour, I object.'

Carolyn ignores him. 'I'm so petrified that my daughters are—'

Judge Nathan cuts in. 'Carolyn, just a second. Just a second. I have to rule on an objection. Grounds?'

'Your honour, it's a narrative and it's—'

Comey cuts in. 'Your honour, an answer he doesn't like is not a narrative.'

'Counsel, both of you need to behave,' Judge Nathan says.

'I'm behaving, your honour. It's a narrative—' Pagliuca says but gets cut off by Judge Nathan again.

'I understand. Just one word objection, please.'

'Four-zero-four (b),' Pagliuca says, referring to the rules of evidence that prevent narrative in cross-examination.

'All right. I'll let the answer in as it is. Next question,' Judge Nathan says.

Comey is back on her feet now. 'Carolyn, what have you been told by the government to do here today?'

'Just tell the truth.'

'No further questions.'

'Could you state and spell your name for the record?' Maurene Comey asks.

'Shawn. S-H-A-W-N.'

It is this moment that I feel most sure that Ghislaine Maxwell will be convicted of her crimes. The moment when Shawn is called to the stand. Some of the time Shawn was driving Carolyn to Jeffrey's house, and when she would return to his car with hundred dollar bills, he was 18, legally an adult. If it could be proven that he either knew or wilfully ignored what was happening inside that house, he could face similar charges to Ghislaine. He could be prosecuted for participating in a federal sex trafficking conspiracy. And despite that risk, here he is, testifying to the prosecution. In the flesh. Willing to tell the truth even though the personal cost could be extremely high.

'When you attended Survivors Charter School, what was the first name of your girlfriend?' Comey asks a few moments later.

'Carolyn.'

Silence descends. I now understand the meaning of 'you could hear a pin drop'.

'While you were dating Carolyn, how, if at all, did she make money?' Comey asks.

'She only had two jobs ever that I know. One was worked at Arby's; and the other, she worked for Jeffrey,' Shawn says confidently.

'Do you know Jeffrey's full name?' Comey asks.

'Yes, ma'am,' he says, more confidently still.

'What is it?'

'Jeffrey Epstein.'

Another moment of silence descended as the corroboration settles across the courtroom.

'Do you know if Carolyn went to Jeffrey Epstein's house?' Comey asks.

'She did.'

'How do you know that?'

'Because I went with her.'

And there it is – an admission under oath that could get Shawn in a lot of trouble. But he does it anyway.

After a few more questions about how Shawn would go with Carolyn to Epstein's mansion, Comey asks:

'After Carolyn and Virginia came back outside, what, if anything, did they have with them?'

'Money.'

'About how often did you go with Carolyn to Jeffrey Epstein's house?' Comey asks.

'About every two weeks.'

Comey goes on to ask how the massages were scheduled, and he says he would often receive calls on his own phone. When asked to describe one of the female callers, he says they sounded 'English and one sounded almost French. English being proper English.'

A few moments later, an unexpectedly spine-chilling

moment occurs during what was otherwise a fact-based conversation about Shawn's memory of how they got to Jeffrey's mansion.

'When you went with Carolyn, how did you two get to Jeffrey Epstein's house?'

'We got a car from her mother.'

'And then who would drive?' Comey asks. The significance hit me like a bullet.

'I would.'

'Why couldn't Carolyn drive herself?'

A pause before the answer:

'*She was too young.*'

I feel the press gallery both freeze and sit up straighter at the same time. Glances are exchanged.

'Other than Jeffrey and Sarah, did Carolyn mention interacting with anyone else at Jeffrey Epstein's Palm Beach house?' Comey asks.

'There was a woman.'

'Did Carolyn tell you that woman's name?'

'Maxwell.'

'Did Carolyn say anything about that woman's first name?'

'She couldn't pronounce it.'

'Why?'

'She wasn't able – she didn't have the reading ability or she couldn't – it was foreign to her; she didn't know it,' Shawn says quietly, sympathetically.

Another silence. The press gallery has already seen Carolyn, looked her in the eyes, heard about the struggles she faced – how she dropped out of education in middle school. Another corroboration.

As I fall asleep that night, I think about how that must have felt for Shawn, to admit what he was part of. How it would have felt for Carolyn, to know that he was willing to show up for her, after all these years.

CHAPTER 15

New York City, 1995

The year Annie Farmer turned 16, in 1995, she was living in Phoenix with her single mother. Money was tight and the family struggled; Annie's father wasn't around and did not help out with child support.

Annie's older sister Maria was an aspiring artist and had left the family home to try to make it big in New York. During one of her first small exhibitions, a young Jeffrey Epstein happened to see her work and asked the gallery to speak to the artist. After speaking with Maria, Epstein knew he wanted to get closer to her. She was 25 at the time, Epstein's oldest victim. He was a donor to her art school and made an offer to the institution: he would buy one of her paintings at a reduced price, but would include in the offer a private artist's residence in one of his mansions in Ohio. Maria agreed, thinking this could be her big break.

For a time before the residency began, Epstein employed Maria to make acquisitions for his private art collection. She had a desk in his Manhattan home, where she reportedly saw underage girls coming and going constantly. When she asked about the girls, Epstein told her they were auditioning to be models, although she did not understand what the financier needed models for.

One day, Maria mentioned in passing to Epstein that she had a little sister, who was bright and full of potential, and that their mother was struggling to find a way to send Annie to college.

'I'd love to meet her,' Epstein said, 'and see if I can help.'

Before long, Epstein had booked and paid for a flight for Annie to visit him and Maria in New York City.

When Annie arrived at Epstein's New York mansion, she was intimidated and overwhelmed by his opulent wealth. He had bought them all tickets to see *The Phantom of the Opera* that night, and Annie was brimming with excitement. She dressed up nicely, feeling excited about seeing her first big theatre show.

Before they left the house, Jeffrey asked Annie some questions about herself.

'What do you hope to achieve in life?' he asked kindly.

'I want to go to college, but I don't know where to go or how,' Annie responded.

'How about UCLA?' Jeffrey asked. 'I think that would be a good fit for you.'

Annie was elated. Did he really think she could get in somewhere like UCLA?

'Do you have any extra-curriculars?' Jeffrey asked.

'Not really, no,' Annie said.

'Well, there's a summer programme I sometimes run for bright young students, to help them with their college applications. Would you be interested in that?'

'Of course,' Annie said, her head swimming with all the new possibilities. A trip over the summer; college in California – the world seemed to be opening up before her eyes.

Annie woke up the next day excited, feeling grown up and full of promise. The plan for that day was that Maria, Epstein and Annie would all go to the movies together. Going to the movies together was something they would do several times.

When they arrived at the cinema, Epstein said he would like to sit in between the sisters. As the movie played, after everything went dark, he reached his hand over and started caressing Annie's hand, then interlocking her fingers with his. Annie was frozen, confused.

He let go of her hand and started rubbing her leg. Annie started to feel nauseous and scared.

Every so often, Epstein would make a comment to Maria, and whenever he did this, he would stop touching Annie, making her feel as though he wanted what he was doing to her to be a secret. This made the 16-year-old even more frightened, and it made her feel very alone.

The movie finished and the lights came back on, and Epstein went back to his normal demeanour, as though nothing had happened. She thought about telling Maria, but she was scared to – Epstein had given Maria her big break in the art world, and she knew that Maria was very protective of him, and Annie didn't want to get in trouble. Plus, as soon as they had left the theatre, Annie wasn't even sure if it had happened at all.

When Annie got back home after that trip, she wrote about it in her diary – a diary she would keep, and from which she would read on the witness stand decades later.

'I went to the movies with Jeffrey,' the 16-year-old Annie wrote. 'It was a little weird. It was one of those things that is hard to explain. He held my hand. It gave me a weird feeling … Maybe it wasn't weird. I don't know. I'm confused … But he is so nice and so generous,' the young Annie continues. 'I didn't, or couldn't, say anything to Maria because she adores him, and I didn't want to portray him in a bad light. I'm just trying to make sense of it.'

―――――――

Hearing Annie's story, I am reminded once again of Dr Rocchio's testimony.

'And can you explain to the jury what "grooming" is?' Moe asks.

'Grooming refers to the process of gaining the trust of a child for the purposes of sexual abuse,' Dr Rocchio says, her body now turned directly to the jury, as if giving a lecture.

Dr Rocchio explains that the currently accepted definition of grooming involves five stages of gaining the trust of a minor.

'The first stage is the selection of the victim,' she explains. 'This involves, firstly, gaining access to the child and slowly starting to manipulate them to gain their trust and attachment … In this stage, the perpetrator will also slowly start to desensitise the victim to physical touch, and will start to assert control over the victim … When selecting a victim,' she says to the jury, 'we know from interviewing both victims and perpetrators that perpetrators often deliberately choose minors who come from vulnerable populations.'

More scribbled notes in the jury box.

'The second stage of grooming involves the perpetrator putting themselves in situations in which it is normal or accepted to have close relationships with children,' Dr Rocchio says.

Four jurors continue taking notes. Ghislaine is taking notes again, too.

'The third stage involves developing a bond of trust and attachment with the child,' Dr Rocchio says. 'This often involves meeting the unmet needs of vulnerable children, such as giving them special attention if they are not given much attention at home.'

'Can gift-giving be a part of this stage of grooming?' Moe asks.

'Yes, gift-giving can be a very powerful inducement for the child, especially if the child has limited resources in their own family … [It] shows the child that they are special to the perpetrator,' she explains. 'The thing with grooming is that victims are being harmed, but they are being harmed by a person they have an attachment to. So the victim will sometimes hold on to certain gifts to remind them of the good parts of the relationship; to remind them that it wasn't all bad.'

The jurors are furiously taking notes.

'Gradually, the perpetrator will normalise touch,' Dr Rocchio is saying now. 'And will slowly start talking about sex – for example, making sexual jokes ... The fifth stage', she continues, 'is all about maintaining the relationship and maintaining control over the victim. This stage involves a relationship of coercive control and entrapment, all of which makes the victim less likely to disclose the abuse.'

Moe nods solemnly and asks: 'Dr Rocchio, could you explain to the jury what "grooming the environment" means?'

'Grooming the environment happens around stages two and three ... What this means is that the perpetrator begins to develop a relationship with the victim's parents, for example, which may include supporting [them] financially ... This means that when the perpetrator starts to spend time alone with the child, it doesn't raise any alarms.'

Dr Rocchio takes a breath. 'Perpetrators often tell us in interviews that they will take the time to figure out exactly what they need to do to gain the trust and support of the adults in the child's life.

'Grooming is an extremely important element of the abuse,' Dr Rocchio says. 'Because it means that the later sexual abuse happens in the context of a relationship of love and trust; it leaves the victim trying to work out what happened, how they were fooled, trying to work out which parts of the relationship were good and which parts were bad.'

'Is the person doing the grooming necessarily always the person receiving the sexual gratification?' Moe asks pointedly.

'Objection.' Bobbi Sternheim stands up.

Judge Nathan starts to say *sustained*, but before she does Dr Rocchio says simply: 'No.'

Moe moves on with her questioning. 'Can you explain to the jury what "coercive control" means?' she asks.

'Yes,' Dr Rocchio says, turning to face the jury squarely again. 'Coercive control refers to a strategic pattern of domination aimed at getting a person to behave in certain ways ... Grooming is designed to establish a pattern of coercive control,' she goes on. '[It] involves interspersing positive or neutral aspects of a relationship with the abuse, which causes confusion in the child about whether the abuse is wrong.'

Dr Rocchio takes another deep breath. I look over at Ghislaine, who is completely still.

'It keeps the hope alive,' Dr Rocchio says.

'And what is the result of coercive control in these kinds of relationships?' Moe asks gently.

'The relationship of trust and attachment means that victims are much, much less likely to come forward about the abuse,' she says. 'And makes it much more likely that they will delay coming forward for a very long time.'

———————

'When you refer to a perpetrator, you are making an assumption, correct?' Jeffrey Pagliuca is now cross-examining Dr Rocchio.

'No,' Dr Rocchio says calmly. 'In our research we have interviewed many perpetrators about their tactics.'

'Grooming behaviours can sometimes be non-grooming behaviours, right?'

'Some of them, yes,' Dr Rocchio nods. 'Grooming is an overall pattern; it is not an individual behaviour.'

'So, for example,' Pagliuca says, 'my grandfather used to take me to the zoo. Was he grooming me? Treating children as special, buying them gifts, that's not always grooming, right?'

'Not always, no.'

Pagliuca then directs Dr Rocchio's attention to a study.

'This study concludes that it's very difficult to identify predatory behaviour when the situation is happening, right?'

'Yes, that's right.'

'So it might be hard for someone looking at a situation while it is occurring and being able to identify grooming behaviour?'

'Yes.'

'No further questions, your honour,' Pagliuca says, keen to end this cross-examination on the point he wants to leave in the jurors' minds, the one that aims to raise the spectre of doubt: *if Jeffrey was so good at grooming the environment, maybe Ghislaine didn't know?*

But Alison Moe is ready.

'Quick redirect, your honour?'

'Go ahead,' Judge Nathan says.

'Dr Rocchio, if someone is in the room while a child is being sexually abused, does that count as grooming the environment?'

'Objection!'

'Sustained.'

Dr Rocchio is not permitted to answer the question, but I can tell that Moe has got what she wanted.

CHAPTER 16

New York City, 2021

Annie Farmer walks confidently into the courtroom in high-waisted black trousers, a floral top and square black glasses. She seems self-assured.

'She's going to be the prosecution's star witness,' Vicky Ward leans over and whispers to me from her seat next to me in the press gallery.

Annie is returning for the final stage of her direct examination.

Laura Menninger stands up and my insides clench. I can tell this isn't going to be pretty.

'You testified that when you were 16 years old, you travelled to New York City to meet Jeffrey Epstein, correct?'

'Yes.'

'Isn't it true that when you spoke to law enforcement about that trip, you told them it wasn't abnormal?'

A pause. 'I don't recall,' Annie said.

'You hoped that Jeffrey Epstein would help you get into college, correct?'

'Yes.'

'My client had no role in organising your trip to New York, right?'

'No, she did not.'

'And you never met my client during that trip?'

'That's right.'

'You didn't even hear about her during that trip.'

'I don't recall.'

At the defence table, Ghislaine is fidgeting, playing with her hands. She leans over and whispers something to Jeffrey Pagliuca.

Menninger is referring to Annie's teenage diary now.

'You testified that you stayed in New York for about a week, right?'

'Right.'

'But there's an entry here dated 7 January, which states, "I got back today," and you were also there for a New Year's Eve party? So that's longer than a week, right?'

'I suppose so, yes.'

'No sexual activity took place at Jeffrey Epstein's New York home, right?'

'Right.'

'There was no physical contact at all in that house, right?'

'That's right.'

'But in 2019, you told the FBI that he held your hand in the movie theatre in New York, right?' Menninger is referring to a series of interviews conducted by the FBI in 2019 when Epstein was finally re-investigated, long after his 2007 sweetheart deal and his luxury stint in prison.

'Yes.'

'Is that because you had refreshed your memory using your teenage diary?'

'Yes.'

'And you didn't write anything in your journal about my client, did you?'

'No.'

'But you did write in your journal entry about New York that you had "such a great time", right?'

'Yes.'

'You wrote that it was "very depressing to be home", right?'

'Yes.'

'You wrote that you "felt comfortable in New York", right?'

'Yes.'

'And you wrote that *after* the movie-theatre incident, right?'

'Yes,' Annie says without hesitating.

'And you wrote in your journal that you found Jeffrey Epstein "down to earth and easy to talk to", right?'

'Yes.'

'And again, you did not write anything about my client, Ghislaine Maxwell, right?'

'That's correct.'

'Is it true that your journal helped bring back some memories that you might not otherwise have been able to recall?'

'Yes.'

'You write in your journal: "It wasn't that weird, it was probably normal, it sounds like I'm trying to justify it but I'm not."'

The 'it' that the journal refers to here, could of course encompass many things: the hand-holding, the movie trips, the friendship with Epstein and Maxwell.

'Yes.'

'So in this entry you say you *didn't* think it was weird, but now you do think it was weird?'

'I thought that then, too.'

'But you use both versions in this journal entry, right? It was weird; it wasn't weird?'

'Yes, I was confused.'

'And you didn't write anything in your diary about the trip to New Mexico.'

'That's right.'

'So we have no way of confirming who invited you on that trip or why?'

'Not using a piece of paper, no,' Annie said confidently.

'So would you agree that it's harder for you to remember what happened in New Mexico than it is for you to remember what happened in New York, because you can't refresh your recollection with your journal?'

'I suppose so, yes.'

'And you never spoke to Ghislaine Maxwell on the phone in the lead-up to that trip, right?'

'Right.'

'And you have very little memory of how that trip was planned, right?'

'That's right.'

'You believe you went to New Mexico in April, right?'

'Yes.'

'But that's a reconstructed memory, isn't it? Because you went on the internet and you checked when [the film] *Primal Fear* came out, didn't you?'

'Yes.'

'And that was when you were speaking with a reporter, Mike Baker from the *New York Times*, right?'

'Yes.'

'And he was confirming these dates with you, right?'

'That's right.'

'And you wrote him back and said that you looked up the release date for *Primal Fear* and also that you checked with your friends when prom was held that year, right?'

'Yes.'

'So you took some *fragments* of your own memory and you compared them to the information you found out about prom, *Primal Fear*?'

'Yes.'

'So this is a *reconstructed* memory, isn't it?'

CHAPTER 17

New Mexico, April 1996

In the spring of 1996, Jeffrey called Annie's mother and asked if Annie could come on an all-expenses-paid trip to his ranch in New Mexico. Jeffrey told Annie's mother over the phone that it was a weekend away for bright students that Jeffrey was mentoring, and he would teach her crucial skills and help with her college applications. It sounded perfect.

The teenaged Annie boarded a commercial flight to New Mexico, alone, a few weeks later. When she disembarked and collected her luggage, Annie was greeted by a man in a fancy suit holding a sign that read 'ANNIE FARMER'. She had never felt so grown up.

The man drove her away from the airport and through vast, empty expanses of New Mexico plains. Eventually, they arrived at a sign that read 'ZORRO RANCH'.

At the ranch, Annie was greeted by Jeffrey and a woman she had not met before. The woman was trim, with dark hair, and very well dressed. She was well spoken and had a thick British accent. The woman introduced herself as Ghislaine Maxwell.

To Annie's surprise, there were no other teenagers there. But, she would say decades later, the fact that Ghislaine – an adult woman who, at that time, appeared to be Jeffrey's romantic partner – made Annie feel confident that what happened at the movies wouldn't happen again on the ranch.

Jeffrey took Annie on a tour of the ranch, which was enormous. She saw horses and met many members of the ranch's staff. She felt special.

After the tour, she sat down with Ghislaine, who seemed to know a lot about Annie. She had been expecting her, Annie would say from the witness box.

Ghislaine was alluring to the 16-year-old; she seemed so put-together, so successful. She was a brilliant conversationalist, and Annie loved listening to the cadence of that accent.

'What are you doing in school at the moment?' Ghislaine asked.

'Well, actually,' Annie said, in a nod to Ghislaine's own heritage, 'I'm currently writing a paper all about British authors.'

'Oh, how wonderful!' Ghislaine said, and they discussed all the writers that Annie was studying. Ghislaine had an intimate understanding of all of them.

'How about I take you into town?' Ghislaine said. 'I'll take you shopping.'

Annie nodded enthusiastically, and soon she and Ghislaine were being driven away from the ranch towards the closest town.

Ghislaine bought Annie hair-lightening cream, to make her dirty blonde hair shine for the summer. She also bought Annie a pair of cowboy boots that cost more than $100 – probably the most expensive things she had ever owned. She was absolutely thrilled.

The next day, Jeffrey suggested they all go to the movies. Annie was immediately nervous, but she agreed, feeling better because Ghislaine, Jeffrey's girlfriend, would be there.

Jeffrey told each of them where to sit, just like the last time. So he was sitting in between them. As the lights went down, Ghislaine and Jeffrey began fondling each other, touching each other everywhere. At one point, Ghislaine tried to pull Jeffrey's trousers down. Annie was terrified.

As the movie continued to play, Jeffrey removed his hands from Ghislaine and put them on Annie's body instead. Just like the last time, he started caressing her hand and rubbing her arm, at one point holding on to one of her feet. Annie could tell that

Ghislaine could see what was happening; Jeffrey wasn't even trying to hide it from her.

The three of them drove back to the ranch with Annie feeling confused and afraid. When they arrived at the lodge that contained all of their bedrooms, Ghislaine announced that it was time for her to teach Annie how to give Jeffrey a foot massage.

Jeffrey sat down on the sofa, and Ghislaine picked up one of his feet.

'You take the other one,' she said to Annie.

Annie complied, picking up his bare foot and bringing it into her lap, as Ghislaine had done.

'Do it like this,' Ghislaine said, rubbing the underside of Jeffrey's foot with her thumb. As Annie started following Ghislaine's lead, Jeffrey started making low, deep groans of pleasure. Annie's insides froze once again. She wanted so badly for it to stop, but she didn't know how to stop it.

Things got worse still.

'Have you ever had a massage, Annie?' Ghislaine asked.

'No,' Annie said.

'Well, it's something you must experience,' Ghislaine said. 'I'm happy to do it for you.'

Before she knew it, Annie was being led by Ghislaine into an adjoining room with a large, green massage table standing in the middle of it.

Ghislaine handed the teenager a sheet to cover herself up with and told her to get undressed. Annie did so anxiously and pulled the sheet over herself as she lay face down on the massage table.

Ghislaine started rubbing her feet and her calves, making small talk as she made her way up Annie's legs. She asked her more about school, about her parents, about her friends.

'Turn over,' Ghislaine instructed after massaging the backs of Annie's legs. Annie complied.

As soon as Annie had turned over, Ghislaine pulled the sheet down so Annie's 16-year-old breasts were exposed. She placed her hands over them and started rubbing.

'I felt completely frozen,' Annie would say at trial. 'It didn't make sense. I just wanted it to be over.'

Annie realised, while lying there paralysed, that the door to the massage room had been left wide open, with Jeffrey still sitting on the couch in the next room. *Can he see me?* she thought to herself in a panic.

Once the massage was mercifully over, Ghislaine and Jeffrey acted as though nothing unusual had happened, so Annie tried to believe this, too. She had never had a massage before, so perhaps this was normal?

Annie climbed into her bed that night feeling afraid and wanting to go home. Eventually, sleep came.

In the morning, as Annie was rousing herself from her dreams, her bedroom door opened slowly, and there stood Jeffrey Epstein.

'I want a cuddle,' Jeffrey said in a low, sleepy voice, and he clambered over Annie's small body, climbing under the covers next to her. With one arm around her waist, he pushed his body into her back and held her tightly.

For a moment or two, Annie was frozen again. But then something overcame her, a need to get away.

'I need to go to the bathroom,' she mumbled and stood up quickly. She walked towards the en suite and closed and locked the door behind her. Sitting on the bathroom floor, barely breathing, Annie waited for the sounds of Jeffrey Epstein leaving the bedroom and closing the door behind him.

Later that day, Annie sat down with Ghislaine, hoping for more of her guidance on school and college. But Ghislaine seemed disinterested now, distant, and shut the conversation down quickly. Annie flew home to Phoenix later that day. She put the cowboy boots into storage and would not retrieve them until years later, when she would start wearing them in order to, in her own words, reclaim her agency over this time in her life.

She didn't write in her journal when she got back. When asked why, years later in court, she would tell the jury: 'I just wanted to put the whole thing out of my mind.'

That summer, Jeffrey offered to pay for a trip for Annie to travel around Thailand and Vietnam, again to help boost her college applications. She felt conflicted and confused when accepting the proposal, but she also felt she should be grateful and take up this offer from her benefactor.

She loved the trip, but she resolved when she got home never to speak to Jeffrey Epstein or Ghislaine Maxwell again. It was a promise she would keep.

On the way back from the airport when she returned to Phoenix from Thailand, Annie's mother noticed that she was pale and withdrawn.

'What's wrong?' she asked, but Annie just shook her head.

Her mother kept pushing. Eventually the 16-year-old blurted out: 'I wasn't raped, and I don't want to talk about it again.' And they never did.

Of course, this fits perfectly with Annie's diary entry. She was – and is – incredibly confused about this experience, as you would expect her to be. She had been excited, elated at this attention from such important people, and then extremely confused when things took a dark turn.

Later that year, Annie met someone. Her first big love. Just like Jane's and Carolyn's first loves, he was the first person she ever told – apart from her teenage diary – about the abuse.

CHAPTER 18

New York City, 2021

'You testified that Ghislaine Maxwell was not surprised to see you when you arrived at the ranch, right?' Menninger asks Annie as the crushing cross-examination continues.

'Right.'

'You met with the FBI in 2006, right?' Menninger asks, referring to the initial investigation that led to Epstein's 2007 arrest. She would later speak to the FBI again in 2019, in the lead-up to his re-arrest.

'Yes.'

'And isn't it true that you told the FBI that originally Maria was going to come on that trip?'

'I don't recall.'

'Did my client ever say anything to you about travel?'

'No.'

'So you have no personal knowledge that she enticed or transported you anywhere, do you?'

'No.'

'You spent a significant amount of time horse riding during that weekend in New Mexico, right?'

'I don't recall going horse riding more than one time,' Annie says.

'Well, you told the FBI in 2006 that it was a significant amount of time, right?'

'I don't recall.'

'And you kept the boots that my client bought you, didn't you?'

'Yes.'

'You kept them for 25 years?'

'Yes.'

'You kept them for *a quarter of a century*?' Menninger is sounding nasty now, but Annie seems unfazed.

'Yes.'

'You wore them, right?'

'Yes.'

'The heels on those boots are worn down, aren't they? The toes are scuffed?'

'Yes.'

'You *chose* to wear the evidence of your contact with Jeffrey Epstein?'

'Yes.'

'You went *dancing* in the boots that Jeffrey Epstein bought you?'

'Yes.'

'You testified that Jeffrey Epstein held your hand in the movie theatre in New York, right?'

'Right.'

'And you testified that you gave Jeffrey Epstein a foot massage, right?'

'Yes.'

'But that wasn't sexualised, was it?'

'I would consider it all sexualised.'

'But isn't it true that you told the FBI that you don't remember the foot massage being sexualised?'

'I don't recall that.'

Menninger shows Annie the FBI notes.

'I see that's what it says here,' Annie says.

'So you remember saying it wasn't sexualised?'

'Objection. Your honour, we've been over this,' Alison Moe says.

'Sustained.'

'It says here in the FBI notes that you had no clothes on during the massage with my client—'

'Objection.'

'Sustained.'

'You told [*New York Times* journalist] Michael Baker that you took off your bra for the massage, but you couldn't remember if you took off your underwear, right?'

'I don't recall that.'

'But now you say you were fully naked – so between 2019 and now your memory has changed, right?'

'No.'

'But isn't it true that between 2019 and now your memory has cha—'

'Objection.'

'Sustained.'

'And you have no journal entry about that massage, do you?'

'Objection.'

'Sustained.'

'You have no written record at all of that—'

'Objection.'

'Sustained.'

Over at the defence table, Ghislaine puts her head in her hands again.

Then, just like she said to the other girls, Menninger asks: 'You put in a claim for the Epstein Victims' Compensation Fund, right?'

'Yes.'

'And you understand that if anything you put in that claim was fraudulent, you could be prosecuted?'

'Yes.'

'In your application to the fund, you were asked about where the sexual abuse occurred, right?'

'I don't recall that question.'

'You said you were abused in New York, right?'

'It looks like that box was ticked, yes.'

'It says here that you were "abused in a movie theatre in New York and New Mexico", right?'

'Yes.'

'Do you really consider *hand holding* to be sexual abuse?'

'All of my experiences were detailed in the claim,' Annie says.

'You never said that anyone touched any of your private parts in the movie theatre, right?'

'No, I have always been very consistent about that.'

'You told the compensation fund that my client "groped" your breasts during the massage, and now you are saying she touched your breasts?'

'Right,' Annie says, sounding confused. I agree with her. Surely these mean the same thing?

'And you told the fund that that was *sexual abuse*?' Menninger says, incredulously.

'Yes.'

'You told this jury that Jeffrey Epstein "pressed his body" against you in bed, but you told the fund that he "rubbed his genitals" against you—'

'Objection. That is simply not inconsistent,' the prosecutor says.

'I agree,' Judge Nathan says. 'Sustained.'

'After all of this happened,' Menninger continues, 'you still accepted the money from Epstein for the Thailand trip, right?'

'Yes.'

'And you now tout yourself as a survivor of sexual abuse, don't you?' I cringe at the way Menninger uses the word *tout*, as if we survivors wear it as a badge of honour, as if going public isn't the hardest thing we have ever done.

'Objection.'

'Overruled.'

'Yes,' Annie says quietly.

'Isn't it true that you told the FBI in 2006 that you did not want Jeffrey Epstein prosecuted for what he did?'

'I don't recall saying that.'

'And isn't it true that the reason you said that is because you knew that no crime had been committed?'

'Objection.'

'Sustained.'

'No further questions, your honour.'

Laura Menninger saunters back to the defence table, clearly pleased with a performance that I have found incredibly distressing. Annie is remarkably composed.

———

Maurene Comey steps up to the podium to begin her re-examination.

'When you spoke to the FBI in 2006, did you have a lawyer?'

'No.'

'Did you tell the FBI about Ghislaine Maxwell touching your breasts?'

'Yes.'

'Did you tell the FBI about Jeffrey Epstein getting into bed with you?'

'Objection.'

'Sustained.'

'Annie, defence counsel just showed you some notes from your interview with the FBI, and they showed you a section where you said that your sister Maria was meant to go with you to New Mexico – do you remember that?'

'Yes.'

'Well, defence counsel didn't show you the next part of the notes – can you read to the jury the very next thing you said?'

'I said that I remember that Jeffrey Epstein and Ghislaine Maxwell were responsible for cancelling Maria's trip at the last minute.'

'When you spoke to the FBI in 2006, did you tell them about the foot massage?'

'Yes.'

'What did you say?'

'I said that Ghislaine showed me how to massage Jeffrey's feet, and that I then continued on my own.'

'And do you remember what you told the FBI about the massage you received from Ms Maxwell?'

'I told them that she seemed eager for me to experience a massage, and that she pulled the sheet down to expose my breasts and that she rubbed my breasts, as I described earlier.'

'How many interviews have you done with the government about this case?'

'Around four or five.'

'And did you tell the truth?'

'Yes.'

'Have you coordinated any of your testimony with other victims?'

'No.'

'Has anyone told you what to say here today?'

'No.'

'Why are you here today, Annie?'

A deep, long breath.

'Because I want to be a part of Ghislaine Maxwell being held accountable for what she did, for the harm she has caused.'

'Defence counsel asked you about the money you received from the Victims' Compensation Fund. Can you tell the jury what that money means to you?'

'It is a significant chunk of money, and it has helped me process what happened to me.'

'Do you have any financial stake in the outcome of this trial?'

'No.'

'Defence counsel asked you a lot of questions about memory. Do you remember Ghislaine Maxwell touching your breasts when you were 16 years old?'

'Yes.'

'Do you need a journal entry, or a piece of paper, to remember Ghislaine Maxwell touching your breasts when you were 16 years old?'

'No.'

'Why does that particular memory stand out in your mind?'

'Because it was a distressing event, and those are the kinds of things you remember.'

On day six of the trial, another tall man in a nondescript suit walks into the courtroom.

'The government called David James Mulligan,' Lara Pomerantz says as she appears at the podium.

'When you were in high school, who, if anyone, was your girlfriend?'

David – Dave's – answer comes quickly.

'Annie Farmer.'

After asking whether Dave recalled a trip Annie took to Thailand one summer, Pomerantz asked if he remembered who paid for that trip.

'Jeffrey Epstein.'

Next, Pomerantz asks whether Dave remembers Annie telling him about a trip to New York when she first met Jeffrey Epstein. Does he remember her telling him anything about what happened on that trip?

'I remember her telling me that Jeffrey was seated between the two sisters and that he reached out and touched her leg during the show.'

'Did Annie tell you at that time how she felt about that?'

'Yes. She said she felt awkward and confused about it.'

This, you will remember, is exactly what she told the court. More importantly still in terms of corroborating evidence, it's exactly what she told her teenage diary just days after it happened.

'Did she tell you why she felt awkward and confused about it?'

'Because Jeffrey Epstein had provided a lot of opportunities for her artistic career, and Annie felt that she couldn't really speak up or say anything, and she really didn't understand, I think, why it was happening in the moment.'

And now, another piece of testimony that I believe, and have been told anonymously by jurors, tipped the scale towards a conviction.

'Did Annie tell you if anyone touched her during the massage?'

'Yes.'

'Who did Annie tell you touched her during the massage?'

'Maxwell.'

'What, if anything, did Annie tell you about where Annie was touched by Maxwell?'

'She told me that she was touched on the breasts.'

'Did Annie tell you who touched her breasts?'

'Yes.'

'Who was that?'

'Ghislaine Maxwell.'

Another sharp intake of breath. I look over at Ghislaine, who is still as a statue. It feels intentional – she is refusing to let her face or body react.

'In 2003 when Annie talked to you about her experiences with Maxwell and Epstein in New Mexico, without going into the details, when did this come up?'

'This came up at a time where we were being physically affectionate with each other.'

As the prosecution asked Dr Rocchio to explain, delayed disclosure usually takes place with an intimate partner first, often when that relationship becomes physical. Matt, Dave and Shawn, without any knowledge of Dr. Rocchio's testimony, told the jury how it happened, exactly as she said it would, in real life.

CHAPTER 19

Paris, 1994

When she was 17, Kate moved to London. She wanted to be a musician. Not long after she arrived, she fell in love with a man twice her age. He was 35 and knew everything about the scene, and she was desperately drawn to him. When he asked her to join him on a weekend getaway in Paris, she was thrilled.

He took her to a swanky bar on their first night there and introduced her to a group of his friends – all of whom seemed remarkably sophisticated and grown up. One of them was Ghislaine Maxwell.

The woman, who was tall, thin and elegant, with a shock of short, black hair, approached Kate not long after she walked into the bar. Ghislaine introduced herself and held out a dainty, jewelled hand. Kate was intrigued.

'What brings you here?' the woman asked her.

'Paul is my boyfriend,' Kate replied.

'Ah!' Ghislaine said. 'We love Paul. How did you meet?'

'We met in London, on the music scene.'

'Oh, wonderful,' Ghislaine said, looking impressed. 'And are you a musician?'

'I'm hoping to be,' Kate said shyly.

'Oh, well, in that case we must stay in touch,' Ghislaine said firmly. 'I can help you. I'd love to be friends.'

Kate let the warm glow of approval fill her up, and she felt excited about her future. When Ghislaine asked her for her number, she gave it gladly.

Back in London a few weeks later, Kate's phone rang.

'Kate, hello, it's Ghislaine Maxwell here – we met in Paris?'

'Of course!' Kate responded. 'Hello!'

'I'd love to catch up – I was wondering if you'd like to come around for tea?'

'I'd love to,' Kate said enthusiastically.

Later that day, Kate thought excitedly about the tea date they had arranged for the following week. Later, at trial, Kate would tell the jury that Ghislaine was 'everything she wanted to be' – sophisticated, elegant, independent. Beautiful. The friendship excited Kate because she liked the way she was reflected in Ghislaine's eyes: as someone worthy of keeping this kind of company.

Kate was even more impressed the next week when she travelled to Belgravia, the well-to-do London suburb where Ghislaine lived and was to have her over for tea. The street was tree-lined and pedestrianised, like something out of a Hugh Grant film.

In Ghislaine's beautiful Belgravia townhouse, Kate felt that warm glow of approval again. Everything was beautiful and in its rightful place, and Ghislaine's gaze made her feel important.

'Tell me about your life, Kate,' Ghislaine said warmly.

'Well,' Kate said, wanting to impress her new, older friend, 'I've just been offered a place to study at Oxford.'

'Oh, how wonderful!' Ghislaine's face lit up; she seemed genuinely excited. 'I went there!'

'Oh, that's great,' Kate said. 'How did you find it?'

'Just *wonderful*,' Ghislaine said. 'I adored it. You'll be great there.'

'Well, actually,' Kate said nervously, 'I'm not sure whether I want to go right now. I really want to focus on my music, but I'm scared to tell my mum that.'

'And why are you scared?' Ghislaine said, leaning forward, inviting intimacy.

'Well,' Kate said, 'my mum's on her own. A single mum. We really struggle at home. There's not much money. Things are really tough at the moment.'

'Oh dear,' Ghislaine said sympathetically. 'I'm so sorry to hear that.'

A pregnant pause settled over them as Ghislaine drew in a breath, as though about to say something, then hesitated, and then started speaking again.

'You know, Kate, I think I know someone who might be able to help you.'

'Oh, really?'

'Yes,' Ghislaine said, rubbing her painted fingers together. 'My boyfriend, he's a philanthropist. He adores the arts, and he gives away scholarships to promising young students who are trying their best to forge careers in music or acting or singing.' Another pause, and then she said: 'I think he'd really love you.'

That feeling of possibility came washing over Kate again.

'Thank you so much,' she gushed. 'He sounds wonderful.'

'He is,' Ghislaine said. 'Shall I arrange for you to meet him?'

It was only a few weeks later that Kate's phone rang again.

'Kate, darling, my boyfriend is in London this weekend. Are you free to come around for tea?'

'Of course,' Kate said, excited.

When Kate arrived at the Belgravia house that weekend, Ghislaine seemed energetic and excited. Decades later, in the witness box, Kate would use the word 'activated' to describe her, which would stick in my mind for months.

Ghislaine greeted Kate at the door and walked her into the same reception room where they had had tea a few weeks before. Kate heard a loud, brash American voice, and soon Jeffrey Epstein came into frame, talking fast on the phone. He looked at Kate, locked eyes with her, and told his correspondent that he had to go.

'This is the girl I was telling you about, Jeffrey,' Ghislaine cooed. 'She's been accepted to Oxford but what she really wants is to be a musician – she's very talented.'

Ghislaine went on to describe Kate as 'very athletic and strong for her size', which struck Kate as strange.

'Why don't you squeeze Jeffrey's arm to show him how strong you are?'

Kate did as she was told.

Ghislaine picked up one of Jeffrey's bare feet and started massaging him.

'You can go ahead and massage my shoulders,' Jeffrey instructed Kate, and she complied.

'Oh, wow,' Jeffrey said in a low voice. 'You really are very strong for your size.'

A few moments later, Jeffrey stood up and the massage was over.

'Right,' he said to Kate. 'Ghislaine and I are going to have a chat about a music producer we know who might be able to help you.'

The two of them went into an adjoining room and spoke in low voices.

Another two weeks passed before Kate heard from Ghislaine again. She had managed to put the discomfort she felt about the shoulder massage out of her mind, but the image of it came roaring back soon after she picked up the phone to Ghislaine.

'Look, Kate, Jeffrey's massage therapist has just cancelled, and we were wondering if you were free? You have such strong hands,' she said.

Kate was confused, but again she complied. When she arrived in Belgravia, Ghislaine and Jeffrey were sitting in the perfectly manicured reception room, but a few moments later, without saying anything, Jeffrey took his leave and climbed the winding staircase up to the second floor. Ghislaine took this opportunity to lean in close to Kate and speak to her in a conspiratorial whisper.

'Jeffrey needs massages *all the time*,' she said. 'It becomes very hard for me to keep up.'

Without waiting for an answer, Ghislaine took Kate's hand and led her up the winding staircase, the same way Jeffrey had gone moments earlier.

At the top of the stairs, Ghislaine led Kate through a bedroom and into a small adjoining massage room. Jeffrey was standing in the room, next to a portable green massage table, wearing a fluffy white robe.

Jeffrey removed the robe and revealed his naked body underneath. Ghislaine was still standing in the doorway when this happened. Kate didn't know it at the time, but this moment would turn out to be crucial for the New York jury that was, almost 30 years later, tasked with deciding how much Ghislaine knew or didn't know about what was happening to teenage girls in those massage rooms.

Ghislaine handed Kate a bottle of massage oil and then left the room, closing the door behind her.

Kate gave Jeffrey Epstein a massage that ended in him sexually abusing her. Kate did not give details of the sex acts he performed or forced her to perform that day, because, given that Kate was 17 – over the age of sexual consent in the UK – they were not technically crimes.

When it was over, Kate walked down the winding stairs on shaking legs.

'Did you have fun?' Ghislaine said with a wide smile that reached her eyes. 'Was it good?'

She seemed happy, Kate would later testify, when asked to describe Ghislaine's demeanour in that moment.

A few days later, Ghislaine invited Kate around for tea. When she arrived, Jeffrey was there.

'You did such a good job last time that Jeffrey wanted you to come back,' Ghislaine said, and as she did so, Jeffrey started making his way up the winding staircase.

Ghislaine motioned for Kate to put her things down, and a few moments later, she led her up the stairs after Jeffrey. This time, when the pair walked into the massage room, Jeffrey was already naked.

'Have a good time,' Ghislaine said with a smile as she left, and closed the door behind her.

When it was over, Kate once again walked down the staircase alone and found Ghislaine waiting in the reception room – but this time she wasn't alone. There was another girl there – blonde, just like Kate, and also around 17.

'Did you have fun?' she said again, and Kate nodded. The blonde girl looked on and said nothing.

Ghislaine seemed very pleased again, Kate would recall later.

'You're such a good girl,' Ghislaine said then. 'He likes you a lot.'

As Kate left, she heard Ghislaine offer the girl a cup of tea and ask her about her dreams.

She heard Ghislaine say: 'I think you'd be a good fit.'

Over the next two years, Kate would visit the Belgravia house around five more times. Each time, the visits would begin with a phone call, in which Ghislaine would chat to Kate for a while – asking about how things were going, if she was dating anyone – and then would invite her over to see Jeffrey.

But even when the visits didn't involve physical contact, discussions about sex would creep in. Over tea in that reception room, Ghislaine started speaking to Kate very explicitly about male genitalia. She opened up about her sexual relationship with Jeffrey, who she then described as her boyfriend.

'I just can't keep up with his appetites,' Ghislaine said one day. 'It's a lot for me.' Then she said: 'Do you know any other girls who would be willing to come over and give Jeffrey a blow job? It would really help me out ... You know what he likes,' Ghislaine said next. 'Cute, young, pretty – like you.'

On another afternoon, Ghislaine confided in Kate that Jeffrey needed to have sex at least three times per day. During these conversations, Kate would recall later, Ghislaine had an almost schoolgirl-like demeanour; she would behave as though she were Kate's peer, or even someone younger than her, giggly and embarrassed.

'Do you like sex?' Ghislaine asked one day, and Kate stammered and changed the subject, unsure how she was supposed to respond.

On another one of her visits, Kate remembers Ghislaine saying it was her 'job' to 'take care of Jeffrey's needs', and also to manage his properties for him. It was the same day, Kate remembers clearly, that Ghislaine bragged to Kate about being close friends with both Prince Andrew and Donald Trump. Not long after that, Ghislaine declared that Kate was one of Jeffrey's 'favourites'.

On her eighteenth birthday, Kate was sent an expensive black Prada bag with a note attached that read, 'From GM and JE.'

CHAPTER 20

New York City, 2021

'Relevance,' Lara Pomerantz says, with anger in her voice. She is referring to a question from Bobbi Sternheim about whether Kate met a man named Kevin and went home with him.

'Overruled,' Judge Nathan said. 'We'll see if it's relevant.'

'Did you have occasion to go to Kevin's house?' Sternheim continues.

'No.'

'Have you been involved in a custody dispute involving your daughter?'

'Yes.'

'And isn't it true that you asked a friend to plant drugs on your daughter's father as part of that dispute?'

'Absolutely not.'

'You didn't ask a friend to help you with that?'

'No.'

With a flourish, Sternheim holds up a piece of paper.

'Your honour, I move for the admission of this defence exhibit, which is email correspondence between this witness and Jeffrey Epstein.'

'Denied.'

'Did you sign one of your emails: "best love always, Kate"?' Sternheim continues.

'Yes.'

'So you don't deny writing these emails?'

'No.'

'And did you attempt to visit Mr Epstein in New York?'

'Yes, I felt compelled to keep in touch with hi—'

'I didn't ask you that. *You* wanted to meet *him*, right?' Sternheim asks, her voice dripping with contempt.

'Yes,' Kate responds in a small voice.

'You even asked to stay at his *place*, didn't you?'

'Yes.'

'But he wasn't in New York when you wanted to visit, was he?'

'No.'

'He was in Paris, right?'

'Yes.'

'So you maintained contact with Jeffrey Epstein?'

'Yes.'

'But there are no emails between you and Ghislaine Maxwell, are there?'

'No.'

'When was your last communication with Jeffrey Epstein?'

'Probably my early thirties.'

'Give me a date.'

'I don't have one.'

'When did you stop contacting Jeffrey Epstein? Was it when you became a mother?'

'Yes.'

'Did there come a time when you met a person called Alexander Hamilton?'

A snigger waves across the courtroom at the name.

'No.'

'Sorry, my mistake – Ray Hamilton?'

'Yes, he's a friend of a friend.'

'You ran into him on a flight to LA, right?'

'I don't recall that.'

'You ran into him on a flight?'

'Yes.'

'And isn't it true that you told him that the Jeffrey Epstein compensation had just "fallen into your lap"?'

'No, I did not say that.'

'And isn't it true that you told him you were going to write a book about it?'

'No.'

'And that you hoped it would be turned into a movie?'

'No.'

'And that you were going to move to Italy?'

Kate laughs now.

'No.'

'Isn't it true that helping the government in this case helped you make your $3.25 million claim to the Victims' Compensation Fund?'

'I didn't know that,' Kate says.

'Isn't it true that you have requested a special visa for people who assist the government?' Kate is a UK citizen and was living in the US at the time, so this question was aimed at undermining her immigration status.

'Yes.'

'Have you begun that process?'

'I've just made an inquiry.'

Sternheim shows Kate a piece of paper.

'Do you recognise this?'

'Objection.'

'Sustained.'

Sternheim tries three more times to ask Kate about the document, which, from the sounds of it, is her visa application. But Sternheim gets knocked back by Judge Nathan each time. When she tries to admit the document into evidence, her motion is swiftly denied, but Sternheim won't drop the question of the visa. It seems to be key to the defence's case that the women taking the stand have been given inducements to lie about what happened to them.

'The current visa you are on, it's for individuals with an extraordinary ability, right?'

'Yes.'

'And what is your extraordinary ability?'

'It's for my music.'

'So any old unlicensed music therapist can get one of these visas?' Sternheim sneers.

'Objection.'

'Sustained.'

'The victim visa is not something you can buy, is it?'

'I don't know the requirements.'

'The only way you can get that visa is if the government says you are a crime victim, right?'

'I don't know.'

'No further questions, your honour.'

Once again, this is a way to suggest to the jury that Kate is lying – this time, the motive they are proposing is not money, fame or attention, but a visa. The suggestion that she is living on a visa that is only given to crime victims was intended to plant in the minds of the jury that she had a reason to make up a story about being a victim of a crime in order to stay in the US.

CHAPTER 21

Palm Beach, 1996

Over the six years that followed Kate's first encounters with Ghislaine Maxwell and Jeffrey Epstein, Ghislaine started asking her to travel with Jeffrey to give him massages. She flew with them four or five times between the ages of 18 and 24, she would later estimate.

Kate clearly remembers the first time she flew from London to Jeffrey's house in El Brillo Way – the Palm Beach mansion that Carolyn and Kate would come to know so well.

Kate was 18 when they flew her there the first time. As she was led through the giant house, she noticed that there were naked photos of women and girls strewn across the walls. 'In almost every room,' she would recall later, at trial.

During that weekend, Ghislaine approached her one afternoon with a schoolgirl outfit clutched in one hand.

'I thought it might be fun for you to go and serve Jeffrey his afternoon tea in this,' Ghislaine said, holding the pleated skirt and white shirt out for Kate. She complied.

'I didn't know how to say no,' she said later. 'I didn't know anyone in Palm Beach; I wasn't sure if they'd make me leave if I said no.'

So, once Kate had changed into the schoolgirl costume, Ghislaine handed Kate a tray with tea on it, and she duly took it upstairs and served Jeffrey, who was in the middle of one of his personal training sessions at the time.

The sexual abuse would continue in London for many, many

159

more years. When Kate was 23, Ghislaine invited her to Jeffrey's private Caribbean island for the first time. While there, the sexual assaults continued. Also while there, Kate saw a very young blonde girl. 'Much, much younger than me,' she would later tell the jury.

During her twenties, Kate became hopelessly addicted to alcohol, cocaine and sleeping pills. Her addictions helped her cope with how she was feeling after the years of assaults, but eventually she recognised that it was becoming incredibly dangerous.

When she was 26, Kate decided to get sober. She made that decision on 1 May 2003. She hasn't had a drink or touched drugs in almost 20 years. I admire her so much, having been a victim of sexual abuse myself and struggled with recovery from substance abuse in its aftermath. As I sit on the wooden benches of courtroom 318, I am full of gratitude for her.

CHAPTER 22

New York City, 2021

'The defence calls Elizabeth Loftus,' Bobbi Sternheim says, and all of our heads turn at once.

Elizabeth Loftus is small in stature but walks with great assurance. She has neatly cut blonde-grey hair, a fringe and striking black glasses that match her black KN95 face mask. A psychologist and professor at the University of California, Irvine, she is arguably the most well-known and divisive memory expert in the US. She has spent 50 years studying the nature of human memory, and says she has proven the existence of false implanted memories – her studies have shown that if you suggest something to a participant enough times, they can sometimes create what they believe to be a genuine memory that is not real.

The study that Loftus often cites is one in which she told a group of participants that their parents had told the researchers that they (the participants) had been lost in a shopping mall as a child. Some participants then recounted memories of this occurring, even though the researchers had invented both the idea and the fact that the parents had relayed it to them.

Loftus has used this science to testify in 150 criminal trials, the court will hear, and in 149 of those trials she testified for the defence. She has developed a second career as an expert witness explaining to juries that victims of crime can be wrong about the things they remember.

Loftus's career has experienced a huge uptick in the era of #MeToo. She has testified or consulted on behalf of Harvey

Weinstein, Bill Cosby, Michael Jackson, Ted Bundy, O.J. Simpson, and many other alleged abusers. She has managed to cement in the public consciousness the idea that memories of abuse can be false, implanted or simply wrong.

Maxwell's defence team has centred its case around the idea that the prospect of financial gain can be enough to plant a false memory. Here's their theory: these victims saw the media coverage of the accusations against Epstein, and then discovered in 2019 when he died in a Manhattan jail cell that his estate planned to dedicate a chunk of his fortune to compensating his victims.

Realising they could make money from Epstein's estate, the women 'made up a story' about Ghislaine Maxwell in order to bolster their claims for compensation from the Epstein fund, the defence argues. They heard about the impending criminal case against Maxwell, the theory goes, and believed that cooperating with the government to help prosecute Maxwell would help them get payouts from the fund. It seems the defence plans to use Loftus's research to try to back up that argument – the backbone of their case.

What's interesting from the perspective of memory is that this trial is the first time Loftus has used her science to support the notion that the desire for cash could cause a human brain to create a completely false – or made-up – traumatic memory.

There is no science or data to support this notion, but the defence team will lead Loftus to suggest it to the jury anyway. When they ask her the question directly, she says, 'I am not aware of any studies on that, but based on my research, it's definitely plausible.'

So this trial is being used to advance a brand-new theory of false memory – one that doesn't appear to be supported by any evidence and plays into a very dangerous gendered stereotype about women who speak out about the bad behaviour of powerful people. And yet the defence team have presented this theory in its opening arguments, its cross-examination of each victim and now, in Loftus's testimony.

'Have you been declared as an expert in the science of memory?' Sternheim asks, and Loftus answers in the affirmative.

'Have you testified with regard to the impact of post-event information on memory?'

'Many times, yes,' Loftus says.

'And have you testified with regard to the construction or reconstruction of memory?'

'Yes.'

Sternheim turns to Judge Nathan, deploying her characteristic omission of the phrase 'your honour'.

'Judge, at this time, I would proffer Professor Elizabeth Loftus as an expert in the field of memory science, the nature of memory reconstruction and the impact of events upon memory.'

Judge Nathan agrees.

'What stands out in your mind with regard to experiments that you have done that have impacted the science of memory?' Sternheim asks Loftus.

'I would say that one of the major contributions is the work that I and my collaborators have done on the misinformation effect on showing that after people see, say, a simulated crime or a simulated accident, and they are exposed to some misinformation about the accident or the crime that they saw, that many people will incorporate that misinformation into their memory and it causes an impairment in memory. It becomes their memory, and their memory becomes inaccurate.

'One – I guess you could call it a classic study, because it's in many of the textbooks in psychology today, is one in which we show people a simulated accident – maybe a car goes through a stop sign that's controlling the intersection. And later, we expose our witnesses to misinformation that it was a yield sign. Many people will now claim that they saw a yield sign instead of a stop sign. So they have succumbed to the misinformation in that new information that was presented to them and adopted it as their own memory. And that study was published in 1978.'

I look over at Leslie. Earlier this morning, I had been telling her about this study. This 'stop' and 'yield' sign study has been used in many sexual abuse trials in defence of those charged with historic crimes.

Loftus is explaining another of her studies now – this is about how language can change our retrieval of memory.

'We showed people a simulated accident. Afterwards, we asked people about the speed of the vehicles involved in the accident. But different witnesses are questioned in different ways. So some witnesses are asked a question like, "How fast were the cars going when they smashed into each other?" And others are asked, "How fast were the cars going when they hit each other?"

'And we found that people estimated the speed as greater if you used the word "smashed" than if you used the word "hit". Also, we had found that if we use the smash word, this leading kind of biased word, it affected what other things ... people remembered. Our witnesses were more likely to remember, for example, broken glass that didn't exist if we had used that word "smashed" in questioning them.'

'Can you please explain to the jury what those stages are in the study of memory science?'

'Yes,' Loftus says, nodding. 'One of the things we know about memory is, it doesn't work like a recording device. You don't just record the event and play it back later. The process is much more complex. [We] study the processes of memory, [and] tend to divide that process into three major stages ... So, typically, we start with the first stage, which is called the acquisition stage. This is a period where some event or events occur.' Loftus has her body turned to the jury, explaining with her hands. 'But after that event or those events are over, now time is passing and we enter the second stage, and this is called the retention stage. After some time has passed, a person might be asked to remember the event or the events, to answer questions, to subject himself to an interview, to testify. These are acts of retrieval where somebody is trying to retrieve information about the event … And so now we enter that third stage, which is the retrieval stage. So our job as researchers in this field is to identify the psychological factors that come into play at each of these three stages that can affect the accuracy of what somebody is telling you,' she explains.

Sternheim asks Loftus about what she calls 'post-event information', which the defence argues can also taint memories or create false ones.

'Post-event information can happen when two people are having a conversation with each other about the past and they can influence each other. Post-event information can be supplied when somebody is being interrogated, particularly if they're being interrogated with somebody who's got an agenda or a hypothesis about what might have happened and communicates that to the person they're interviewing, even inadvertently.

'The media is a source of post-event suggestion that we've actually studied where people are sometimes interviewed on the media, or media personalities will supply some suggestive information that can contaminate memory.'

'Does the fact that someone reports a memory with vivid detail mean that the memory is accurate?' Sternheim asks.

'No, because of false memories. Once they're constructed in somebody's mind, either by external suggestion or by auto-suggestion, [they] could be very vivid, detailed. People can be confident about them, people can be emotional about them, even though they're false,' Loftus says.

'So if somebody believes that they had an experience and describes that experience, there is no way of proving that that actually occurred?'

Lara Pomerantz stands up.

'Objection.'

'Sustained,' Judge Nathan says, without a second's pause.

165

'Outside of the laboratory, is there any way of proving that someone has an actual memory?' Sternheim presses.

'Objection.'

'Sustained.'

The objection is an obvious one – Sternheim has been hoping to get Loftus to say that no memory is ever, under any circumstances, proveably 'real'. There is no evidence to suggest this.

'Does an experience that may contain some trauma make a memory more reliable than one that does not?' Sternheim asks.

'Traumatic experiences compared to maybe more neutral ones might be associated with certainly remembering, you know, the core of what happened. You know that what you saw was a plane crash and not a warehouse fire and maybe some core details, but even traumatic experiences can be subjected to post-event suggestion that can exaggerate or distort or change the memory.'

Without knowing it, Loftus has just said something that the prosecution will seize on again and again in their closing arguments, and which my interviews with jurors will show was very important to the ultimate verdict: Loftus is admitting that even though traumatic memories can be subject to post-event information, a witness will usually remember 'the core of what happened'.

'And in looking at memory, is there any way for you to tell, based upon your training, experience and research, whether a memory is real or the product of post-event information?' Sternheim tries again.

'Objection.' Lara Pomerantz is on her feet.

'Sustained.'

'May I have a moment, judge?' asks Sternheim

'You may.'

Sternheim is asking for a private conversation with the judge to try and sway her to overrule the objection. Sternheim and

Judge Nathan take a moment to confer, while white noise plays so the press and the jury cannot hear.

After consulting with her team, Sternheim returns to the podium.

'Thank you, Professor Loftus,' she says, indicating that the testimony is over, and that Sternheim lost her argument with Judge Nathan behind the white noise.

Lara Pomerantz, looking determined, now gets up to begin the prosecution's cross-examination.

'I believe you testified that in addition to being a researcher, you often serve as a consultant, right?'

'Yes.'

'And that entails consulting with lawyers about cases, right?'

'Yes.'

'And you've consulted with attorneys hundreds and hundreds of times, right?'

'Yes.'

'Okay. And of those hundreds of times, you've consulted with the prosecution about five or six times, right?'

'That's approximately the number of times I've been called by prosecutors to consult, yes.'

Pomerantz holds up a book for the jury.

'You wrote a book called *Witness for the Defense*, right?'

'Correct.'

'You haven't written a book called *Impartial Witness*, right?'

The gallery snickers.

'Objection,' Bobbi Sternheim says.

'Overruled.'

'I have not written a book with that title, no.'

Later in her cross-examination, Pomerantz brings up something that the prosecution will use again and again in their closing arguments.

'One of your experiments involves Bugs Bunny, right?'

'Yes.'

'And in that experiment, you tried to get people to think that they met Bugs Bunny at Disneyland, right?'

'Correct.'

'That experiment involved an advertisement for Disneyland that includes a picture of Bugs Bunny, right?'

'That was involved in that study, yes.'

'And that would be impossible because Bugs Bunny is [a] Warner Brothers [cartoon], right?'

'That's exactly why we did the study, yes.'

'And then you ask people in this experiment whether they had met Bugs Bunny at Disney, right?'

'On a childhood trip to Disney, yes.'

'And in that experiment, about 16 per cent of people went along with the suggestion, right?'

'Well, I don't – it's been a while since I've looked at the actual data. I don't remember the exact number, but some percentage claim that they met Bugs Bunny at a Disney resort.'

Of course, Loftus not remembering the exact figure doesn't matter, because Lara Pomerantz is holding a copy of the study. And you can sense that everyone in the room is taking in the fact that 16 per cent is, by any measure, a relatively low figure. It means 84 per cent of participants were *not* susceptible to the implantation of false memories.

Let's pause on Bugs Bunny for a moment. This study was not chosen by chance. A memory of Bugs Bunny is a typical benign – usually even happy – childhood memory. It is in a completely different category, neurobiologically, to traumatic memory. I know this, as I sit here in the press gallery, because I have written two books about traumatic memory, but the jury doesn't know it yet; although the prosecution will use this later to argue that Loftus's research does not properly account for the fact that the core facts of traumatic memories, as opposed to benign memories, are seared into our brains in a different way. Pomerantz continues:

'Isn't it true that studies have shown that in the extreme case where participants are given blatantly contradictory suggestions, they are sometimes not susceptible to suggestion or misinformation at all?'

'We did a study where we tried to give a blatantly false suggestion and people resisted it, yes,' Loftus says.

'You're familiar with a study conducted by Kathy Pezdek, in which Pezdek presented 20 subjects with one true memory and two false memories, right?'

'Well, I know about that study, yes.'

'And one of the false memories was being lost in the mall, right?'

'Yes.'

'And the other false memory was receiving something called a rectal enema, right?'

'Correct.'

'And I'm not going to ask you to describe a rectal enema, but it's fair to say that that's an intrusive bodily procedure, right?'

'Yes.'

'Three of the 20 subjects remembered having been lost in the mall, right?'

'Something like that in her study, yes.'

'And none of the 20 subjects remembered the rectal enema, right?'

'None of the 20 remembered the scenario that they were presented with involving a rectal enema. But they weren't told they even saw it.'

'Pezdek tried to instil a false memory of subjects of having a rectal enema, but she did not succeed in doing that, right?'

'She did not; correct.'

The implication is clear. The idea that four separate women could have been implanted with completely false memories of sexual abuse is simply not supported by the science – because those memories are more akin to a memory of a rectal enema.

'This is not a case about Bugs Bunny,' Alison Moe would argue on closing.

'I want to talk about memories of trauma. The core memory of trauma is stronger than other types of memory, right?' Moe says now, in cross-examination.

'There are studies that show typically people can remember a core event and some core details, [so there is] support for that proposition, yes.'

'People tend to remember the core or essence of trauma events, right?'

'They can, yes.'

'People may forget some of the peripheral details of a trauma event, right?'

'That can happen, yes.'

'But the core memories of a trauma event remain stronger, right?'

'I probably agree with that.'

I probably agree with that. The prosecution team has got what they wanted.

––––––––

Later that night in my hotel room, I am thinking about Elizabeth Loftus, and about why she has dedicated her whole career to this idea of the possibility of false memories. I find an old profile of her in the *New Yorker*.

Loftus says in the interview that she has not seen evidence to support the experience that abuse survivors often report, in which memories that have been repressed then return to their minds without warning. 'She could find little experimental evidence to support the idea that memories of trauma, after remaining dormant for a decade or more, could abruptly spring to life,' *New Yorker* writer Rachel Aviv explains.

Later in the same profile, during a completely unconnected

anecdote, Loftus is recounting one of her experiences on the witness stand. A prosecution lawyer asked several questions intended to draw out the fact that she has never practised as a therapist and therefore has never treated a single traumatised patient.

'So, you really don't know anything about childhood sexual abuse, do you?' the prosecutor asked.

After a pause, Loftus said: 'I do know something about this subject because I was abused when I was six.'

Recalling that moment later, she wrote: 'The memory flew out at me, out of the blackness of the past, hitting me full force.'

CHAPTER 23

New York City, 2021

In what comes as a surprise to all of us in the press gallery, Bobbi Sternheim informs Judge Nathan that the defence is almost ready to rest its case, after only a handful of witnesses. Their star witness is Elizabeth Loftus, and with good reason – her testimony alone has worked wonders in previous trials. But still, it feels sudden. What was slated to be a six-week trial will now barely last four weeks.

But, Sternheim says, there is an emergency witness they'd like to call, and they'll need an extra few days to fly him from London.

'He's an 80-year-old man,' she explains. 'It's going to be diffi-cult to get him here.'

'Well,' Judge Nathan says. 'This trial has been on the court calendar for 12 months. Surely that's enough time to arrange travel?'

'Your honour, we weren't planning on calling this witness – he's a rebuttal witness,' Sternheim says.

'Who is this person?'

'He owns the Nag's Head pub in London,' Sternheim says.

Both sides are entitled to call last-minute rebuttal witnesses – that is, witnesses that they only realise they need after certain testimony has been given by the other side. Unfortunately, Judge Nathan doesn't buy it.

'It's funny that you say that,' she says in her dry, deadpan voice. 'Because I remember, a few weeks ago, when you cross-examined the witness we are calling "Kate", you asked her if Ghislaine's Belgravia home was opposite the Nag's Head pub. Am I remembering that correctly?'

Sheepishly, Sternheim says, 'Yes, judge.'

'Well, you see, the funny thing about that is that I remember thinking at the time, *Oh, what a strange question – the only explanation could be that the defence is planning on calling a witness from the Nag's Head pub.*'

The press gallery jitters.

'So that means this is not a rebuttal witness, Ms Sternheim, nor is it a surprise witness. Motion denied.'

The press gallery openly laughs this time.

———

It is a Saturday, but court is sitting today due to the recent discovery that the trial will wrap up at least two weeks ahead of schedule. Because of this, Judge Nathan wants to try to fit everything in before the New Year, so she has arranged for court to sit on a Saturday to hold what is known as the 'charging conference'. This is where the lawyers argue over Judge Nathan's jury instructions – the instructions she will give them after closing arguments and right before they deliberate. A judge's instructions refer to the part of the trial right before the jury retires to deliberate, and it is a crucial day in any trial. Its purpose is for the judge to explain the law to the jury on each count. So, for example, what they need to be satisfied of in order to determine that Maxwell legally 'knew' what was happening.

Jury instructions are always important, but here they are particularly so, because Maxwell is charged with six different federal crimes that are all quite complicated and difficult to understand.

Those six counts are made up of three 'pairs' where one is the substantive count and one is the conspiracy count. Counts two, four and six are the crimes, whereas counts one, three and five are counts of conspiracy to commit those crimes.

> Count one: Conspiracy to Entice Minors to Travel to Engage in Illegal Sex Acts
>
> Count two: Enticement of a Minor to Travel to Engage in Illegal Sex Acts
>
> Count three: Conspiracy to Transport Minors with Intent to Engage in Criminal Sexual Activity
>
> Count four: Transportation of a Minor with Intent to Engage in Criminal Sexual Activity
>
> Count five: Conspiracy to Sex Traffic a Minor
>
> Count six: Sex Trafficking of a Minor

Counts two and four include the phrases 'to engage in illegal sex acts' and 'to engage in criminal sexual activity'. The question, then, is what exactly those criminal sex acts are, i.e. what the illegal activity intended by Maxwell was. The prosecution has listed those criminal acts as 'sexual abuse in the third degree'.

According to New York Penal Code § 130.55, third-degree sexual abuse may be charged if a person has imposed sexual contact on another person without that person's consent.

Under that law, 'sexual contact' means any touching of the sexual or other intimate parts of a person for the purpose of gratifying the sexual desire of either party. It includes the touching of the victim by the actor, whether directly or through clothing, as well as the emission of ejaculate by the actor upon any part of the victim, clothed or unclothed.

For counts two and four, the prosecution has to prove that Maxwell encouraged or organised the travel of the girls with the intention that sexual abuse in the third degree would occur as part of that trip. They do not have to prove that the crime was in fact committed – only that this was Maxwell's intention.

A conspiracy charge is a separate crime. It alleges that a person was part of a plan to break the law, and it requires that Maxwell had an understanding with one or more other people that they were going to break the law together.

Conspiracy also requires that a member of the conspiracy took at least one active step towards putting the plan into action. This person does not have to be Maxwell – just one member of the conspiracy needs to have done *something* in furtherance of that conspiracy. This element of conspiracy requires that the plan 'went beyond the mere talking stage'.

Here's how Judge Nathan describes conspiracy: 'A conspiracy is a kind of criminal partnership – an agreement of two or more people to join together to accomplish some unlawful purpose … To show that a conspiracy existed, the government is not required to show that two or more people sat around a table and entered into a solemn pact, orally or in writing, stating that they had formed a conspiracy to violate the law and spelling out all of the details. Common sense tells you that when people, in fact, enter into a criminal conspiracy, much is left to the unexpressed understanding.'

Judge Nathan went on: 'In determining whether such an agreement existed, you may consider direct as well as circumstantial evidence. The old adage "Actions speak louder than words" applies here.'

Importantly, the prosecution does not have to prove that the plan was successful, or that any law was actually broken, in order to prove the conspiracy charges in counts one, three and five. The illegal act here is simply the making of the plan to break the law. So, in this case, it does not matter if the sexual abuse or even the transporting of a minor for sexual abuse actually occurred – only that the conspirators intended that it would happen and took at least one step towards making it happen (e.g. arranging an appointment, inquiring about plane travel).

Conversely, counts two, four and six are the actual crimes that were the object of the conspiracy: enticing a person to travel for the purposes of sexual abuse, transporting a minor for the purposes of sexual abuse and sex trafficking. For those counts, the prosecution has to prove that those crimes were actually committed.

In this case, if the jury is not satisfied with the evidence of the sexual abuse itself, or is not satisfied with the evidence that Maxwell enticed the victims to travel for the purpose of sexual abuse, or is not satisfied that she helped transport the victims for the purpose of sexual abuse, they can still convict her on counts one, three and five if they are satisfied that she planned for these things to happen and that at least one person in the conspiracy took an active step towards making them happen.

For the substantive counts – counts two, four and six – the jury must be satisfied that the following occurred. The following criteria are known as the 'elements' of each count. The jury must be convinced of every single element of a count beyond a reasonable doubt in order to convict on that count. As you'll see below, some of the counts relate *only* to Jane and some relate *only* to Carolyn. This is very common in conspiracy cases spanning decades and with multiple victims. For example, below are the elements of count two, which relates solely to Jane:

That Maxwell enticed, persuaded or coerced an individual (Jane) to travel.

That Jane did in fact travel.

That Maxwell acted with the intention that Jane would engage in criminal sexual activity.

That Maxwell knowingly transported an individual (Jane) in interstate commerce.

That Maxwell transported Jane with the intent that she would engage in illegal sexual activity.

That Maxwell knew Jane was under the age of 17.

That Maxwell knowingly recruited, enticed, harboured,
   transported, provided or obtained a person.
That Maxwell knew that the person would be caused to engage
   in a commercial sex act.
That Maxwell knew the person was under the age of 18.
That Maxwell's actions were in or affecting interstate
   commerce.

The 'overt act' that must be proven to have taken place as part
of the conspiracy does not have to have been committed by
Maxwell, it just has to have been committed by a member of the
conspiracy. So it's open to the jury to find that the overt act was
committed by Epstein.

Importantly, the different substantive counts relate to the testimony of different victims. Counts two and four relate solely to
Jane and count six relates solely to Carolyn.

But the conspiracy counts relate to 'multiple alleged victims' –
that's because for the conspiracy counts to be proven, we do not
need to have evidence of travel, or evidence of sex trafficking.
We only need evidence from the victims that they were part of
a broader plan by Epstein and Maxwell that would eventually
involve those things.

For example, Carolyn testified that she never travelled with
Maxwell and Epstein because she didn't have a passport. But she
testified that Maxwell asked her to travel to the private island –
that's enough for conspiracy to transport a minor.

To simplify what is needed to prove the substantive counts
for Jane and Carolyn respectively: to convict on counts two
and four, the jury has to be satisfied that Jane travelled between
Florida and either New York or New Mexico (as she testified)
for the intended purpose of sexual abuse.

To convict on count six, the jury must be satisfied that
Carolyn was recruited to engage in a commercial sex act –
that is, the massages that involved sexual abuse, for which

she was paid by Maxwell/Epstein. The requirement that this commercial sex act involved interstate commerce just means that money or goods flowed between state lines at some point as part of the commercial sex act – so, for example, Carolyn testified that Epstein sent lingerie from New York to Palm Beach for her. That would be enough to satisfy the interstate commerce element.

Just to make things even more complicated, there's one more thing I think is vital when it comes to convicting on the substantive counts.

The law believes that a person does not have to personally carry out each element of a criminal offence in order to be found guilty of that offence. This is known as 'aiding and abetting'. Basically, the jury can still convict Maxwell on the substantive counts even if they don't believe she, for example, personally arranged Jane's flights from Palm Beach to New York, but believe that she 'aided and abetted' another person in engaging in the criminal act.

Maxwell can be convicted on counts two, four and six if she, while not herself committing the crime, assisted another person or persons in committing the crime.

The law says that in order to be guilty of aiding and abetting, a person has to 'aid, abet, counsel, command, induce, or procure' the commission of an offence.

As Judge Nathan told the jury, a person aids or abets a crime if he or she knowingly does some act for the purpose of aiding or encouraging the commission of that crime, with the intention of causing the crime charged to be committed.

The prosecution must prove that Maxwell wilfully and knowingly associated herself in some way with the crime committed by the other person and wilfully and knowingly sought by some act to help the crime succeed.

The key question in this case would become: does it matter what Ghislaine knew?

The short answer is yes, despite what the defence would go on to claim in their closing arguments.

The substantive counts all require that Maxwell 'knowingly' enticed, persuaded or coerced someone to travel, or 'knowingly' transported a minor for the purpose of sexual abuse, or 'knowingly' sex trafficked a minor.

The conspiracy counts require that Maxwell 'knowingly' participated in the conspiracy. Aiding and abetting the substantive counts requires that she 'knowingly' associated herself with the criminal venture and participated in it.

So Maxwell's knowledge is an important element in every single count. But what exactly does it mean to say that Maxwell knew?

This was Judge Nathan's definition:

'An act is done knowingly when it is done voluntarily and intentionally and not because of accident, mistake or some other innocent reason. Now, knowledge is a matter of inference from the proven facts. Science has not yet devised a manner of looking into a person's mind and knowing what that person is thinking. Whether Ms Maxwell acted knowingly may be proven by Ms Maxwell's conduct and by the facts and circumstances surrounding the case.'

The defence asked several witnesses during cross-examination how old Jane and Carolyn appeared to them. Many witnesses, such as pilot Larry Visoski, said they believed the girls were 'over 18', introducing the idea that if the girls looked older, it's possible that Maxwell didn't know for sure that they were underage.

But, importantly, there is another way you can prove knowledge in these offences. Knowledge does not have to mean whether Maxwell actually knew for certain that her conduct was illegal, that the girls were underage. In this case, the judge has instructed the jury that they can decide that Maxwell 'knew' based on a concept called 'conscious avoidance'.

Conscious avoidance involves a person purposefully avoiding finding out whether their actions are illegal.

It's also sometimes known as 'closing your eyes to the truth'. If you believe that someone had reason to suspect that something illegal was going on, but deliberately did not make further inquiries – i.e. purposefully did not specifically ask the girls their age – the jury can decide they acted 'knowingly'.

Judge Nathan explained: 'If a person is actually aware of a fact, then she knows that fact. But, in determining whether the defendant acted knowingly, you may also consider whether the defendant deliberately closed her eyes to what otherwise would have been obvious.'

PART TWO

The Verdict

CHAPTER 24

New York City, 2021

'Ghislaine Maxwell was dangerous,' Alison Moe says forcefully. 'She was a grown woman who preyed on vulnerable kids – young girls from struggling families.'

Alison Moe is poised like a woman on a mission as she gives the prosecution's closing statement, as if this is the fight of her career. And it is.

Moe has become increasingly passionate in her arguments as the trial has progressed; I've noticed it in her objections and in her arguments with Judge Nathan and with the defence team. But most of all, I've seen it in her redirect examinations of the accusers after they have had their credibility attacked for hours and hours during cross-examination.

'She targeted a girl whose father had just died. She targeted a girl whose mother was an alcoholic. She targeted a girl with a single mom who was struggling to raise her daughters. Maxwell was a sophisticated predator who *knew exactly what she was doing.*'

Moe emphasises these last words; a nod to the defence's twin suggestions that either Ghislaine, too, was manipulated by Jeffrey Epstein, or that she did not in fact know that he was sexually abusing the girls she found for him.

'She ran the same playbook again and again and again,' Alison Moe is saying now. 'She manipulated her victims, and she groomed them for sexual abuse. She caused deep and lasting harm to young girls. It is time to hold her accountable.

'Over the last few weeks, you've heard from witnesses from all walks of life. You heard powerful testimony from women who told you about traumatising events from their childhoods. You heard from people they spoke to years ago about those events, who corroborated their testimony.

'Ladies and gentlemen, this summation is our opportunity to explain how all of that evidence fits together. The proof is in. It's clear, it's consistent, and it points to only one conclusion: Maxwell is guilty.'

There is something very interesting about the few occasions on which prosecutors choose to refer to Ghislaine as simply *Maxwell*. They will most often use 'the defendant', or, when they do use her name, they say 'Ms Maxwell', as is court etiquette. But there are times when they drop the honorific, and this one seems important. *Maxwell is guilty.*

Moe continues. 'You know Maxwell knew exactly what she was doing when she recruited and groomed young girls for abuse. Maxwell and Epstein were partners. They were partners in crime who sexually exploited young girls together … They were the best of friends. A couple for 11 years. Great partners. Rarely apart. Best of friends. Close partners who operated together. When you're with someone for 11 years, you know what they like. Epstein liked underage girls. He liked to touch underage girls. Maxwell knew it.'

Leslie and I exchange a look here. *When you're with someone for 11 years, you know what they like. Epstein liked underage girls.* She's not mincing words anymore.

'Maxwell was crucial to the whole scheme,' Moe continues. 'Epstein could not have done this alone. A single middle-aged man who invites a teenage girl to visit his ranch, to come to his house, to fly to New York, is creepy. That sets off alarm bells. But when that man is accompanied by a posh, smiling, respectable, age-appropriate woman, that's when everything starts to seem legitimate. And when that woman encourages those girls to massage that man, when she acts like it's totally normal for the man to touch those girls, it lures them into a trap. It allows the man to silence the alarm bells and get away with molesting those girls. Maxwell was the key to the whole operation.'

This is what I will hear from victims again and again over the year of reporting that will follow this trial. She was the one they trusted. She was the one who made them feel safe. None of this would have worked without her. Maxwell told workers in the Epstein house to see nothing, hear nothing and say nothing. And in that house, behind closed doors, Maxwell and Epstein were committing horrifying crimes.

Moe changes tack. 'You also know that Maxwell … ran the same playbook over and over and over again. The similarities between what happened to Jane and Annie and Carolyn and Kate are incredibly powerful evidence of the defendant's guilt.'

I am reminded of Bobbi Sternheim's opening arguments. She was right, this trial hasn't featured a whole lot of documentary evidence, but that's not the same as a lack of *corroborating* evidence. When four different women, who don't know each other, recall experiences at different times and in different parts of the world that all sound remarkably similar, that should count as corroboration.

'Maxwell touched these girls' bodies,' Alison Moe continues. 'The relationships that Maxwell cultivated with these girls were essential to the scheme. Jane didn't become Epstein's so-called goddaughter by accident. Maxwell helped establish a close relationship that became a cover for sexual abuse.

'Now, the defence cross-examined Jane about why she didn't immediately tell someone about the abuse she suffered when she was 14 and 15 and 16, as if that would have been easy … And, in fact, when the defence points out that Jane wasn't able to tell people what really happened to her, they're actually pointing to what makes this a textbook case of child sexual abuse.'

I look over at Leslie again. As Dr Rocchio's evidence confirmed, this is a fundamental truth about child sexual abuse. The fact that Jane and Annie and Kate and Carolyn didn't come forward until they were adults doesn't mean this didn't happen – statistically, it makes it more likely that it did.

'How else do you know that Jane told you the truth?' Moe adds. 'It's because her testimony is corroborated by the testimony of Annie and Carolyn and Kate. It's not a coincidence ... The evidence tells you that Jane told you the truth at this trial because you could see and hear her yourself. You met Jane. It was a powerful testimony and it was difficult to hear, but you know from your direct observations that she was telling you the truth.'

This is crucial. In a trial that has revolved so heavily around the idea of *dis*crediting victims, it is interesting for the prosecution to raise this important point: you, the jury, get to decide for yourselves whether they were credible. You saw them, you heard them, you looked them in the eye. Did you believe them?

'You learned that Annie got away,' Moe says. 'Ladies and gentlemen, Maxwell lost interest in Annie because her scheme didn't work. When Annie wouldn't cuddle with Epstein, when they couldn't take things further, Maxwell dropped the act. After that, Annie never spoke to Maxwell or Epstein again.'

I think of the boiled frog metaphor. If a frog is placed in a pot of boiling water, it will always immediately jump out and save its own life. But if a frog is placed in tepid water that is boiled slowly, it won't notice, and will boil to death.

All the traumatic events in Jane's and Carolyn's and Kate's lives before they met Maxwell and Epstein were moments in which the heat of the water they were swimming in was gradually turned up. And with each temperature hike, they adjusted, as humans are built to do. They became used to surviving in more and more desperate circumstances. By the time they met Maxwell and Epstein, their instinct to save themselves didn't kick in. Maxwell and Epstein knew that; it's why they chose them.

But they miscalculated with Annie. Something went wrong. Perhaps because she had not experienced as much childhood trauma as the other victims, she almost immediately jumped out of the pot and got away. They saw this in her, that she couldn't be groomed as easily as the others, and so they let her go.

'Ladies and gentlemen, what Carolyn told you is powerful evidence that Maxwell was conspiring with Epstein to abuse underage girls. Maxwell sent a teenage girl into a massage room with an adult man. She knew exactly what she was doing. If you believe Carolyn's testimony, the defendant is guilty on counts one, three, five and six,' Moe says. 'In her opening statement, defence counsel said something to you about Maxwell being blamed for something a man did. Let me be very clear. The evidence at this trial showed you that Ghislaine Maxwell made *her own choices.*

'At the beginning of this trial, the defence said to you that this case was about manipulation, money and memory. And you know what? Defence counsel was exactly right, but not in the way she meant. This case was absolutely about manipulation. You learned about how Maxwell manipulated young girls, making them believe that she was their friend, making them feel special, all so they could be molested by a middle-aged man. And you heard from Dr Rocchio, an expert psychologist, and you learned about how perpetrators manipulate their victims in a process called grooming. The evidence in this case overwhelmingly shows you that that's exactly what Maxwell did to these girls.'

This, too, is absolutely crucial. Dr Rocchio's testimony about the stages of grooming was, to my mind, one of the most powerful pieces of evidence presented at trial. When Alison Moe says this, I watch the jury closely. Four jurors are nodding along.

'And make no mistake,' Moe continues, 'this trial was absolutely about money. The evidence showed you that Maxwell and

Epstein were a wealthy couple who used their privilege to prey on kids from struggling families.

'This trial was also about memory. When the witnesses took that witness stand, they told you about searing memories of childhood sexual abuse, traumatic memories that they've carried with them for years. That is what the evidence at this trial showed you.

'So next, the defence has repeatedly attacked Jane, Annie, Carolyn and Kate, claiming that they are liars or that their memories are faulty, or maybe it's both. They argued both to you during this trial. They are doing that because the testimony of the witnesses in this case is devastating evidence of Maxwell's guilt; because if you believe these women, that's it. Ghislaine Maxwell is guilty.'

That's a line I will come back to again and again; a line that speaks to exactly what this historic trial is testing: is collective testimony enough?

If you believe these women, that's it. Ghislaine Maxwell is guilty.

'Common sense tells you that only one of three things can be true about Kate, Jane, Annie and Carolyn: either they are all misremembering the same thing, or they're outright lying, or they're telling the truth.'

Either they are all misremembering the same thing, or they're outright lying, or they're telling the truth.

If you believe these women, that's it. Ghislaine Maxwell is guilty.

––––––––––

It is almost exactly midday when Judge Nathan asks the defence to give their closing argument. The argument will be presented – to my great surprise – by Laura Menninger, the attack dog of the defence team.

As she walks to the podium, an attack dog is exactly the energy she embodies.

'Ghislaine Maxwell is an innocent woman wrongfully accused of crimes she did not commit.'

Menninger is angry and defiant; you can see in her face and body that she cares about her client, that she believes what she is saying – and that she anticipates that the jury will believe it, too.

'The evidence presented at trial has established exactly what we told you it would during openings, that the stories relied on by the government are the product of erroneous memories, manipulation and money. But, in this case, the order is reversed. The money brought the accusers to the FBI with their personal injury lawyers sitting right there next to them. The lawyers manipulated their stories, and the government accepted those stories at face value without ever testing them or corroborating them or checking with other witnesses to see if they were accurate. And suddenly, the women recovered memories years later; they recovered memories that Ghislaine was involved, that Ghislaine was there, that Ghislaine is the culprit.

'The government spent a lot of time focusing on Epstein, on his character, on his lifestyle, on his flaws, and they certainly proved to you that Epstein had abused his money and his power … They proved to you that he was a master manipulator. That has nothing to do with Ghislaine and everything to do with Jeffrey Epstein.

'We are not here to defend Jeffrey Epstein; he is not my client. Ghislaine is not Jeffrey Epstein … They said: her, too; her, too. Ghislaine was there, she must have known. You've seen them together. She must have known,' says Menninger.

'Ladies and gentlemen of the jury, you heard that the government seized somewhere near 38,000 photographs,' she goes on, 'and they brought you a handful of Jeffrey Epstein and Ghislaine Maxwell together. Where are the other 37,960 photographs?

Who were in those photographs? Was it other girlfriends? Was it other women? Who was it? You don't know. They didn't bring you those photos.

'These women, with their lawyers, walked into the US Attorney's Office, they filed their civil lawsuits at the same time, and the lawyers, like Boies Schiller LLP, helped set up the Epstein Victims' Compensation Fund.

'On that fund application, it asked you, *Are you cooperating with a criminal investigation? Have you filed a civil suit? Because if you are, we'll just assume you're a real victim, even though we, the fund, aren't going to ask you any questions or put your story to the test.*'

I remember wondering, in court that day, whether this was true – whether in fact the compensation fund failed to test any of the victims' claims before they paid out. It isn't.

'And all of these ladies had lawyers' – *ladies* – 'went to the FBI, and filed a civil suit and filed a civil claim with the fund, and they each took home millions, and now they are stuck with the stories that they told,' Menninger says. 'That's the money piece.'

Now Menninger targets Jane.

'The prosecution opened with this: this is the story of Jane. It was just that, *quite a story*, like an actress who forgot her lines.'

One of the other reporters and I share a quick glance.

'Let's talk about her memory. She demonstrated a very poor and inconsistent memory about things that, if they were true, she would have remembered. Her memory is the underpinning of this entire case, because the government has to prove to you beyond a reasonable doubt that she was travelling, enticed to travel, encouraged to travel, transported while she was under the age of 17, in order to find Ghislaine Maxwell guilty of counts one through four.

'They try to tell you she was too scared to disclose the facts about what happened to her. Well, you could judge for yourself her lack of discomfort in talking about it on the stand.'

Again, I am taken aback by the brazenness of this. Menninger is accusing Jane of lying about feeling uncomfortable disclosing graphic details of sexual abuse because she ultimately agreed to disclose those details at a federal criminal trial. Her *lack of discomfort on the stand* feels like a sentence from a parallel universe – her extreme distress on the stand was plain as day. Jane had said that telling the jury about what happened to her was one of the hardest things she has ever had to do.

'Let's turn to Annie Farmer now,' Menninger continues. 'She's saying that ... she was bought these boots by the people who sexually abused her; Maxwell bought her these boots. And she said that she kept them in the closet, and then the government didn't ask for them in 2006 ... You'll have the boots with you back in the jury room, and you can see for yourselves how worn those boots are.'

Those boots again.

'[The] government finally got those boots in June of 2021, even though they'd met with [Annie] repeatedly, and she never told them anything about wearing these boots; she just said they bought her these boots, and then when they finally got them and looked at them and saw that she's been wearing boots from the people that she says sexually abused her, she came up with a new story, and that story was that she wanted to reclaim the boots. And that's the story she told for the first time right before trial and what she told you on the stand.'

Now Menninger turns on Kate: 'I'm not really sure why Kate testified here. Kate traded up from one prominent gentleman to the next. Kate told you about her life, where she was abusing cocaine and sleeping pills and alcohol for more than ten years. That's the kind of information that Kate shared with you about her life.

'She was above the age of consent. She maintained contact with Epstein into her thirties. He was in prison, and she was writing and sending him emails, offering to send him pictures while he was in prison, while she was in her thirties. Use your common sense. Is that someone who was abused by Epstein?' Menninger asks.

'You heard from the government that Ghislaine was Epstein's right-hand woman; that she controlled everything in his life; she knew everything, she saw everything, she did everything; she's to blame for his sins. That's not what the evidence showed you at all. Everyone knew that Jeffrey was keeping secrets from Ghislaine, except Ghislaine.'

As Menninger is making this compartmentalisation argument – that Jeffrey deceived Ghislaine, tricked her into thinking he wasn't committing these crimes – I think of the exchange between Alison Moe and Dr Rocchio weeks earlier, the one that drew a ferocious objection from the defence.

Dr Rocchio, if someone is in the room *while sexual abuse is happening, does that count as grooming the environment?*

No.

As I tune back into the room, Menninger is talking about Professor Loftus.

'And what she told you is that memory is malleable. Memory weakens over time. And memory can be impacted and corrupted by post-event contamination. She talked about times when false memories can be planted in a person's mind, and that the person could then become just as emotional about these created memories as other individuals who truly had the experiences.

'And contrary to what most people think, memory doesn't work like a recording device; you can't just push play and it all comes back later. Memories can be impacted by post-event information that comes from all different sources. Interviews that use words that are suggestive.

'She told you about the three different stages of memories, and that one thing that can happen is what's called autosuggestion ... And post-event information can impact a memory at any one of those stages. If you're under the influence of drugs or alcohol at the time you acquire the memory, that affects the quality of the formation of the memory in the first place. The older a memory gets, the more susceptible it is to post-event information. And news media in whatever form can include re-dramatisation.

'And what does reasonable doubt mean? I expect the judge will instruct you [that] reasonable doubt is a doubt based in reason, arising out of the evidence in the case or the lack of evidence. In other words, if you have such a doubt as would reasonably cause a prudent person to hesitate to act in matters of importance in his or her own affairs, then you have a reasonable doubt, and in that circumstance, it is your duty to acquit Ms Maxwell of that charge.

'Would you hesitate to act in a matter of importance to yourself based on the word of *Carolyn*?' Menninger asks the jury. 'Would you hesitate to act in a matter of importance to yourself based on the word of Jane? Did they demonstrate to you that their stories were credible? I submit to you that they did not.'

This is something I would talk about in detail with the jurors I later interviewed about their deliberations – the nasty tone in Menninger's voice when she said: *Would you hesitate to act in a matter of importance to yourself based on the word of* Carolyn?

'As we have said from the beginning,' Menninger continues, 'Ghislaine Maxwell is not Jeffrey Epstein. She's being tried here for being with Jeffrey Epstein. Maybe that was the biggest mistake of her life, but it was not a crime.

'Please only consider the evidence against her. Don't be fooled by the government's smoke and mirrors and big fancy houses and bank accounts. What was the evidence that pertains to her? The evidence on the law, the burden of proof, justice, demand that you acquit Ghislaine Maxwell of every single count with which she is charged. Thank you for your time.'

———

I don't know it yet, as I sit here in the courtroom, but the next 20 minutes will, in my opinion, change the course of this trial. Of history. Of my own life.

From day one of the trial, Maurene Comey has been professional, austere, reserved and calm. She has been serious and understated, as all good prosecutors are. I've been wildly impressed by her composure – and I realise now that every minute of that makes what we are about to hear from her even more powerful.

Maurene Comey is upset. She is angry. She heard the same defence closing argument that I did, and her response is written all over her face. When she opens her mouth, anger is dripping from her voice, too. I have never heard her like this.

'I want to start off by making one thing very clear: this case is about *that woman*.' Comey turns her whole body towards Ghislaine Maxwell, throws an arm towards her and points right at her. The press gallery, more or less in line with where Comey is pointing, takes a slight but perceptible collective in-breath.

'This case is about *Ghislaine Maxwell*, the crimes *she*' – Comey points directly at her again – 'committed.'

She breathes, resets herself, draws in her emotion and regains composure. But it's too late – the jury has seen it. That she cares. That she believes this happened. And, as I will find out later from my interviews with the jurors, this means everything to them.

'The defence are trying to get you to think about anyone other than the defendant ... The defence tried to suggest that even if Jeffrey Epstein did engage in sexual contact with Jane, Kate, Carolyn and Annie, Maxwell didn't know about it. She just had no idea that her boyfriend and best friend for more than a decade had a thing for teenage girls. Ladies and gentlemen, that suggestion is borderline laughable. *Of course she knew.*

'The defendant ran every aspect of Jeffrey Epstein's life for the better part of a decade. She travelled with him constantly. She shared a bed with him, inside a bedroom they can't get to without walking past a photo of a young girl pulling down her underwear. She had a bathroom off of that master bedroom. She referred to her homes as his home. She was the lady of the house. So of course she knew what was going on.

'Of course she knew that her boyfriend, when he was spending time with teenage girls like Jane, like Carolyn, like Annie, like Virginia Roberts, she knew that he was doing it because he was attracted to them, because he wanted to have sex with them. The suggestion that she didn't know borders on the absurd.'

Comey went on: 'The sexual abuse of children is not the kind of crime that leaves paper evidence. The victims are the evidence … The defence attacked Jane, Kate, Carolyn, and Annie, and it's obvious why they did that. Those four witnesses gave you the most damning testimony in this trial. If you believe those women, then that's it; the defendant is guilty,' she repeats for emphasis.

'The defence's own expert, Professor Loftus, confirmed that the core memories of trauma are solid. Peripheral details make it a little fuzzy, but those main memories, those events that are at the centre, are implanted. Some things you never forget because they're seared into your brain forever.

'You remember key moments, moments that change your life, like Jane remembering the defendant touching her breasts, Carolyn remembering the defendant touching her breasts, Annie remembering the defendant touching her breasts, Kate remembering the defendant standing right next to her in the doorway the first time she sees Jeffrey Epstein naked, frozen with fear.

'There was nothing peripheral about the defendant. She was the core memory; she was essential to this scheme.

'And you know Jane was 14 when she met Maxwell and Epstein. She vividly remembers being 14 years old when that abuse began. It was within a year of her father dying. That's an anchoring way for her to hold on to that memory and know she was 14. It's also what she told [her boyfriend] Matt a decade ago, long before this trial. And there are documents to confirm she's right ... You saw the Interlochen records putting her and the defendant and Epstein all at Interlochen [in] the same summer of 1994. You saw the flight records putting Maxwell and Epstein there that summer. It is so clear that Jane was 14 when she met these predators.'

Comey is not letting this point go. 'And hypothetically,' she adds, 'let's just say the defence was right. Let's just say that she got the timing of her first meeting [with Maxwell and Epstein] wrong, that it was actually that last summer when she turned 16 in 1996 – and you know that she knew them by the time she was 16, because you saw the flight records putting her on those planes with the defendant and Epstein going to New York when she was 16. So the best argument the defence has is she was 16, not 14, when the abuse happened. That is not a defence. It is still illegal. It is not a defence to say, "Oh, no, no, no, she was 16, not 14, when I touched her breasts." It's still a crime.'

Now Comey moves on to Carolyn's evidence. 'Carolyn vividly remembers the first time she met the defendant,' she says. 'That first day was a scarring memory for Carolyn, and she remembers Maxwell as a fixture in her experiences at the Palm Beach house – like the stuffing at Thanksgiving, there every time.

'And why is the defence focusing so much on these peripheral details? Because they desperately want you to ignore the fact that Carolyn has consistently remembered Maxwell as one of the people involved in her experiences at that house. They want you to forget that she mentioned Maxwell not once, but twice in her 2009 deposition. Without prompting, Carolyn named Maxwell as one of the two people who would call her to schedule these massages with Jeffrey Epstein ... She named her as one of the two people she would talk to when she called herself, begging to come over because she needed the money. And Carolyn told [her boyfriend] Shawn that she met a woman named Maxwell, whose first name she couldn't pronounce.

'Now, back then there was no reason for Carolyn to go into more detail about what was happening with Maxwell, especially not in a lawsuit that was about Sarah and Epstein. But when she was asked more detailed questions, she remembered the core events, and she'd already mentioned Maxwell, without prompting, long before there could be anything to contaminate her memory.'

Comey's next target is the defence's arguments on memory. 'The defence suggests that somehow these clear memories of Maxwell got implanted into the brains of Jane and Kate and Carolyn and Annie. The defence seems to suggest that this implantation happened from the media, greedy civil lawyers and the FBI.

'Starting with the media, you heard absolutely nothing at this trial about any of these witnesses consuming media in this case. Turning to the lawyers: there is not a shred of evidence that a group of lawyers got together, made up a story about Maxwell and then implanted it into these witnesses' minds. Remember, each witness had a different lawyer. So for this theory to work, four different attorneys had to come up with this story and separately manipulate their clients into perjuring themselves at a federal trial, all so they could get a cut of the Epstein Victims' Compensation Fund. That makes no sense.

'Annie mentioned [the abuse] to Dave Mulligan, her high-school boyfriend, and the FBI in 2006. She told both of them how Maxwell touched her breasts during a massage. Jane told Matt, her boyfriend from a decade ago, about the woman who would make her feel comfortable in the room. Carolyn mentioned meeting the woman with short black hair and an accent to the FBI in 2007. She mentioned Maxwell twice in her deposition, and she told Shawn that she saw Maxwell at the house at that time, way before there was a compensation fund or any incentive to add in Maxwell if it wasn't true.'

Comey goes on: 'Before he died in 2019, Epstein was the big fish; he's who you go after if you're going to make up a story. So all of the things that these witnesses said about Maxwell before 2019 were not part of some frame-job for the defendant. Even under the defence theory, there was zero reason to make up her involvement with these women, disclosed years ago.

'Really, the whole memory thing makes no sense at all. There is no way that Jane, Kate, Carolyn and Annie just misremembered the defendant's core role in abusing them. So what does that leave the defence with? They are all liars. In order for the defence to be right, witness after witness after witness must have lied to you.

'And all of the witnesses who backed them up must be lying, too. The ex-boyfriends – Matt, Dave, Shawn – they must be lying. Why would they come here and lie to you? ... Jane, Kate, Carolyn and Annie have no motive to lie at this trial. There's nothing pending. These women have already received millions of dollars. They are not getting a penny more.

'If Jane, Kate, Carolyn and Annie really believed that making up a story about Maxwell would somehow benefit them, you better believe they would have told much better lies. If they wanted to frame Maxwell, they would have said that Maxwell was in the room every single time Jeffrey Epstein initiated sexual contact ... That's not what happened. These women put themselves through the hell of testifying at this trial, even though they have nothing to financially gain. They exposed the darkest, most traumatising events of their lives to the world at this trial ... They sat on that stand and went through excruciating and humiliating cross-examination. Why would they let themselves be attacked like that? You know why. They did it for justice, for the hope that the defendant would be held accountable for her role in shattering their lives.'

Maurene Comey is more emotional with every word. Next, she says the thing that will take up residence on repeat in my head.

'The defendant never thought that those teenage girls would have the strength to report what happened to them,' she says, her voice breaking. 'But the defendant didn't count on those teenage girls growing up into the women who testified at this trial; women who would be willing to take that stand and tell the truth about what happened.'

The defendant didn't count on those teenage girls growing up into the women who testified at this trial.

'And she didn't count on you,' Comey says, rounding on the jury. 'She didn't count on a jury who would see past the nonsense that she tried to throw up, who would look at the evidence, clear-eyed, and see her for the predator that she is.

'Ladies and gentlemen, you know what happened here. Four incredibly brave women came forward and told you what happened to them. They opened themselves up and shared their horrifying experiences. Jane, Kate, Carolyn, Annie, they each told you how the defendant played a pivotal role in the worst events of their lives.'

You know what happened here.

'Now it is time to hold her accountable. If you use your common sense, stay focused on the evidence and follow Judge Nathan's instructions on the law, then you will reach the only verdict that is consistent with the evidence, the verdict that justice demands: the defendant is guilty.'

Leslie, Jess, Julie, Vicky and I all exchange glances. We find out later that we are all thinking the same thing: that closing argument could have transformed a possible acquittal into a certain conviction.

CHAPTER 25

New York City, 2021

It is the first full day of jury deliberations in *USA v Maxwell*. The mainstays of the press gallery in courtroom 318 – myself, Leslie, Jess, Julie and Vicky – all trickle in as usual during the morning, between around 2am and 7am, and take our places in the line. We talk about what we can expect, and, of course, what we think the verdict will be.

Recently, I relistened to the interviews I conducted with prominent journalists during the trial – because I was one of so few reporters on the ground, I was hired to work as a field producer for a documentary about the trial – and in each recording I noticed a trend: all of them seemed to be preparing either the audience, or themselves, for an acquittal. They said things like, 'This was always going to be a hard case to prove,' and, 'The government lost a few important arguments early on.' It reminds me that during the trial, we all believed that this prosecution would fail. As we were witnessing it in real time, it seemed to us that the prosecution simply hadn't done enough, that even though we – or, at least, I – were completely sure that these events had happened, it might still be the case that she got away with it.

Of course, my memory is now coloured, in part, by what I know the outcome to be. But when writing about these idle days of verdict-watching, it's important to remind myself that we were at some points sure that this one last attempt at justice would go awry.

'So, what do you think it'll be?' Julie asks me outside the courthouse that morning.

'Honestly,' I remember saying, 'I don't know. At the end of the prosecution's case, I would have said she'll be acquitted, because their case just wasn't that strong. But then her defence was such a mess that when the defence rested, I would have said she might be convicted.'

'Yes, exactly!' Julie said. 'That's what I was thinking.'

'But I think everything changed after closing arguments,' I say. 'I don't know if it's just me, and my personal emotional investment in these kinds of crimes – but when Maurene Comey spoke to the jury yesterday, I think something changed.'

'Absolutely,' Julie says, nodding.

When we file into courtroom 318 that morning, we don't really know what to expect. Courts have their own ways of dealing with awaiting a verdict in different jurisdictions, and we all have varying experiences of covering trials all over the world. But here's what it ended up looking like in the Southern District of New York: we arrive and take our usual seats in the gallery. And then we just wait. We sit there all morning, with nothing to do – no phones, no laptops – and no one to talk to but one another.

Speaking to the other reporters and the security guards, I learn that the way to identify when a verdict or a note is imminent is that there will be flutters of movement around the idle courtroom. The stenographer will be called, and she will have to come into the courtroom. Then the lawyers will be called, and they will file in from the dedicated offices in which they are posted, waiting for the verdict.

We sit and we chatter, sometimes about the trial and sometimes just about our lives. The hours stretch on and on and we grow hungrier and hungrier. Around mid-morning, I take a quick trip to the bathroom, and as the lift doors open to deposit me back on level three, I hear the *ping* that indicates that the second lift is arriving at the same time. I look to my right to say hello to whichever press colleague is arriving, but instead I see Bobbi Sternheim.

Our eyes meet, and she knows immediately that I know what it means that she is here. She gives me a half-smile as we approach the courtroom door. She holds it open for me. 'After you,' she says, still smiling.

I hurry to take my seat and I pull on Leslie's sleeve.

'Bobbi's here,' I said. 'Something's happening.'

We each scramble to get out our notebooks and pens. Sure enough, about two minutes later, Christian Everdell appears with Laura Menninger. Just behind them is Maurene Comey, and a few moments behind her is Alison Moe. The rest of the lawyers follow shortly after.

Judge Nathan enters the room. 'We have a note,' she says flatly, and her no-nonsense tone jars with the buzzing anticipation that is flowing between the bodies in the press gallery.

Judge Nathan unfolds a piece of paper and reads: 'Could we please have copies of the testimony of Jane, Carolyn and Annie Farmer?'

I turn to Julie, Jess, Vicky and Leslie.

'They want to go over the victims' testimonies more closely,' I say. 'What does that mean?'

'Do you remember all those times Jane said "I don't recall" in a row, just again and again?' someone worries aloud, and I can tell that we all simultaneously cast our minds back to that day – a day that feels like decades ago now – when Jane was being cross-examined.

A silence settles among us. We all agree – silently – that this jury note is bad news for the prosecution. I will learn later, from interviews with jurors, that we are wrong.

As we sit in silence, I ponder what I think this means. It means that this will not be a quick or instinctive verdict – it will not be made based on an intuitive sense that *she must have known* or *she did this*. It means that the jury is taking their job seriously and will rake over the exact testimony and facts of the case before reaching a decision.

I have Alison Moe's voice ringing in my ears: *If you believe these women, that's it. Ghislaine Maxwell is guilty.*

A few hours later, Lara Pomerantz appears at the door of the courtroom and everything repeats itself. The stenographer arrives, the lawyers trickle in, and finally Judge Nathan appears. 'We have a note,' she says, in exactly the same flat tone as she used earlier that day.

'Can we have a look at the notes from Carolyn's interview with the FBI?'

Everyone seems to shift in their seats.

The defence relied heavily on handwritten notes from interviews some of the victims did with the FBI – which the defence argued included contradictions in the victims' stories, and which they used to boost one of the central tenets of their argument: that these victims' stories have changed over time; that they included Maxwell in their stories after the fact because there was suddenly some secondary benefit in doing so.

The defence was allowed to question the victims about these notes because they were presented as 'impeachment evidence', or evidence that can be used to contradict something the witness said on direct examination.

The impeachment rule allows attorneys to present evidence that would otherwise be hearsay – which these notes are, because the jury did not hear directly from the FBI agent who wrote them. Without the person who created the document coming forward and testifying that it is an accurate record of the interview, the document itself is hearsay – which is why Judge Nathan didn't allow any of the FBI notes to be admitted into evidence.

So, this question from the jury sparks furious debate among the lawyers. Of course, the defence wants to be able to show the jury these notes, and the prosecution does not – because, as they argued through the witnesses, the notes are a rushed, handwritten, inaccurate record of an interview that was done very early on in the Maxwell/Epstein investigation.

Judge Nathan is firm that her answer to the jury's question is 'no', and the defence – including Ghislaine – is visibly upset by this.

When Judge Nathan leaves, the group of us reflect on what this question means. It means, we all agree, that the jury is focused very heavily on the victims' testimonies, and on their credibility. *If you believe these women, that's it. Ghislaine Maxwell is guilty.*

CHAPTER 26

New York City, 2021

It's verdict day, but we don't know it yet. The wind is bitingly cold. I arrive at 2am and have paid a line sitter to be there from 9pm the night before. Things are getting more and more competitive when it comes to those four spots in courtroom 318. Reporters who haven't been in the room for the whole trial desperately want to be there on verdict day – they want to see Ghislaine when the verdict is read, want to see the jurors' faces when everything finally ends.

Leslie is changing over with her line sitter at around 6am, and when she arrives we do our Starbucks coffee run together. We have done this for each other every morning, but on this morning we go together; we are feeling nostalgic about this incredible connection we have formed in such a short period of time. As we cross the square, bracing ourselves against the cold, we reflect on the last few weeks.

While our coffees are being made, we snap a selfie. We will send this photo back and forth over the next few months, marvelling at how strange it is that we didn't know, when we were taking it, what would happen later that day.

At around 9.30am, I notice Liz Stein, another of Epstein's and Maxwell's victims, near the courtroom door.

I can see that she's speaking with one of the security guards and asking to be allowed into the courtroom. I can see that he's shaking his head. Suddenly I feel full of uncontrollable rage at this indignity – this indignity after decades and decades of other indignities.

'Hi there, sorry to interrupt,' I say to the security guard. I motion to myself: 'Lucia, we've spoken a few times – I've been here every day.'

'I know,' he says. 'Hi, Lucia – everything okay?'

'Well, I just wanted to come over and ask what's going on – I know that Liz is a victim of the crimes charged on the indictment in this trial, and I'm fairly sure that entitles her to a seat in the courtroom.'

'Well, as I was just explaining to Miss Stein, it's not that simple,' he says. I can tell he expects this to be enough for me and is surprised when I am still standing there ten seconds later.

'Go on,' I say, after a pause. 'How is it more complicated?'

'Well, Miss Stein did not actually testify at this trial so she's not *technically* a victim.'

'Oh, come on,' I say to him. 'We are talking about a trial involving one of the largest and most heinous sex trafficking rings in history. Surely you know that there will be victims who don't testify at trial but still want to assert their right to have a seat in court?'

'In my mind, she's not a victim,' the man says, motioning to Liz as though she is not even there.

'Excuse me?' I say, angry now. 'How dare you say that in front of her.'

'I'm sorry, but she's not.'

'Don't speak about her like she's not standing right there.'

The security guard is completely unfazed. 'I don't know what you want me to do. We originally had one seat reserved for victims, but then about halfway through the trial we took it away.'

'Why?'

'I don't know.'

'Well, you used the word "we" – *we* took it away. So that implies you were involved somehow.'

'Well, yes, the court administration took it away.'

'And are you part of the court administration?'

'Yes.'

'So why was the victims' seat taken away?'

'I don't know.'

'Okay, how about this,' I say. 'Liz and I will swap. She can have my seat. I've got the spot on the far right of the fourth bench back.'

'No, ma'am, that's not possible.'

'What?' I stammer. 'W-why?'

'Because it's first come, first serve, miss. You got here at 2am, so you get the seat. She didn't get here at 2am, so she doesn't get the seat.'

'*Please*,' I say. 'Stop talking about her as though she's not there.'

I sneak a glance at Liz, who is tearing up.

'Let me get my boss,' the security guard says, and he brings over a man named Joe, who I know by now is the head of the court administration office.

'Hi, Joe, how are you doing?' I say in my sweetest, most professional voice.

'Hi there, what's the problem?'

'Well,' I say. 'This is Liz Stein. She's a victim of Ghislaine Maxwell. She's been commuting to trial every day from inter-state, so she's not able to arrive at 2am to get to the front of the line to get into the main courtroom. But given that she's a crime victim, I'm fairly sure that the CVRA protects her right to have a seat in this courtroom,' I say, referring to the Crime Victims' Rights Act.

'She's not a victim,' Joe says, with the most alarming lack of sympathy. I can feel my mouth hanging open.

'Yes, she is,' I say. 'She applied to the Epstein Victims' Compensation Fund.'

'Well, she's not registered with my office as a victim, so she's not a victim.'

Liz cuts in here. 'Look, I can prove it if you need me to—'

Joe cuts her off, raises his voice. Lifts his arms up threateningly. *Yells* at her.

'Look, if you haven't registered with my office, you are not a victim.'

'Excuse me,' I say. 'This is a place of business. You can have your rules – that's fine – but there is absolutely no excuse for yelling at a traumatised person while she waits for a verdict for her abuser in a federal sex trafficking trial.'

Julie Brown arrives from the elevator in this moment, and immediately clocks that something is happening.

'What's going on?' she says.

'Joe has just yelled at Liz that she's not a true victim.'

Joe raises his voice again.

In that moment, Julie has the same idea as me. 'Look, she can have my seat, okay? I'll swap with her.'

'I already offered,' I say, turning to Julie. 'They said no.'

'*What?*' Julie says, indignant.

Joe, furious now, repeats what his colleague has said. 'You two got here early enough, so the seats are yours. They are non-transferable,' he says flatly, as though the seats in this federal courtroom were digital tickets to a Taylor Swift concert.

Julie doesn't know what to say. 'I'm going to speak to the judge.'

She walks purposefully into the courtroom, beyond the press gallery and up towards where Judge Nathan would usually sit, looking around for her deputy, Miss Williams.

Joe looks as though he may explode.

'EXCUSE ME,' he screams at Julie, chasing her. '*YOU CANNOT BE THERE. I AM CALLING SECURITY AND I WILL HAVE YOU REMOVED FROM THIS COURTHOUSE PERMANENTLY.*'

Joe approaches her threateningly and Julie, alarmed at his aggression, raises her hands in surrender. 'I just want to speak to the judge,' she is saying as he violently ushers her outside and walks off in a huff.

Julie and I catch one another's eyes, sharing a look of *what the hell was that?* We look around for Liz, but she is gone.

'I'll go find her. You stay here and let me know if he comes back,' Julie says, motioning to the exit that Joe has just marched out of, and then she is gone, too.

I sit and wait for her to come back, debriefing Jess and Leslie on what has just happened.

About ten minutes later, Julie reappears, shaking her head furiously.

'She's distraught,' Julie says. 'She's going back to Philly on the train. Said she can't be here anymore.'

I feel crushed under the weight of the injustice of that. I can tell that Julie is feeling the same.

We sit down together on two chairs that are usually used by security guards, but which are sitting empty today.

'I just got yelled at by the courthouse administrators' office when I called them just now,' she said.

'What do you mean?'

'They said, "You're a journalist, not an advocate for victims – you shouldn't be calling us about victims' seats in the courtroom."'

She is striking on something which, of course, all of us who do this kind of work have thought about: what should our role be? Were we wrong to get involved in what just happened with Liz?

'And what do you think about that?' I ask, sincerely. She hears the earnestness in my voice and knows I want her answer.

'I think that it absolutely is part of my job as a journalist to stand up for people like Liz. Journalism is about giving a voice to the powerless – this is part of that.'

And this is the ethos I know I will carry with me for the rest of my journalism career.

By mid-afternoon, Leslie, Jess and Julie and I are all flagging. The exhaustion, both emotional and physical, that we have been desperately trying to keep at bay over the last five weeks is threatening to swallow us whole.

At a few minutes past four, there is movement. Christian Everdell appears at the door of the courtroom, then Bobbi Sternheim.

We look at the clock and consult each other. It's late, and the jurors are probably exhausted. Around this time every day, they've sent a note to the judge about what time they'd like to finish for the day. We assume this will be another of those.

But then one of the top court administrators walks in. He is not wearing a suit. I have seen him almost every day for a month, but I barely recognise him without the suit. He is wearing jeans. My interest piqued, I move closer to where he is standing and talking to a colleague. I only catch a few words, but it is enough.

'Already on the subway home … next stop … ran back.'

I lean over to Leslie again.

'It's a verdict,' I say and gesture towards the court administrator in his jeans. Her eyes widen.

Behind me, five FBI agents that I have never seen before file into the back of the courtroom and stand to attention. Leslie, Jess, Julie and I all notice them.

'This is it,' Leslie says. We all breathe in deeply and wait.

Both legal teams have arrived now, looking flustered. Judge Nathan walks in and takes her seat behind the bench.

'We have a verdict,' she says. 'Bring in the jury.'

A knock at the adjoining door that leads to the jury room, and Judge Nathan's deputy walks the 12 jurors into the room as we all stand. For the first time in the whole trial, Ghislaine Maxwell turns to face them as they enter. Her first act of humility.

The foreperson stands up with a microphone.

'Have you reached a unanimous verdict?' Judge Nathan asks.

'We have,' the foreperson replies, and hands up the verdict sheet.

'I will now read the verdict,' Judge Nathan says quietly.

No one breathes.
'Count one: guilty.
'Count two: not guilty.
'Count three: guilty.
'Count four: guilty.
'Count five: guilty.
'Count six: guilty.'
If you believe these women, that's it. Ghislaine Maxwell is guilty.

CHAPTER 27

New York, 2021

After the verdict is handed down, Leslie, Jess, Julie and I all rush outside to post about the news and to wait for the attorneys to walk down the courthouse steps and give their statements. In the moment when the foreperson read the verdict, Leslie and I had just looked at each other, eyes full of feeling – sadness, relief, catharsis, exhaustion.

Now, standing outside the building, we keep catching each other's eye with that same expression. But also, we have to work: Leslie is updating her followers and I am recording an interview for a documentary I am working on about the trial. Everything feels a bit surreal.

After a long wait, Bobbi Sternheim appears and gives her statement, followed by the prosecutors and the survivors' lawyers. When it's all over, Leslie, Jess, Julie, a few other trial friends and I go to a restaurant in Lower Manhattan where we sit together and decompress. I say to Julie that she's the only reason this trial even happened, that any semblance of justice was delivered, and I really mean it. She waves off the accolade – that's not what she does this for – and suggests we FaceTime Liz Stein, because we are both thinking of her, both heartbroken that the treatment she received from the court administrators earlier that day – could that really have been today? – forced her to get on a train back to Philadelphia and miss the verdict, this crucial moment in her own life.

Liz picks up the phone immediately from bed. She is crying

happy, cathartic tears. Speaking to her makes my night, and I can tell it makes Julie's, too.

As the night ends, Leslie and I are the last ones left. We are standing on the New York City street, her waiting for my Uber to arrive to make sure I get home safely before she starts her journey back to New Jersey. We both cry. We hug each other. The enormity of our closeness, of what we have just been through together, of what we have simultaneously witnessed, sits in the air between us and neither of us knows what to say.

I arrive back at my hotel room just after 1am and my whole body collapses into the sheets. I can think only of Jane, Annie, Kate and Carolyn. *If you believe these women, that's it. Ghislaine Maxwell is guilty.* And they did. They did believe them. And so, from this night on, it is official: Ghislaine Maxwell is guilty.

I fall asleep wondering how that must feel, for the four victims who testified, but also for Liz Stein, and Sarah Ransome, and potentially the hundreds of other victims of Ghislaine and Jeffrey who were glued to the news tonight, waiting to see if their pain would be validated. And it was. It's not everything – I am now close to enough of Maxwell's and Epstein's victims to know that; but I also know that for them, it's a start. For them, it really means something.

———

The next morning, I sleep in. I let my body feel the effects of five weeks of 1am alarms, of 2am arrivals at court. I breathe.

I pull myself out of bed just in time to walk from my hotel just off Wall Street up to midtown to get my rapid Covid test to ensure I can board my red-eye flight to London tonight.

The test is negative, so I sit in my hotel bar at 4pm with a glass of wine watching rolling news coverage of the verdict until my taxi driver picks me up to take me to John F. Kennedy Airport. I check my bags in and find a bar. I sit and text all my trial friends a photo of me at the airport, on the way home. We all say goodbye.

It's 7am on New Year's Eve when I land back in London and take the Piccadilly Line all the way to Finsbury Park. I haven't seen my partner or my cats in almost six weeks. I missed Christmas with them, and almost New Year's Eve. I am thrilled to be home, and also can't shake the feeling that something important in my life has shifted, that I am not the same person I was when I left.

I open Instagram and someone I don't know has sent me a message. There is no text in it, just a link to a profile. I open it up. It belongs to someone called Scotty David, and as I scroll, wondering why I've been sent this profile, I see a close-up of his face. It's a juror I recognise from the top-left corner of the jury box.

I open up his latest post to read the caption and, sure enough, he has just posted that he was on the Maxwell jury. I DM him immediately and ask if he wants to talk.

Scotty looks at my profile, follows me back. Not long afterwards, he messages me in reply: he does want to talk.

Scotty David, who wishes to be identified by his first and middle name, told me that he believed all the victims. All the accusers corroborated each other and were backed up by other evidence, he said.

Scotty said he is proud to be part of holding Maxwell accountable for her crimes.

'This verdict is for all the victims,' Scotty told me. 'For those who testified, for those who came forward and for those who haven't come forward. I'm glad that Maxwell has been held accountable.

'This verdict shows that you can be found guilty no matter your status.'

Scotty told me that he found all the accusers who testified to be believable and credible, despite the defence's many attacks on their credibility and their attempts to poke holes in their memory.

'They were all believable. Nothing they said felt to me like a lie,' he said.

Scotty then told me something that would change both of our lives: he knows that sometimes you can misremember small details of traumatic memories without ever doubting the core of the memory. He knows that because he is himself a survivor of sexual abuse.

'I know what happened when I was sexually abused. I remember the colour of the carpet, the walls. Some of it can be replayed like a video,' he said. He explained this to the jury.

'But I can't remember all the details, there are some things that run together.'

So he knew that some misremembered details doesn't mean the memory itself didn't happen.

There were also questions from the jury about why the girls didn't come forward earlier. But Scotty said he knows what that's like, too. 'I didn't disclose my abuse until I was in high school,' he said.

The jury room went dead silent when he shared his story, he told me. Scotty believes this helped the jury understand that it's possible that these women were telling the truth. You might forget some things, he said, but the core of a traumatic memory stays with you.

There were also questions about why the girls kept going back to Epstein and Maxwell, why they accepted their help.

'We are not here to judge these victims,' Scotty told me. 'We are here to judge whether we believe their stories, but we are not here to judge the decisions they made or didn't make.

'We cannot judge what they did or didn't do afterward,' he said. 'It doesn't change that it happened.'

Scotty felt that the defence were continually attacking the accusers on the stand, and he said these attempts did little to change his mind.

At one point, Carolyn threw her binder of evidence down

beside her because she was so distressed by the questioning she was being subjected to.

'It just made me feel more compassion for her,' Scotty said.

The juror said that, ultimately, the jury found that all the victims were credible.

The defence team focused strongly on its memory expert, Professor Elizabeth Loftus. Loftus testified about experiments that had been conducted in which researchers had successfully implanted a false memory into the mind of research subjects. In one study, the researchers were able to change a detail of a memory about witnessing a car accident. They were able to convince participants that the scene featured a stop sign rather than a yield sign.

But that didn't sway the jury either, Scotty said.

'None of that relates to traumatic memory,' he said. Loftus said herself that she had never conducted a study on whether these tactics would work with memories of sexual abuse, Scotty recalled.

Since the trial, there has been speculation that the fact a juror had been a victim of sexual abuse could be used by Maxwell as grounds for appeal. Speaking separately to the MailOnline, Scotty said he could not remember the details of the fifty-question pre-trial questionnaire each potential juror was asked about whether they were a victim of sexual abuse or a relative or a friend of a victim, but felt he had answered all questions honestly.

Scotty told the *Independent* that the accusers' testimony was corroborated by a significant amount of evidence.

He specifically mentioned Kate – an accuser who testified but was not allowed to be considered for the actual charges because she was over the age of consent in the UK when she was abused – and said her testimony powerfully corroborated the other accusers' stories.

'She was able to show us that this was a pattern,' Scotty said. 'We knew we couldn't use her testimony to convict Maxwell, but she showed the pattern of how those girls were groomed. She showed us the pattern that happened to all of these girls.'

'It was about confusing their boundaries,' he said. 'For Jane, it started with seeing Maxwell topless. For Annie Farmer, it started with Maxwell showing her how to give Epstein a foot massage. The pattern is that Ghislaine talks to you like she is also a teenager. Then it moves into massage. She tries to make you comfortable, to see what they can get away with.

'What she did was wrong.'

Annie Farmer's story was backed up by her teenage diary, as well as her high school boyfriend. That was important to the jury, he said.

Carolyn's story was backed up by Shawn, her ex-boyfriend, who testified that he used to drive her to Epstein's Palm Beach mansion.

Jane's story was backed up by her high school boyfriend, who remembered being told about Epstein when they were younger.

The accuser's stories were backed up by flight logs which placed Jane on at least one flight with Maxwell, Scotty said.

Their stories were backed up by Maxwell's 'little black book' – an address book found in Epstein's home that listed the names of 'masseuses' including Jane and Carolyn.

Scotty said the little black book also gave the jurors clues about how Maxwell and Epstein had evaded accountability in the past. There were names of several Palm Beach police officers listed on a first-name basis in that book, Scotty said.

'Those girls' names and phone numbers were listed next to the words "mom" and "dad",' he said. 'Professional masseuses do not need their parents with them.'

Many speculated that the jury chose to acquit Maxwell on count two because that count related solely to Jane, and that Jane was less credible than other victims.

But Scotty told me that wasn't the case.

'We simply didn't see enough direct evidence to convict on count two,' he said. 'It wasn't about not believing Jane.'

Count two was a substantive charge that required proof that Maxwell 'enticed' Jane to travel across state lines. Scotty said there just wasn't any direct evidence for any specific trip that Maxwell took any action to entice Jane to get on those flights.

'I personally was willing to find her guilty on count two,' he said. 'But we all decided in the end that there wasn't enough evidence.'

Scotty also explained that he was convinced by the closeness of Maxwell and Epstein's relationship and the key role she played in his life.

We hang up, and I type up the interview. An hour or so later, I send it to him to check all the quotes, and he signs off on it.

The editors who are publishing the story have got lawyers involved to check everything, and we hit publish. By this time, Scotty has already given his second interview to the *Daily Mail*, but ours ends up being published first.

It doesn't take long for the articles responding to the interview to come in. They suggest that Scotty's comments about his own sexual abuse could lead to a mistrial if he didn't disclose the abuse on his juror form. I had asked Scotty if he'd disclosed his abuse on the form, and he said he couldn't remember being asked about it but that he'd answered all the questions honestly.

All of the papers are suggesting that you cannot serve on a jury for a sexual abuse trial if you yourself have been sexually abused. But that's not true; it's not an accurate representation of the law at all. In fact, jurors are seated all the time who have experiences akin to the stories on trial.

Scotty hires a lawyer, who tells him not to speak to me, or any reporters, until the situation is ironed out. I understand that, of course, but I think about him every day.

Before long, the defence has filed a motion for a retrial based on Scotty's comments, claiming that he showed bias. As I read this, I can think only of his words: *I believe so strongly in the concept of innocent until proven guilty. I went into every day of that trial assuming she didn't do it.*

Everyone on my social media platforms immediately starts demonising Scotty for lying. But we haven't yet confirmed that he has 'lied' – and weren't we now, yet again, just assuming that an abuse victim is dishonest?

I ask the court for Scotty's juror form to see his answers, but the court administrators refuse to give it to me. Soon, it transpires that there was a question about being a victim of abuse, and Scotty answered 'no'. The internet lights up again with allegations that he has misled the court. But I am the only one who has spoken to him, who heard the tone of his voice when he realised he might have mistakenly not disclosed his abuse. I know, in a way that no one else can know, that he didn't lie – he made a mistake.

The question asked of the jurors, in full, read: 'Have you or a friend or family member ever been the victim of sexual harassment, sexual abuse or sexual assault? (This includes actual or attempted sexual assault or other unwanted sexual advance, including by a stranger, acquaintance, supervisor, teacher or family member.)'

Scotty ticked the box for 'no'.

There are two issues here, though, and both of them bother me. The first, of course, is the fact that Scotty answered 'no' when asked if he had been an abuse victim. That is worthy of consideration – and I'll get to that in a second. But what bothered me more was that the overwhelming sense from the public was that people genuinely believed that sexual abuse victims are not fit to sit on juries in sexual abuse trials – which just isn't true, and is not said about victims of burglary or fraud.

Everyone who wrote to me, commented, called me, seemed to think that once a person has been a victim of abuse, they can never again be fair or rational. This seems far too close, in my opinion, to suggesting that they are fundamentally damaged in some way that victims of other crimes are not, and that they should be excluded from participating in certain aspects of societal life as a result.

I decide to investigate. I call up Dominic Willmott, an expert in legal psychology at Loughborough University in England, who has dedicated his career to researching jury decision-making in rape trials.

Willmott tells me that his many years of research on this topic have told him two things. First, there is no well-established scientific literature that sexual abuse victims lean one way or the other when deciding whether to convict or acquit a defendant accused of sexual crimes. Second, there is incredibly persuasive evidence that what does sway jurors is not whether they have experienced sexual violence, but their attitudes towards it – something that is not asked about on the questionnaire.

'We conducted two studies looking at whether people with experience of sexual victimisation are more likely to convict or acquit a defendant on trial for sexual crimes,' Willmott explains. 'In the first study, 75 per cent of jurors who had been sexually victimised returned a guilty verdict, and 25 per cent returned a not-guilty verdict – so that one indicated a tendency to convict,' he explained. 'But in the second study, 100 per cent of jurors who had been victims of sexual crimes returned a not-guilty verdict – indicating a tendency to acquit.'

The conclusion? Willmott says there is just not strong enough evidence one way or the other.

Willmott notes that the predominant process for jury selection in the US is typically referred to as 'scientific jury selection', but the notion that sexual abuse victims are biased jurors is just not backed up by a rigorous body of scientific research.

'If that's what we are calling it, then we should be looking at the science,' he says. 'Assuming, without a well-established evidence base, that victims are more inclined to vote one way or another is simply not scientific, and therefore we should not be excluding anyone based on that supposition.'

He tells me that recent multi-country research from the World Health Organization suggests that one in three women globally have been, or will be, sexually victimised during their lifetime. Other figures suggest one in ten men will also experience sexual abuse over the course of their life.

After noting that the question on the Maxwell jury questionnaire asked jurors not only whether they themselves had been sexually assaulted, abused or harassed, but also whether a friend or family member had been, Willmott says this question would exclude almost everyone.

'When you widen the question out to your social network, realistically almost everyone would have to answer yes to that question if they were being truthful,' Willmott says. 'So that leaves you with an incredibly small jury pool.'

Next, I call Paul W. Eastwick, a professor of psychology at the University of California, Davis, who agrees that there seems to be a different set of rules for sexual abuse victims.

'I would note that it is just as reasonable to suggest that jurors without sexual abuse history are also biased, just in a different way,' Eastwick says. 'In other words, all jurors will bring their own experiences with them into the deliberations, and – from a social science perspective – there isn't an official standard that makes one set of experiences the normative default and a second set of experiences the "biased" ones.'

Bette Bottoms, professor emerita of psychology at the University of Illinois, Chicago, tells me she has a study that does indicate victims of abuse are slightly more likely to have empathy with victims in a sex crime trial – but she does not believe this means that we should not have abuse victims on juries.

In fact, Bottoms echoed Eastwick's point – if anything, the evidence suggests that people who have not been abused have a bias that should be considered as well, and that there shouldn't be a special category for abuse victims.

'We do not believe our study supports the argument that these abused jurors should be struck from the jury during jury selection. Instead, we argue that their experience with abuse is just one among thousands of experiences that make jurors individuals, and just one more piece of experience they should draw from while deliberating a case,' Bottoms says.

'Why do we think it is fair to strike the abused jurors, but not those who were not abused?' she adds.

'Consider describing our results a different way,' she says. 'We found that jurors who were not abused did not have as much empathy for the victims. They did not find defendants guilty as often. That is indeed a bias.'

In general, Willmott has found that personal characteristics and experiences are not strong predictors of bias. What is a strong predictor of bias, on the other hand, is what he calls 'attitudes' – long-held beliefs, based on societal stereotypes, about certain crimes. Rape beliefs are – according to the science – the most important predictor of bias in rape trials, Willmott explains to me.

'In our studies, sexual victimisation was not a significant predictor of jury decisions. In fact, when considered alongside a number of other juror characteristics, the only factor that was a consistent predictor of verdict choices was rape myth beliefs – the extent to which you believe misconceptions or endorse stereotypes about sexual violence.'

Rape myths are defined as beliefs about sexual violence that are factually incorrect but widely believed. They include beliefs in inaccurate statements such as: false allegations of rape are common; any delay in reporting rape is suspicious; people who get voluntarily intoxicated are at least partly responsible for their rape; if the complainant did not scream, fight or get injured, then it is not rape; and an encounter is not rape if a complainant fails to sufficiently communicate lack of consent to the accused.

'Nearly all of the research conducted over the last 40 years shows us that the degree to which you believe in these rape myths directly contributes to whether you will convict or acquit a perpetrator accused of a sex crime,' Willmott says.

The idea that our attitudes towards factually incorrect but widely cited beliefs about rape have a detrimental impact on jury decision-making is incredibly well demonstrated by scientific evidence, he says. 'And yet we do not screen for that, and we focus on whether the juror has themselves been victimised when we have no well-established evidence base that this would affect their decision-making.

'The truth is that we apply a separate set of rules and standards to victims of sexual violence throughout the whole criminal justice process, and that's why we need radical reforms regarding how we treat victims and manage the impact of bias upon jury outcomes,' Willmott says.

He also tells me that as someone who studies attitudes towards sexual abuse victims, he is very disappointed by the public's reaction to Scotty David's story.

Now, the issue of Scotty's incorrect answer on the questionnaire.

To ensure I am exercising balance, I call up a criminal defence attorney. Lisa Wayne, the executive director of the National Association of Criminal Defense Lawyers, tells me that from the perspective of the defence, it is crucial to be able to explore a juror's personal history in these kinds of cases.

But Wayne adds that it doesn't seem in this case that the juror with a history of abuse intentionally misled the court – the problem arising in this case was that lawyers were not able to delicately explore the question of any past history of abuse.

Wayne says the phrasing of the question in this case could have given rise to error.

'This could easily have been a misunderstanding on the part of the juror as to what he was being asked,' Wayne says. 'It's not a very good question.'

She adds: 'It seems very possible that this juror never intentionally misled anyone.'

Wayne says that in sexual assault cases, she would always expect to see a question about whether jurors had been victims of assault themselves – but not questions as complicated as this one.

'We try to make them very simple and straightforward in order to avoid this kind of confusion,' Wayne tells me. 'You don't want these long, run-on sentences with multiple-choice answers … This is the perfect example of the kind of question that causes problems,' she adds.

Wayne also says that in her extensive experience as a criminal defence lawyer, she has found that it is extremely unusual for jurors to intentionally mislead the court during jury selection.

'I've tried hundreds of jury trials,' she explains. 'And I know that jurors take this incredibly seriously. They do not intentionally mislead the court. The only issue is whether you are able to ask the right questions.'

Wayne says the issues that have arisen out of this trial demonstrate how important it is for courts to be careful about the way they deal with sexual abuse histories in jury selection.

'This just shows how important it is to get this right,' she says.

Wayne notes that it is a 'delicate area of questioning' and jurors have said 'that they were sexually assaulted 30 years previously and forgot about it' until they were being questioned.

These screening questions should be asked in-person and not through written questionnaires, she says.

'It is so important to be able to carefully and delicately explore very personal and traumatic experiences that people have repressed. And that wasn't allowed to happen here.'

My head spinning, I await Judge Nathan's decision on the retrial. I cry several times a day as I consider that an article I have written could undermine the entire trial. I think over and over about what I should have done: should I have killed the story, in case this happened? Or was it right to publish?

I call up Julie Brown, who will forever be my go-to for questions of journalistic integrity.

She answers the phone immediately, and enthusiastically congratulates me. I am baffled.

'What for?'

'You got a great scoop, and you revealed something important and true.'

'But it could have terrible consequences,' I stammer.

'Lucia,' she says, serious now. 'If you are only going to report stories when you are certain what the outcome will be, you are not a journalist, and you are not up for this job … You have to be able to tell the truth when you have no idea what will happen. You cannot control the outcome of your stories. If you try, you will not be doing your job.'

'But maybe I should have killed the story. Maybe that would have been the morally better thing to do.'

'Was the story true? Did he really give you those quotes?'

'Yes,' I say definitively. 'Of course.'

'Then you had no choice but to report it. If you'd done anything else, I'd be extremely disappointed in you.'

A pause.

'Plus, now we are going to have a conversation about the system and how it questions jurors and why it's asking questions like this on a jury form,' she says. 'And that's what journalism is for.'

Then she asks me: 'Do you think it's right what people are saying, that sexual abuse survivors should never be allowed to sit on juries for sexual abuse cases?'

'No,' I say. 'I don't.'

'Well then, go and report on that story. You've started the conversation – don't be afraid to finish it. Ask experts. Report on what you find. Give us the information we need to analyse this issue. That's your job, and you can't shy away from it now.'

I sniffle, and she can hear in my voice how upset and worried I am.

'Stop crying and get to work,' she says, in her characteristic no-nonsense way.

'Okay,' I say, my voice steadying. 'You're right.'

'And Lucia?' she says, before I hang up.

'Mmm?'

'I'm proud of you.'

Judge Nathan orders an evidentiary hearing to examine the issue of Scotty's juror form. An evidentiary hearing basically means that Scotty will have to come to court and the judge personally will ask him questions about his answers on the form.

Of course this is extremely worrying, and the stress devours me. But Judge Nathan does say something interesting when she orders the hearing.

'To be clear, the potential impropriety is not that someone with a history of sexual abuse may have served on the jury. Rather, it is the potential failure to respond truthfully to questions during the jury selection process that asked for that material information so that any potential bias could be explored.'

So, I think to myself, we really are going to have this conversation. I do what Julie says and I get back to work.

Scotty attends the hearing and explains to Judge Nathan that the reason he mistakenly checked 'no' on the questionnaire was for all the same reasons we explored together at trial – the memories are difficult to think about and he often tries to push them out of his mind. The question was confusing and he was answering it quickly, he explains, not thinking that he would actually be seated as a juror.

He explains that his personal experience in no way interfered with his ability to assess the case fairly.

For weeks and weeks, we await Judge Nathan's ruling. When it arrives, it is 11pm in London and I am already in bed with my cats. It is 1 April 2022.

> This Court has presided over a murder trial in which a juror who had a family member murdered was not struck for cause. So too victims of fraud serve faithfully in fraud trials and individuals who have been discriminated against serve fairly in discrimination cases. And survivors of rape have and can serve impartially in trials charging the crime of rape. In this case, Juror 50's responses at the hearing to the questions regarding his ability to be a fair and impartial juror, even in light of his past experience of sexual abuse, established that he too could serve fairly and impartially ...
>
> So the critical question, as for any juror, is whether the juror has the ability to decide the case based only on the evidence presented in court, not extraneous information, and without bias, prejudice, or sympathy. See U.S. ex rel. *Owen v. McMann*, 435 F.2d 813, 818 (2d Cir. 1970) ...
>
> Juror 50 repeatedly and unequivocally affirmed his ability to do just that. And for all the reasons articulated above, the Court found that testimony credible.

And, the most important part of Judge Nathan's ruling:

> To imply or infer that Juror 50 was biased – simply because he was himself a victim of sexual abuse in a trial related to sexual abuse and sex trafficking, and despite his own credible testimony under the penalty of perjury, establishing that he could be an even-handed and impartial juror – would be tantamount to concluding that an individual with a history of sexual abuse can never serve as a fair and impartial juror in such a trial. That is not the law, nor should it be.

That is not the law, nor should it be.

That night, I sleep through the night for the first time in three months.

PART THREE

The Stories You Didn't Hear at Trial

CHAPTER 28

New York City, 1991

Jessica Michaels danced with MC Hammer and Aretha Franklin.

Jessica's life felt like a movie that year. At 21, she had finally made it as a professional dancer. She had moved to New York City to dance, and had left her old life behind. In the summer of 1990, she had just been offered a dance contract in Tokyo that paid her thousands of dollars – more money than she could have dreamed of as a child. The contract led her to more connections to modelling agencies where she made tens of thousands of dollars. She modelled during the day and danced in the show at night.

Earlier in 1990, Jessica was commuting to the city from her family home in Connecticut, and the travel was taxing. But during her first dance contract of 1990, she made friends with a girl called Christine, who was slightly older, more experienced and kind. The two became fast friends, and Christine asked Jessica if she wanted to move into her apartment in Brooklyn. Jessica was thrilled.

The Brooklyn brownstone was warm and inviting, on a tree-lined street that felt like home.

The two girls didn't see each other very much that year, because both of them were dancing and modelling profession-ally all over the world. Jessica had just come back from a dance contract and lots of freelance modelling job in Tokyo, and she still remembers the feeling she got when she boarded a subway in Yokohama and saw her own face on the ad inside the train, surrounded by busy commuters packed like sardines.

When she arrived home from that trip, Christine was excited. She had met someone, and she had that air about her, that brimming sense of possibility, that feeling that a new life was on its way to her.

'So I've been working with this guy,' Christine said as the two girls sat together in their living room.

'Tell me more,' Jessica said, enjoying the glowing sense of camaraderie that comes with these shared confidences.

'Well, he's very rich,' Christine said. 'He's a millionaire.'

Christine's boss had travelled all over the world, she told Jessica, and he knew every single gold standard massage technique from across the globe.

'He's training me in massage,' Christine said proudly.

Christine started travelling more and more with her new boss. Jessica noticed that she would drop everything to travel overseas with him – to Europe, to Asia – for a week at a time. These moments seemed incredibly enticing to Jessica, as they would to anyone.

When Jessica asked why Christine travelled with him, she explained that he really liked to receive hand and foot massages whenever he was in the air, because he got uncomfortable swelling in his extremities at altitude.

'But listen,' she said. 'When I travel with him for a week, I do maybe two or three massages, and the rest of the week is my own – and I get paid for all of it.'

That sounds like a really good deal, Jessica remembers thinking to herself.

'He's really flexible and he knows we are all dancers, so he'll always let me prioritise my auditions,' Christine said. 'He's so supportive of artists; he *loves* dancers.'

One day, after two months of hearing about this man, Christine told Jessica that she needed to go away and was looking for a substitute massage person for him, and would Jessica be interested in meeting him? Thirty years later, Jessica will reflect on the fact that it was her friend's confidence, her friend's trust, in this man that made her feel safe enough to meet him.

'This was the first time I was offered the opportunity and I jumped at the chance. By then, I'd only been hearing all of these incredible things about her work, all she learned about the body, her travels, and how she could still audition whenever she wanted. I was jealous of this great job she had so I did not hesitate because I trusted all she was telling me for months,' Jessica tells me in 2023.

Thirty years later, when sharing her story with professionals, Jessica came to understand that these two months of Christine bragging about Jeffrey constantly, making the job feel enticing, was actually grooming.

'Do you wanna go meet him?' Christine asked.

By this time, Jessica was convinced.

'Yeah, for sure,' she said.

The man's name, of course, was Jeffrey Epstein.

Christine made the arrangements and passed on the details to Jessica. In 1991, in a day planner that Jessica *still has with her* to this day, she wrote down: 'Meet Jeffrey Epstein. Madison Avenue.'

Jessica's first thought when she arrived that day was that the office was nowhere near as impressive as she expected. He's a millionaire, she thought to herself, but his office is so basic. The desk looked like the ones Jessica's teachers had in high school in Connecticut, she remembers thinking to herself.

A young woman took her name and then ushered her through another door. That was the first time she laid eyes on Jeffrey.

'So,' he said, stony-eyed, looking at her searchingly. He bombarded her with questions about the body, massage techniques, how long she'd been doing massage, where she had trained.

Jessica immediately felt thrown by this, and, feeling as though she was on the back foot, started questioning herself.

Jeffrey seemed unsure and disappointed.

'Come over here,' he said, beckoning her over to the desk. He opened a drawer in the metal teacher desk and showed her piles and piles of copies of the same book about massage.

Oh wow, Jessica remembers thinking to herself, *he's really serious about this.* She felt nerves prickle in her throat. *Maybe I don't know as much about the body as I thought I did.*

'Take this one,' Jeffrey said, handing her a thick textbook. 'And study it. And let me think about it,' he said, suggesting that he would consider giving her the job but was unsure.

Jessica nodded shyly and understood she was being dismissed. She took the book from his hands and vowed to herself that she would learn every last technique it had to teach her.

She went to a local bodega on the way home and bought herself a five-subject notebook. She has always been a perfectionist. Jessica took the book home with her and studied it voraciously. Every model in it was nude, but she didn't take much notice.

'I am learning everything in that book, wrote everything down – I still have that notebook,' Jessica tells me, more than 30 years later.

Not long after that, Christine got a call from Jeffrey.

'He really liked you!' Christine said. 'He wants you to come for an appointment next week.'

Jessica called the number that Christine gave her and made an appointment with Jeffrey for 9 July, 1991. She knows this because it's written in her 1991 day planner, which she would hand over to her attorneys. She would also try to give it to the FBI, but they never looked at it.

CHAPTER 29

Lower Manhattan, 9 July, 1991

Jessica was directed to go to a different building than the one she had met Jeffrey in the week before. She arrived at the address in the Upper East Side and stared up at a looming, modern-looking building.

A doorman accompanied her in the elevator, because the penthouse – where they were headed – needed a special key card. The man used a special key, hit the PH button and the climb began.

The elevator doors opened into an entryway. It was almost a small foyer. In front of her was a dark wooden wall that she had to walk around to see the rest of the apartment. When she got to the other side of that wall, she almost felt her jaw drop.

Wall to wall windows looking out over the city. A glittering Manhattan skyline that stretched on and on in every direction. A sunken living room. Jessica remembers this because she had never seen one in real life before that day.

Okay, Jessica remembers thinking to herself. *He really is a millionaire.*

The room is empty, no sign of Jeffrey. He then walks out into the living room in a white bathrobe.

Jessica wants to present as very capable, smart professional. She wants to seem unafraid to ask the question:

'Jeffrey, why do you hire dancers to do massage when you can hire professionals?'

'Well,' Jeffrey said, smiling. 'Think about it – dancers know the body *so well*, they are always in shape, they are the best masseuses.'

By way of example, he said: 'You wouldn't hire a fat personal trainer, would you?'

When Jessica and I speak 30 years later, she tells me that she can now see the way that he played up to her ego in this moment, her knowledge of the body, her good shape. She tells me that she felt relaxed.

But then, Jeffrey suggested they do a trial massage. He drops his robe and is completely naked.

Jessica is taken aback, and he ignores her reaction completely.

'And dancers are comfortable with nudity,' he said, smiling.

Christine didn't say anything about nudity, she thinks to herself.

She takes a breath, convinces herself this was all just part of the job. Jeffrey picked up a white towel, totally naked, and placed it on the carpeted floor and laid down, face down.

Jessica prepared herself to regurgitate everything in her five-subject notebook.

She notices herself nervously chatting to him, telling him about all the hand positions she had learned. 'I still felt like everything was okay,' she tells me in 2022.

But then, just as she had this thought, Jeffrey turned over.

'In other countries, they are much less uptight,' Jeffrey was saying now. 'In some of the places I've been, you wouldn't just have one masseuse.'

He paused here.

'You'd have three – one for the head, one for the feet and one right in the middle,' he said, and she could hear the smirk in his voice.

'So that was when the sexual jokes started,' Jessica tells me.

After about 45 minutes, Jeffrey's whole demeanour changed and he raised his voice at her, seeming annoyed at her for wasting his time: *You're doing it wrong!*

He seemed annoyed. He said, 'Look, the only way I'm going to be able to show you is if I show you on your body.

'Take off your dress.'

When she gets to this part decades later, she says: 'And that's when I felt something inside me switch off.'

Jessica was wearing a sundress. She remembers the exact one.

'It's fine, we're both professionals here,' he said, and she felt unable to say no – particularly because he'd already set up this expectation that *real* dancers are okay with nudity. So she complied.

'I laid naked on the white towel he had put on the floor. He started at my shoulders. Then massaged my breasts showing me how he wanted his massaged. He showed me how to massage his stomach in a clockwise direction for "better digestion",' Jessica tells me.

'He took his time moving down each part of my body, giving "instruction". Then he went down to my legs, parted them and kneeled between them massaging my inner thighs up to my genital areas – not touching them at first – just slowly inching his way there over time. Then he said, "It's okay if you become sexually aroused".

'My body was frozen. My voice was mute. My brain is echoing back to me, saying "I don't want to be here" but some reason I can't get up. Everything gets foggy. I can't tell him to stop. I can't kick him. I can't roll away and run out of the apartment. He has hands on me, then fingers in me, and I can hear the rhythmic movements of him masturbating and his breathing changes. I hear his breathing escalate to sort of these grunts and then it all abruptly stops. He is up off the floor and I hear the sound of crumpled paper.'

She looked up and saw that he had thrown money for her on the table.

Jessica thinks long and hard about how much detail to share when it comes to what you've just read. But she has chosen to do so because she wants the world to understand just how powerful the freeze response truly is.

This is why the freeze response is so important to understand – it is the body's survival response kicking in even when you are being told you are safe. But the body knows you are not.

'It took months of discussions with my trauma therapist for me to grasp the freeze response was automatic and involuntary,' Jess tells me now. 'The lightbulb moment happened for me when she explained my body froze automatically just like when your hand pops off of a burning hot stove automatically. We don't have to strategise about what to do when our hand lands on a hot stove.

'That understanding released me of so much self-blame for not fighting or screaming. Because I was incapable of doing either.'

'Call my secretary to make an appointment for next week,' he said cheerily, and walked out of the room. He was gone.

'I don't remember putting on my dress,' she tells me now. 'I don't remember how long I sat on the floor, holding my dress in front of me. All I remembered was picking up the money and feeling like I was going to throw up. I wanted to leave the money behind, I didn't want it, but I also did.'

Jessica walked out of the door sometime later, and remembers passing the doorman, and feeling like everything had changed since the last time she saw him when she entered that building.

Everything was foggy in Jessica's mind. She raced out of the building and to the subway. She got on the train going the wrong direction.

In 2023, Jessica looks back on this confident, brave, tenacious 22-year-old who was not afraid to speak up for herself. She was not weak. She was not fragile.

'To then freeze, and be unable to help myself in a moment of terror, and be unable to speak or move, that was such a moment of identity crisis for me,' Jessica tells me now. 'I thought to myself: *I'm not brave. I'm not smart. I am unable to keep myself safe in the world. I'm wrong about who I was.*'

When she finally got home, she picked up her day planner, the one that said *meet Jeffrey Epstein* in the square for 9 July

1991 – the one she still has – and scrawled the word ASSHOLE next to his name.

The next thought that Jessica remembers having is this: there is no way that Christine would still be working for him if this was happening, so it must only be me.

Jessica and Christine barely saw each other again after that.

The next day, Jessica was due to take part in the work-study part of her scholarship programme at Steps On Broadway. When she arrived, she saw her friend Joanne.

Joanne asked Jessica how she was doing, but she asked the question three times, because she could sense that something wasn't right. Jessica kept looking at her but was in shock and couldn't get anything to come out of her mouth.

Joanne grabs her and pulls her into a nearby office and Jessica breaks down. She tells her a fraction of what happened. She couldn't tell her all of it.

Joanne grabbed her shoulders. 'We have to go to the police.'

Jessica thought to herself: *I'm a 22-year-old dancer and he's a wealthy Wall Street guy with a plane. No-one is going to believe me. And I walked right out past that doorman and I didn't say anything. I didn't say no.*

'What we knew in the nineties about rape was that, to prove it, you have to protest, you have to fight back – and so in my mind I didn't qualify. I just decided it was my fault.

'There was one thought that just kept ringing around in my head, over and over: *I am so stupid and I will never trust myself again.*'

Jessica punctuates this staccato, for effect, and it rings in my head for weeks.

I. Will. Never. Trust. Myself. Again.

The night before Jessica went to that appointment with Jeffrey Epstein, she received her cheque for a job she did as a back-up dancer for Aretha Franklin.

'My whole life was on this trajectory. I was about to leave in two weeks for a job in Tokyo.'

But everything fell apart after that day. She developed cystic acne all over her face within two weeks.

Three months later, Jessica felt scared to live in the city; she felt frightened all the time. She experienced insomnia, anxiety, brain fog, deep feelings of doom and dread, depression all within the first three to six months after the assault. She felt like a completely different person to the one she had been just months before.

'So I just gave up on living in New York City. I was too scared. I moved to Atlantic City and took a job at a casino, went downwards in my career trajectory.'

Within six months, Jessica had lost so much weight that she could pull on size zero jeans without unbuttoning them.

About a year later, Jessica's boyfriend of two weeks asked her to marry him. She said yes – because she felt that with a wedding ring on her finger, she would be safer.

The next thing Jessica heard about Christine was her friend Heather, who was still friends with her.

'Heather would tell me during that time about how Ghislaine Maxwell would call the house, and no matter what Christine was doing, she would drop everything and go to them,' Jessica tells me now.

As far as I can tell from my research and reporting, this is the earliest reference to Ghislaine Maxwell playing an active role in Jeffrey Epstein's abuse ring. The trial you have read about in this book charges her with offences beginning in 1994 – but Jessica says she was communicating with Christine as early as 1992.

Because this is an important detail, I decide to try to corroborate it. I asked Jessica if she could put me in touch with Heather, who lived with Christine that year. Within a few days, Heather and I are on the phone to one another. Heather confirms that

Ghislaine used to phone their apartment all the time, and that Christine would often speak about Ghislaine. She confirmed that Ghislaine was involved in procuring girls for Epstein as early as 1992.

Heather remembers hearing that Ghislaine was trying to mentor Christine, Jessica tells me – helping her manage her money, encouraging her to get health insurance, trying to get her to be responsible now that she had all this extra money.

Jessica had not heard from Christine for seven years, until she heard that Christine showed up at Heather's wedding in 1998. But she had to leave early – because she was travelling later that day with Jeffrey Epstein.

'That's the last I heard from her,' Jessica tells me, talking about Heather's wedding. But she tells me that Heather had kept in touch with her throughout the nineties and another mutual dancer friend heard from her up until 2010.

Christine never reached out or asked what had happened, why Jessica wasn't calling. Jessica assumes that she didn't ask the question because she already knew the answer.

'She was Ghislaine before Ghislaine.'

Years later, when Jeffrey's name came up in the news in his capacity as a billionaire financier, Jessica's stomach turned. It was in a piece by Julie K. Brown called *Perversion of Justice*. It was the first time she'd seen his face in 30 years. She had a panic attack and cried for 24 hours straight.

She called a friend of hers, a private investigator.

'Jeffrey Epstein,' she said.

'Yes, I heard. What about him?'

'He raped me. He raped me in 1991.'

After expressing her shock and concern, this is what her friend said next: 'You do not want to be on this man's radar. Tell no one else. Do not go to the police. Don't go to the FBI. You don't know who is in whose pocket. These are very powerful people.'

And so that's what she decided to do.

But then, in 2019, when Jeffrey was finally re-arrested for his crimes and the news alert came up on Jessica's TV, she happened to be sitting on her sofa with that same friend.

Without missing a beat, the friend turned to Jess and looked her dead in the eye and said: 'Now you can speak.'

Jessica asked me to help her look for Christine. *The things she might know*, she said to me. And more importantly: *The things she should be held accountable for.*

Jessica sends me an email with everything she knows and remembers about Christine, and any hints she's heard from her dancing circles about where she might be.

It includes a picture of her from the 1990s; the way she looked the last time Jessica saw her. It's a promotional image for her dancing career. She is in her early twenties, blonde. High cheek-bones that slice through the air around her face. Crossed legs, ballet shoes, pointed toes. The email gives the address of the flat that Jessica shared with Christine 31 years ago, and as I look it up on Google Earth I think – as I have thought again and again and again during this investigation – how different Jessica's life could have looked if she'd never met Christine. If Christine hadn't offered for Jessica to move into that Brooklyn brown-stone with her. If she wasn't home that day when Christine asked her. If she'd been out of town.

And I wonder what Christine knew, then. How involved she was with Jeffrey's plan. If she hadn't asked Jessica that summer, would it have been someone else? How many other dancers did Christine recruit? Did she know what she was sending them into?

And, the question that is most important to me, because it is most important to Jessica: *where is she now?*

What did Christine think when Jeffrey was re-arrested in 2019? What did she think as she saw on the news that he'd died in jail? When Ghislaine was arrested in the summer of 2020, after hiding from the FBI for 12 months? Did it occur to her that justice may soon come knocking on her door, too?

The rest of the email reads:

Christine massaged Prince Andrew twice (that I know of) in Martha's Vineyard in the early 90's.

After I left NYC, Christine lived with a mutual friend of ours, Heather, who said Ghislaine Maxwell would call the apartment and Christine would drop everything she was doing, and go to them. Christine tried to recruit Heather. But she wasn't interested.

Christine & I were both professional dancers and I have no doubt Christine recruited many 90's dancers in NYC as she frequented Broadway Dance Center, Steps on Broadway, and David Howard Studios.

Christine danced in CATS in Germany at one point and lived in Italy as well so I'm thinking she absconded to either of those two countries she knew. Though she did fly with Epstein all over and spent a month with him in Europe at one point.

You'll find Christine's name on flight plans starting in 1991.

It hits me, again, that as far as Jessica knows, Christine worked for Epstein from 1991 until at least 1999. That is at least eight years of evidence; I feel determined to find her.

I employ all my usual tricks; skills that I learned while working in an investigative journalism newsroom in California back in 2014, skills that I have built upon during all my years of reporting since then; skills that I learned while investigating cases at a law firm that I worked at between 2015 and 2018.

Jessica didn't testify at trial. Not because she didn't want to, or wasn't willing to. In fact, she desperately wanted to.

Jessica contacted the FBI several times to try and hand over her information about Jeffrey Epstein and Christine. She contacted them in 2019, 2020 and 2021.

She asked the FBI to look over all her information about Christine, and to try and find her so that Christine could be questioned at trial. She told them that Christine could have vital information about the earliest years of Ghislaine's involvement with this pyramid scheme of abuse.

She called the FBI, she sent emails. *I have information*, she said again and again. *Don't you want to see it?*

The answer, it seems, was no. They never collected her information.

'I reached out to the FBI multiple times,' she tells me now. 'A New York agent assigned to talk to me but ultimately said "it was 30 years ago what do you want us to do?", so I called the Southern District of New York directly who kept saying if I don't hear back from him in two weeks call back (I did that for six weeks), and *finally* my number was passed on to Special Agent Amanda Young,' Jessica explains as my heart sinks.

'She called me and scheduled time for an interview on March 19, 2021 – a year and a half after the first time I contacted the FBI,' Jessica continues. 'I didn't know who she was – that she'd been working on this case for five years – and so when she called I was pissed and rattled off my list of all of the times I called or emailed or tried to get information to someone and no one was responding.

'Special Agent Amanda Young very kindly apologised, said that should never have happened, and that she was willing to listen to anything and everything I wanted to share,' Jessica tells me. 'So I told her everything. She asked me if there was anyone else in Epstein's apartment when I was there, did I know if there were any cameras? I did not know the answer to either of those questions. I apologised for not coming forward in 1991 but I really believed it was my fault.'

My heart sinks again hearing this from Jessica, who has had to be so brave, not only to her abuser but to the government agency that is meant to protect her.

'Amanda Young said, "Jessica, it wasn't your fault. It was designed that way – for you to think it was only you."

'I told her I could not imagine I was the only one to tell them about my roommate Christine as she'd worked for him for eight-plus years. Did the FBI have her? Know where she was? Was she cooperating with the prosecution? She said she couldn't tell me that but legally she had to tell me that my statement would be included in the prosecution's case against Ghislaine Maxwell. They would hold all of the victim statements until the last possible moment, my name would need to be shown, but all identifying information would be redacted. And did I understand that? Yes. I understood.

'I emailed Amanda Young all of the information I had on Christine that she had requested.'

The information she sent Amanda Young was the same information she would send me not long after; the email you just read.

Jessica approached me with her information because the federal government wasn't interested. They told her that her statement would be used in the Maxwell trial, but it wasn't. I know, because I was there. But do you know who delivered that news to her? It wasn't the FBI, who never told her they'd decided not to use it. It wasn't a victim support officer. It wasn't any law enforcement officer. It was me. She did not know until I told her that I attended every day of the trial and I promised her it was never used. How could that be?

Jessica reached out to Amanda Young again – using the number Amanda had personally given her – because she wanted to ask if it was okay for her to share her story while the Maxwell trial was ongoing. But she never heard back.

Unfortunately, this became a theme in my reporting. I met several victims who have important, compelling evidence and testimony against Jeffrey Epstein and Ghislaine Maxwell and who approached the federal government in the lead-up to the

Maxwell trial, hoping that their evidence could be used in the case against her. This is true for Liz Stein, and many other victims I have spoken to. But you did not hear from them at trial, because, for reasons I am still trying to understand, their evidence was ignored.

CHAPTER 30

New York City, 1994

Liz was on her way to her job at Henri Bendel's flagship store in Manhattan. It was a dream come true, if she was honest with herself, and there was a spring in her step every day when she arrived at the store.

Growing up in Pennsylvania, Liz had always known she wanted to work in fashion, wanted to learn everything she could about design. As soon as she turned eighteen, she applied to the Fashion Institute of Technology, one of New York's preeminent fashion schools. She knew it was a long shot, but she was ambitious and driven.

In the spring of 1991, Liz found out that she got in. *She got in. She was going to New York.*

She had arrived full of excitement and possibility that fall, and started her freshman year. She took to fashion school like a duck to water, and she felt immediately that she was in the right place.

Liz had visited New York a lot growing up and she had always dreamed of living there. When that dream came true, she loved it. By her senior year, in 1994, she had landed a part-time job doing fashion and merchandising as a stylist at Henri Bendel.

She had been working there for a while when we meet her in this story, on this morning in the fall of 1994. She felt comfortable there, she knew the ropes. She helped high-end clients shop for high-end accessories, such as scarves, gloves, handbags and belts, and would allow them to regale her with stories of the black-tie fundraisers they would be wearing them to.

The morning passed easily, because Liz was busy and happy. Just after lunch, a woman came in and looked around the section as though hunting for something. She was complaining that her personal shopper was off sick that day, and asked if Liz could help her.

They started talking and it felt easy. The woman spoke about her father, about how he had recently died. She said she was in real estate. She talked about a man who seemed to be either her boss or her boyfriend, Liz couldn't tell. She asked Liz for salon recommendations. Then she asked if Liz had ever gotten a massage in the store, and Liz said that she usually gets her massages at Elizabeth Arden.

As Liz tells me this in 2022, she stops and says: 'I'm seeing it now, in my mind. I'm seeing the stairs. I'm seeing her standing there.'

She was tall and thin; she looked like a model. She was immaculately dressed, and Liz could tell from a mile away that she was one of the store's high-end clients. Could tell from the way she walked; the way she held her shoulders back as if held up by a piece of invisible string that ran all the way down her straight spine; the way she carried her expensive handbag, flung casually over a thin, dainty wrist.

The woman had short, jet-black hair and impossibly dark eyes that smiled when they caught Liz's.

Liz could hear the accent clearly now: the woman was speaking the Queen's English. The British accent was thick and dripping with wealth. Liz felt intrigued, but also immediately drawn to this woman, whose presence was 'electrifying', as she would describe it to me, decades later.

'I'm Ghislaine,' she said, smiling broadly. 'A pleasure to meet you.'

Liz remembers asking how you spell that, and she remembers thinking it sounded like the French word for *gasoline*.

Liz spent the rest of the morning helping the woman pick out a selection of very expensive accessories for a series of events she was planning to attend. Liz got the impression that she was a socialite of some description, a member of New York's high society.

'You look like a young Elsa Klensch,' Liz said, smiling. Ghislaine smiled and said that her father knew Elsa, and pointed out that she was Australian, not British.

In 2022, Liz says to me: 'You're too young to know who that is, but Elsa was a style icon back in the 80s and 90s, she had her own show on CNN.'

When Liz finished finding accessories for Ghislaine, Ghislaine said that she and her boss-boyfriend needed some holiday gifts.

The bill came to thousands of dollars by the time she had found everything she wanted. Liz would sometimes offer to deliver packages to high-end clients after work, so that clients didn't have to carry everything across town with them.

'Would you like me to deliver these to you?' Liz asked at the till. 'I can drop by after work and drop them off.'

Ghislaine seemed impressed by this offer, and nodded enthusiastically.

'Well, that would be divine,' she said.

'She gave me a phone number to call her office to arrange for delivery. I was told to bring them to the concierge at the St. Regis,' Liz tells me in 2022.

Liz nodded, and Ghislaine thanked her and walked out of the store's huge double doors. Liz had no idea that this would be the sliding doors moment that would define the rest of her life.

The rest of the shift continued as usual. When she finished up at around 6pm, she bundled up all of Ghislaine's purchases, double-and triple-checked everything and set off towards the St. Regis.

Liz walked up to the concierge.

'I have a delivery for Ghislaine Maxwell from Henri Bendel,' she said.

'I was told that Ghislaine was in the bar and wanted to introduce me to someone. I took the packages into the bar,' Liz tells me now.

'I'd like you to meet Elizabeth Stein,' Ghislaine said with that winning smile. And that was the moment that Liz met Jeffrey Epstein.

'A pleasure to meet you,' the man said in a New York accent. 'I'm Jeffrey.'

'The concierge came over and let them know their room was ready. I didn't understand, because I knew they lived in the city,' Liz tells me.

Before having a drink, Jeffrey suggested that they move up to his and Ghislaine's hotel room to discuss some more details about Liz's fashion career. That's when they sexually assaulted her for the first time.

Liz left the hotel room that night, trying to pretend that everything was normal, but she knew deep down that everything had changed. She had always done well academically until this point, but her grades began to slip after the assault. She failed a compulsory course at FIT that semester and had to retake the whole unit.

'I started to crack,' she would say to me, thirty years later.

Later that semester, someone in management at Henri Bendel took her aside. Liz was offered a full-time position, but it would have meant her leaving school early and not finishing her degree. Liz had by then decided she wanted to go to law school and knew she needed her undergraduate degree for that, so she declined.

Liz was contacted by Ghislaine and Jeffrey shortly thereafter, who asked why she declined the job. It was then that she realised that it was they who had arranged the job. They took her decision as a lack of gratitude.

'It got really nasty,' Liz tells me now. She made a promise to herself to get away from them.

But not long after that, Ghislaine turned up at Liz's new work-place – she was working as a manufacturer's line representative at Bloomingdale's – and was charming and apologetic.

'After she found me at Bloomingdale's, she began to invite me out socially again,' Liz tells me now. 'I tried to resist, to make up excuses for why I could not hang out with them but they were relentless. I knew that I couldn't resist her requests.'

'After what happened at Henri Bendel, I knew I had to placate them,' she says. 'Satisfy them just enough while trying to keep myself as safe as possible. I began to go out with them socially, only going to public places where there would be other people, in case I needed to get away.'

'After they made me feel comfortable going out with them in public, Ghislaine invited me to a dinner party taking place at Jeffrey's residence,' Liz tells me. 'Initially, I tried to deflect the invitation but Ghislaine let me know that there would be important people at the party that she wanted me to meet.'

There's a pause. 'I didn't realise that I was going to be the entertainment. I was assaulted that night, for the second time,' she says. 'The sex acts stopped just short of penetration because I used the one act that I knew would make it stop: I started vomiting. Nobody wants to be around someone who is sick, and vomiting is especially unsexy.'

The following New Year's Eve, Jeffrey and Ghislaine invited Liz to join them to celebrate the all the possibilities that 1995 could bring, and she agreed.

Liz, who was 22 by this time, was in a long-term relationship with her high school sweetheart. But Jeffrey and Ghislaine were always telling her to leave him; she could do better, they would introduce her to celebrities and millionaires who would fall in love with her and change her life. This man, on New Year's Eve, could have been one of those people, they explained.

Liz was introduced to a man, whose name escapes her now, and Jeffrey and Ghislaine escorted her from the hotel ballroom, where the party was taking place, up to the hotel room they were staying in. She could leave her coat, hat and gloves up there, they explained, and return to the ballroom in her gown.

Instead, when she got to the hotel room, they took turns with her.

While they were on top of her, Jeffrey joked about the fact that Liz caught the train to meet them that evening: 'She thinks she knows what a train is, but we're going to show her what a train is tonight.'

Later that evening, Liz noticed it was one minute to midnight. Despite everything, she wanted a midnight kiss. She noticed that her 'date' had got up and left the table very abruptly.

'Where did he go?' Liz asked Ghislaine softly. 'It's nearly midnight.'

Liz will never forget the look in Ghislaine and Jeffrey's eyes in that moment: pity, yes, but mostly amusement, with a touch of cruelty.

'He's calling his wife, of course,' she said, smirking.

Terrified, Liz got up from the table.

'I realised what they had done to me by setting me up. I knew I had to get away but I knew they weren't going to let me leave. So I excused myself to the ladies' room. On the way, I passed the date on the phone at a booth in the lobby and brazenly told him that what he did was the biggest mistake of his life,' she tells me now.

'In the ladies' room I tried to gather myself and think, but Ghislaine came in just a few minutes later trying to get me to go back to the party. I again started vomiting because I knew it would make her leave. When she did, I fled,' she says.

She flagged down a yellow taxi to take her to Port Authority: she lived in New Jersey at the time and needed desperately to get home as soon as possible. But it was New Year's Eve in New York City, and all the roads around Times Square were blocked off. The driver couldn't take her any further.

She got out of the cab. She remembers looking around – the big city lights, the Times Square billboards, the New Yorkers celebrating the New Year. It was something she'd pictured – exactly this scene. But by the time it came true, everything about herself and her life had been irrevocably changed.

She couldn't figure out what to do, everything felt blurred, dissolving around her – the people, the billboards, the fireworks. Somehow she made it to Port Authority and found her way home.

After the New Year's party, Ghislaine reached out to her once again, acting as if what happened on New Year's Eve was nothing more than an unpleasant date with an incompatible suitor.

She invited Liz to get away with them in Florida: there were people she wanted Liz to meet and after all, Maxwell said, Liz deserved a vacation. She arrived at the airport.

'The driver, who was holding a sign that said "Ms. Maxwell," met me in the baggage claim area. I expected to check into my hotel and get settled, but instead the driver took me directly to the party.'

Jeffrey's mansion on El Brillo Way was enormous and sprawling. It had a pool house with photos of semi-clothed young girls everywhere.

There was one night in Florida when Liz had been abused by them and eventually fell asleep. She was woken up at 4am and tried to refuse the requests. She was punished for it.

This led to extreme violence.

Liz was due to fly back to New York that Sunday night, because she had work first thing on Monday morning. But when Sunday night came around, Jeffrey said he wanted her to stay. Liz realised in that moment that her travel, her itinerary, was completely in their control. There was nothing she could do. If Jeffrey wanted her to stay, then she had to stay.

Jeffrey assured her that everything would be fine, that he'd call Bloomgindale's and arrange for Liz to be absent from work. But he didn't: it was another lie to make it impossible for Liz to say no to the request. When she returned to work, Liz was fired.

Liz now had no job and no source of income and was entirely reliant on Jeffrey and Ghislaine.

'Seizing on this new vulnerability, they began trafficking me to their friends. By that time, I was trapped,' she would say, thirty years later.

For the next several months, Liz was sexually assaulted, raped and trafficked countless times to many, many different men. Liz moved to different cities and states several times to try and escape Jeffrey and Ghislaine, but they always found her and entrapped her once again.

At one point Liz became pregnant. To this day, she does not know who, of all the men she was trafficked to, is the father of her child.

They insisted on and arranged for her to abort the pregnancy and she did. In a beautiful piece of writing that Liz would share with me in 2022, immediately after the US Supreme Court repealed Roe vs. Wade, Liz described the day she had her abortion: 'To paint a picture of what happened next would be too gruesome. My bedsheets were covered in blood and I was gutted in pain. I thought I was going to die, and what was worse was that I actually wanted to. Being pregnant by a man who raped me was a fate worse than death.'

She continued: 'I cannot imagine being forced to carry that pregnancy to full term and to give birth to a child created under such horrific circumstances. It was a decision I would make again – at any cost. To not have had that legal right is almost unthinkable to me. But it is now a reality for women living in a post-Roe America.'

Liz moved again, this time to Philadelphia, where she lives now, thirty years later. She planned to start law school. She thought it was finally time to start over. But she was wrong.

Strange things started happening. She noticed that she was being followed around Philadelphia when she was out in public. When an electrician came around to install cable TV into her new home, he said – ever so casually, while he was working – 'you know I'm very well connected.'

In our interview, Liz tells me that I must think she's crazy. But of course I don't – in what universe would an electrician, a person uniquely positioned to access the inside of your home, say something like that unless they were sending you a message from Jeffrey, the master manipulator? *I'm still watching you. I know where you live. In some ways, I'm in your house right now.*

'He just needed me to know,' she tells me in 2022. 'He needed me to know that he could always find me.'

Jeffrey still called. She was terrified because she thought she had gotten away. Not long after Liz became re-entrapped in Epstein's spider's web, she started throwing up constantly every time he demanded sex from her. This might seem like an instinctive bodily reaction to trauma, but in fact it wasn't – it was a survival skill. Liz was doing it on purpose. She believed that if she let Jeffrey see these horrific bodily betrayals, he would lose sexual interest in her.

Liz had used this trick before. Like so many of Epstein's victims, Liz had been abused as a child – a child much younger than the one she was when she met Jeffrey. From the time she was a young girl, she was sexually abused. Back then, without even thinking this through cognitively, she used to race to the bathroom when he approached her and make herself vomit. It worked; he never touched her after she'd been sick.

And so, fifteen years later, she used the same survival technique with Jeffrey. It's amazing the way we learn to save ourselves.

And the trick worked on Jeffrey, too.

'I just became too much of a hassle,' she tells me in 2022. 'The game wasn't fun anymore.'

But then she performed another important act of survival: she had a nervous breakdown. She was in long-term inpatient psychiatric care. She was hospitalised around thirty times.

In 2009, Liz started having seizures that no-one could understand and started pursuing DBT therapy. She would black out at random moments and wake up on the floor, seizing. She lived alone, so the seizures were incredibly dangerous. She would wake up on the floor, not knowing how she got there, with her cat, Serena – who I have met many times on FaceTime and is absolutely beautiful – licking her face, trying to wake her up.

The worst seizure happened one night when Liz was at home with her then-boyfriend, watching *Pulp Fiction*. It was a film she had watched once with Jeffrey, but she thought that enough time had passed by then. But not long after the movie started, she lost consciousness and had the worst seizure she's ever had. Her boyfriend rushed her to the emergency room, where the doctors informed them both that her heart had stopped for more than thirtyseconds while they were monitoring her. In more ways than one, those memories nearly killed her.

She was admitted to hospital and the seizures continued. The doctors hooked her up to all sorts of machines to try to understand what was going on neurologically, but they kept coming up short. Tests showed that Liz's heart was stopping, but they couldn't tell her why. But, of course, Liz knows now that there wasn't one: not in the way the doctors were looking for, anyway. Liz was having seizures because that is one way the brain copes with intolerable memories. Liz wasn't sick. She was traumatised.

'I knew I wasn't crazy,' she tells me now. 'But no one even mentioned the word trauma. Imagine how different my life could have been if someone had intervened in the way that I needed them to.'

Not long after this, Liz was diagnosed with Chronic Regional Pain Syndrome – a debilitating and incurable neurophysical disorder that causes constant pain all over the body. By the end of her stay in hospital, the pain was so bad that Liz could no longer walk or use her legs. She spent the next six months learning to walk again.

In 2019, Liz was sitting at a friend's house watching the news when a breaking story interrupted the broadcast, showing images of a swarm of FBI agents at Teeterboro Airport arresting Jeffrey Epstein as he disembarked his now-famous private jet. Then the newsreader read the charges – decades of sex trafficking of minors.

There are tears behind her eyes when Liz says what she says to me next, in 2022: 'I genuinely always thought it was just me.'

By the time I would meet Liz in 2021, she had managed to create an amazing life for herself despite everything that was taken from her, and her resilience astounds me. She still struggles every day with her physical health. She still has gowns that Jeffrey and Ghislaine bought for her while she was being trafficked, to remind herself that it was real. That it happened.

In June 2022, Liz and I would spend a few days together in New York after Ghislaine Maxwell's sentencing. She would invite me to come with her to the St. Regis Hotel for a drink – because she was determined to reclaim that memory.

Liz was willing to testify against Ghislaine Maxwell. Liz *wanted* to testify against Ghislaine Maxwell. In fact, Liz travelled to Manhattan from Philadelphia every single morning of the trial – a two hour commute – just to witness her abuser being brought to justice.

But Liz didn't testify – because every single call she placed to the FBI offering to help them with their investigation went unanswered.

She called both the numbers listed on the FBI's call-out for victims to come forward. She said she was a victim.

Next, she called the FBI's tipline number and said the same thing. She was promised an investigator would get in touch to collect her evidence. No one ever did.

She called James Margolin – one of the people listed as the FBI's victim contacts – one final time. All he said was, 'I think they've got their case sorted now, no need for more evidence'.

All through the trial, my press gallery colleagues and I kept asking ourselves and each other: why did only four victims testify? We know from successful applications to the Epstein Victims' Compensation Fund alone that there are *at least* 150 victims. So why didn't more of them testify? Well, safe to say that my reporting over the last twelve months gives us a pretty good answer to that question.

Liz was trafficked to countless men during the years she was entrapped by Jeffrey Epstein – whom she is, with good reason, afraid to name because she has been promised multiple times that if she ever did, she would be killed within days. So when we talk in 2022, she says: 'What about those men? What about those trials? Why is there no accountability for them?'

And then she says something about the Maxwell trial that every single piece of my reporting over the last twelve months has led me to believe: 'It was a show trial. They just wanted everyone to think it was over, we could move on from this story. But it was a sham'.

PART FOUR

The Sentencing

CHAPTER 31

New York City, June 2022

Ghislaine Maxwell's sentencing date is nearly here. I sit at Heathrow Airport awaiting my 3pm flight to John F. Kennedy Airport – the first time I will be back in New York since the trial ended. The night before my flight, I speak to Liz Stein on the phone at length. Her lawyers, Bob Lewis and James Marsh, are currently petitioning the court to allow her to give a Victim Impact Statement at sentencing. She is anxiously awaiting the judge's ruling. She and I have agreed to meet the day after I land, a Sunday, to spend some time together before the Tuesday-morning sentencing.

I land in New York City and go straight to have pizza with one of my oldest and best friends, who lives in a beautiful apartment in Brooklyn and works as a housing rights attorney in the Bronx. We sit on her new outdoor furniture in the beautiful summer night air and we drink wine and I feel the same excitement about being in New York as I did all through the trial.

The next night, I meet Liz and her best friends at a restaurant in midtown. Her closest girlfriends have all travelled to New York from Philadelphia to support her at the sentencing. Her new partner, Brian, is here, too. She's told me so much about him during our long conversations over the last six months, and she's so excited for me to meet him. He is wonderful.

I ask Liz how she's feeling, and she takes a big breath in and out.

'Like something's finally ending,' she says. 'But let's talk about something else tonight.'

And we do. I chat to her girlfriends about Philly, about their kids, about their lives. The gang tells me stories about all the different road trips they've taken together, how they didn't even think twice about turning the sentencing into a girls' trip to make sure Liz had her nearest and dearest around at every moment.

Even though I've seen Liz's face countless times on FaceTime over the last few months, I haven't seen her in three dimensions since the day she was yelled at by the courthouse staff and left the trial crying just hours before the verdict. And she looks completely different – so much more settled in her skin. She is effervescent and chatty and full of hope.

'Tomorrow afternoon we are going for a drink at the Pierre Hotel,' she tells me, referring to the hotel where Ghislaine Maxwell first introduced her to Jeffrey Epstein almost 30 years before. 'We're going to reclaim it, make new memories. Want to come?'

'I'd love nothing more,' I say.

The next day, however, I am struck down with a flare-up of my autoimmune disease and cannot get out of bed all day, so I have to miss the trip to the Pierre, but when I see Liz and the girls the next day they tell me how wonderful it felt, and I am so happy for them.

That afternoon, while I am resting on a sea of painkillers, I get a notification on my phone. Judge Nathan has decided that both Liz Stein and Sarah Ransome will be allowed to read their Victim Impact Statements at sentencing the following day. I text Liz immediately.

Scotty and I meet before sentencing the next day and walk up to the court line together. At around 8am, we are ushered into courtroom 318, and my mind reverberates, being back in that room again. I am separated from Leslie and Jess, because for the sentencing they are asking the press and the public to sit in different galleries. The press are assigned to sit in the jury box – which is, of course, now empty. I have introduced Scotty to Leslie and Jess, and he sits with them in what was, during the trial, used as the press gallery. I reflect on the fact that last time we were in this room, on verdict day, he was in the jury box and I was in the press section, and now we have swapped.

From my new seat in the jury box, I cannot see the courtroom door, but I hear a distinctive 'good morning' ring out, and I know that Bobbi Sternheim has arrived.

The rest of the attorneys arrive next. Jeffrey Pagliuca, with his signature backpack; Laura Menninger, looking flustered. Christian Everdell does not show up. On the prosecution side, I recognise the towering silhouette of Maurene Comey, and Alison Moe next to her.

Two bailiffs appear at the back courtroom door and I know that Ghislaine's arrival is imminent. A moment or two later, she appears. It is the first time I have seen her in her orange prison jumpsuit. Her eyes are downcast; her entrance nothing like those during the trial. I remember the day after her birthday, when trial resumed after Christmas, and the chorus of her attorneys saying, 'Happy birthday, G!' and her giving and receiving hugs like we were at her cocktail party. This is not the Ghislaine standing in front of me now.

Two loud knocks on the door and everyone in the room gets to their feet as Judge Nathan enters.

'Good morning,' she says to the room in her idiosyncratic manner, one that manages to be both direct and very warm.

'Is counsel ready?' she asks.

'Yes, your honour,' Alison Moe says, and I notice that she is sitting in the first chair, meaning she will be giving today's sentencing submissions on behalf of the government.

'Yes, judge,' Bobbi Sternheim says in her characteristic way.

Judge Nathan invites Alison Moe to come forward and give her submissions.

Alison Moe approaches the podium with purpose and takes a deep breath.

'Ghislaine Maxwell first met Jane in August of 1994. Jane was only 14 years old. What Ghislaine Maxwell did in the years that followed was almost unspeakable, but the truth came out in this case,' she says.

'The kids that Ghislaine Maxwell targeted – their pain is real and it matters.' She speaks slowly, making sure every word lands squarely. Occasionally, she looks over at Ghislaine, who is looking straight ahead.

'Her victims were vulnerable kids who were sexually exploited by adults who promised to help them,' Moe says.

Now, she looks directly at Judge Nathan.

'I urge the court to take an unflinching look at her actions and think about what kind of person she really is – about what kind of person would use their privilege and power in this world to prey on vulnerable children.

'Before the court today is a defendant who was *indifferent* to the suffering of other human beings.' Moe's intonation, always so measured and lawyerly, becomes passionate as she emphasises the word 'indifferent'. 'Those choices were hers, and they have to have consequences.

'To Ghislaine Maxwell, there are two types of people in the world: those that are disposable and those that matter,' Moe says. 'Ghislaine Maxwell's actions had serious consequences for her victims. Those victims have shown the world what the meaning of true bravery is by coming to this court and telling their stories.'

Alison Moe now turns her attention to the federal sentencing guidelines – the rules which direct judges to a range of available sentences for different crimes. But judges also have discretion to impose what's called an 'above-guidelines' sentence, if there are factors that warrant a harsher punishment.

One of these factors, which the attorneys discussed at length with Judge Nathan earlier this morning, before the sentencing began in earnest, is if the law has changed since the offence took place to reflect changing societal attitudes to a particular crime.

A basic principle of the justice system is that offenders must be punished based on the law that was in place at the time the crime was committed. This is because a central philosophical tenet of the legal system is that it must be knowable and accessible – that is, that offenders must know what the punishment for different crimes is when they commit them, and that they shouldn't be subject to legal changes that they could not have predicted when they committed the crime.

However, this philosophical principle can be overridden in some cases – for example when society acknowledges that the severity of a crime went underrecognised by the law for much of our history.

This, Alison Moe is about to argue, is exactly the case here.

'There are only a small number of true above-guidelines cases that come before the courts,' she says. 'But this is that case … Our country finally recognises how serious sex crimes against children really are, and Ms Maxwell's sentence should reflect that. The breath-taking scope of this wrongdoing, the number of crimes that Ms Maxwell committed, the vulnerability of her victims, the way she psychologically preyed on children, all point to an above-guidelines sentence.'

Moe pauses for a long moment here.

'We ask for the court to send a message that no one is above the law. That it is never too late for justice.' She pauses again.

'Thank you, Ms Moe,' Judge Nathan says, and I notice how much her tone has changed as Moe was speaking. Her voice is softer and noticeably more sombre. I've never heard her like this before.

'The first Victim Impact Statement comes from Annie Farmer, and it will be read by her attorney, Sigrid McCawley,' Judge Nathan announces.

Sigrid, who is tall and blonde and sporting a smart black skirt-suit, approaches the podium.

'Judge Nathan,' Sigrid begins, reading Annie's words from a binder set upon the podium. 'For a long time, I wanted to erase from my mind the crimes that Ghislaine Maxwell and Jeffrey Epstein committed against me and pretend they hadn't happened … Beyond my initial description to my boyfriend and family of what occurred when I was with them in New Mexico, I didn't talk about it for years,' Sigrid says. No one in the courtroom moves or breathes. 'It was the type of dark memory that feels safest to keep locked away, and so I did the best I could.

'One of the most painful and ongoing impacts of Maxwell and Epstein's abuse was a loss of trust in myself, my perceptions and my instincts. When predators groom and then abuse or exploit children and other vulnerable people, they are, in a sense, training them to distrust themselves.'

When I hear this in courtroom 318 on 28 June 2022, I have not yet met Jessica. But typing up these words from my notebook now, I can think only of those words she uttered in staccato, the thought she had after leaving Jeffrey Epstein's New York home after she was raped: *I. Will. Never. Trust. Myself. Again.*

'When a boundary is crossed or an expectation violated,' Sigrid is saying now, 'you tell yourself, "Someone who cares enough about me to do all these nice things surely wouldn't also be trying to harm me?" This pattern of thinking is insidious, so these seeds of self-doubt took root.

'For years these memories triggered significant self-recrimination, minimisation and guilt. I blamed myself for believing these predators actually wanted to help me. I felt tremendous survivor guilt when I heard what other girls and young women had experienced at the hands of Maxwell and Epstein. That sickening feeling that made me want to disappear.

'The ripple effects of trauma are undeniable,' Sigrid says after taking a long breath. 'A young person on the path of pursuing her dreams was pulled in by Maxwell and was abused and exploited. Maxwell had many opportunities to come clean, but instead continued to make choices that caused more harm. Once arrested, Maxwell faced another choice. She could admit her participation in this scheme, acknowledge the harm caused or even provide information that could have helped hold others accountable. Instead, she again chose to lie about her behaviour, causing additional harm to all of those she victimised. For me, it meant having to be involved in this nearly two-year legal process that involved reliving this painful experience over and over again.

'Then, during the trial, my memories were repeatedly called into question, and I was publicly grilled on the details of the trauma she perpetrated. Given the shame and self-doubt that these injuries had already caused, this all felt like a retraumatisation – one that could have been easily avoided had she told the truth.'

Again, sitting in the courtroom that day, my reporting had not yet led me to Juliette; I hadn't met her and I didn't know her story. But typing this up now, her voice is in my head – words she has said to me so many times in our many, many conversations over the last six months: *the truth will set you free.*

Sigrid closes her binder slowly and returns to her seat.

'Thank you, Ms McCawley,' Judge Nathan says, again in that new, solemn tone. 'We will now hear a statement from the witness we are calling "Kate".'

I look over at the public gallery and I see the striking blonde woman I remember from trial stand up and take to the podium. She is dressed in black, with a black headpiece in her bright blonde hair.

'I began writing this statement on Mother's Day, because, it has been my experience that it was only in becoming a mother, to a daughter, that gave me the courage and impetus to speak out about the abuse I had suffered and made me understand the gravity and horror of what had taken place,' Kate says.

'The need to protect innocent children is even more important now, as a woman's right to make choices about her own family are being stripped away in this country,' she says, referencing the overturning of *Roe v. Wade* just days before.

'The many acts that were perpetrated on me by Epstein, including rape, strangulation and sexual assault, were never consensual and would have never occurred had it not been for the cunning and premeditated role Ghislaine Maxwell played,' the woman, now 45, says in a steady voice.

'Being around her was like being spun fast in a circle and then trying to maintain balance. It was like a roller-coaster ride, designed to disorient and disempower me.'

Kate takes a long, deep breath.

'The best way to imprison someone is to make them create the prison bars in their own mind, to instil enough fear to make sure they never risk leaving or disobeying and make the bars invisible to everyone, so that no one can see their cage or hear their silent screams.'

I. Will. Never. Trust. Myself. Again.

'The consequences of what Ghislaine Maxwell did have been far reaching for me. I have struggled with, and eventually triumphed over, substance-use disorder. I have suffered panic attacks and night terrors, with which I still struggle. I have suffered low self-esteem, loss of career opportunities ... I have battled greatly with feeling unable to trust my own instincts in choosing romantic relationships. I have had a hard time identifying dangerous people or situations. I have also suffered periods of disassociation.' Kate's voice is cracking now.

'We will not stop fighting for justice. I hope this chorus of our voices rings in the ears of those who are still being victimised and gives them strength ... I became what I am today in spite of Ghislaine Maxwell's attempts to make me feel insignificant. I am no longer afraid.'

'Thank you,' Judge Nathan says. 'We will now hear a statement from Ms Sarah Ransome.'

I look around at Sarah, who is sitting in the public gallery next to Liz, her partner, Brian, and her lawyer, Bob Lewis, who is wearing a distinctive bow tie.

I didn't know Sarah well that day, but in the six months between sentencing and writing this, we have become very close. We have spent many days together, talking through everything that happened to her all those years ago, poring over photos, emails, documents, contracts.

'It has been a long journey to bring Maxwell to justice,' she says when she reaches the podium. 'I frequently experience flashbacks and wake up in a cold sweat from nightmares reliving the awful experience. I am hyper-vigilant, experience dramatic mood changes and avoid certain places, situations and people. I will sometimes start crying uncontrollably and without apparent reason. I have worked hard with several mental health professionals who have diagnosed me with extreme symptoms of anxiety, depression, low self-esteem, PTSD [post-traumatic stress disorder] and tendencies to self-harm.'

At this juncture, Sarah begins the part of her statement that hits me hardest – the part that, over the course of my reporting and getting to know these victims, is probably the most important story in this book.

'Despite my earnest effort, I have not realised my God-given potential professionally or entered healthy personal relationships. I have never married and do not have children, something I always wished for, even as a little girl. I shy away from strangers and have difficulty making new friends because

I fear they could be associated with Epstein, Maxwell and their enablers.

'To this day, I attend AA meetings, but I have had numerous relapses and know that only by the grace of God do I continue to live. I have attempted suicide twice since the abuse – both near-fatal.

'I am grateful that the jury believed the victims and returned a guilty verdict. But a question still tears at my soul: after all of this, how can she continue to maintain her innocence? Who and what institution enabled this sex trafficking ring to continue? Why haven't the institutions and important people that enabled them been exposed and brought to justice? Reflecting on it, I know the answers to my questions.

'Maxwell is today the same woman I met almost 20 years ago – incapable of compassion or common human decency. Because of her wealth, social status and connections, she believes herself beyond reproach and above the law. Sentencing her to the rest of her life in prison will not change her.

'As for the important, high-profile enablers – governmental institutions, politicians, and very wealthy friends of Epstein/Maxwell here and abroad – so far, their stature and power have protected them. I hope that one day they will be exposed, and we will be able to say that the United States truly is governed by the rule of law and not by powerful people.

'To Ghislaine I say: you broke me in unfathomable ways. But you didn't break my spirit.'

Judge Nathan now calls Liz Stein. As she walks to the podium, I think about how relaxed she seemed at dinner two nights before, surrounded by friends – and about how terrified she looks now, walking towards her abuser to finally say her piece.

'I was assaulted, raped and trafficked countless times in New York and Florida during a three-year period,' she says. 'At one point I became pregnant (by whom I am unsure) and aborted the baby. Things happened that were so traumatising that to this day I'm unable to speak about them; I don't even have the vocabulary to describe them.

'In the most literal sense of the word, Epstein and Maxwell terrified me. They told me that if I told anyone, nobody would believe me and if they did, they would kill me and the people closest to me. I believed them. I was once bright, fun, outgoing and kind. I loved life and people genuinely enjoyed being around me. After meeting Jeffrey Epstein and Ghislaine Maxwell, it felt like someone shut off the lights to my soul.

'My secrets became too much for me to handle, and I began doing whatever I could to try to get away from Maxwell and Epstein. I changed jobs, apartments, cities and even states to try to get away. I was hospitalised with a nervous breakdown. It would be the first of over two dozen hospitalisations in the decades following my involvement with Epstein and Maxwell,' Liz tells the court.

'I was diagnosed with complex regional pain syndrome and was primarily bedbound for over a year. CRPS is a rare neuroinflammatory disorder characterised by intense, relentless physical pain. Both CRPS and PTSD are psychophysical states in which the sympathetic nervous system is engaged and remains inappropriately hyper-aroused. There is no cure. The mind and body are interconnected. Despite all of this, I immersed myself in DBT [dialectical behaviour therapy] and repaired my emotional health. I began physical therapy and regained my physical mobility. I started to rebuild my life,' she says.

'The arrests of Epstein and Maxwell in 2019 and 2020 respectively helped me immensely. For the first time, I was finally able to disclose their abuse to close friends and medical providers. Twenty-five years after meeting them, my experience was validated. I could finally see the possibility of closure.

'This past November and December, I commuted almost every day from my home in Philadelphia to attend Ghislaine Maxwell's trial in Manhattan. For weeks I sat in the courtroom anonymously, only revealing my identity the day before the verdict. I had to see justice for myself.

'At the age of 48, I feel as if I'm just starting my life. All those things I assumed I would have in life, the things that my siblings and friends have achieved – a career, success, a partner, family, a home, a legacy to be proud of leaving behind – were jeopardised for more than two and a half decades.'

My heart cracks open as I hear my friend say these words. *At the age of 48, I feel as if I'm just starting my life.* I cry for Liz, my friend. I cry for Sarah, who will soon become my friend. I think – and it's important for me to be honest about this – I cry for myself, too.

But now here is Liz, having wrested her life from the jaws of defeat again and again; having survived, again and again, the consequences of her abuse.

I feel these next words like a punch to the gut.

'For the past 25 years, Ghislaine Maxwell has been free to live a life of wealth and privilege that is almost incomprehensible. Meanwhile I have had virtually none of the life experiences I might have had, had we never met. For over two and a half decades, I felt like I was in prison.'

Liz pauses for a long moment.

'She's had her life,' she says. 'It's time to have mine.'

———

It is now Bobbi Sternheim's turn to speak. She is holding herself differently, more cautiously. Her voice is soft and serious.

Instead of facing the judge, she turns around at the podium to face the gallery where the victims are sitting.

'I want to acknowledge the courage you showed in coming forward,' she says. 'I want you to know we acknowledge your pain. We hope that the end of this chapter gives you some solace, and the sanctity that you need to move on.

'I know that what we heard at this trial does not beg sympathy for my client. But these are the circumstances of her life, and I want to share them with you.

'Giant clouds have cast long shadows over my client's life,' Sternheim says solemnly. 'She had a narcissistic, brutish and punitive father who overwhelmed her adolescence,' she adds. 'Then, the manipulation of Jeffrey Epstein overshadowed her adulthood.'

This is the closest Ghislaine's lawyers will ever come to making one of the arguments that the public speculated they might: that she, too, was a victim of Jeffrey Epstein.

The argument is over as quickly as it began.

'My client poses no further danger to the public. She is being sentenced for terrible conduct, but she has the ability and the desire to be law abiding for the rest of her life and to do good.'

With that, Bobbi Sternheim sits down, and I can't help but feel her heart wasn't really in it. A few weeks later, she will sue Ghislaine Maxwell and drop her as a client over unpaid fees – but I wonder, secretly, if she no longer believes in her as much as she has told us she does.

But my thought is interrupted.

'Ms Maxwell, you have a right to be heard. Would you like to make a statement?'

'Yes, your honour,' Maxwell says, and the room shifts, fidgets; intakes of breath can be heard. No one expected this.

There is a soft *clink-clink-clink* as Maxwell stands and shuffles towards the podium. It is a set of heavy silver chains tied around her feet.

She puts on her glasses slowly and begins.

'It is hard to address the court after listening to the pain and anguish of these women,' she says in that accent that all the girls described falling for all those years ago. 'The terrible impact of Jeffrey Epstein's crimes on the lives of so many women is difficult to hear. I want to acknowledge that suffering and I want them to know that I empathise.

'I acknowledge that I have been convicted of helping Jeffrey Epstein. It is the greatest regret of my life that I ever met him. I believe he was a manipulative, cunning and controlling man.

'But this is not about Jeffrey Epstein,' Ghislaine says. 'To all the victims who came and spoke here today and at trial, I am sorry for the pain you have experienced. I hope my conviction brings you closer to [finding] some peace. May this day help you travel from darkness into the light.'

The next day, Liz tells me what she thinks of this apology. '*I am sorry for the pain you have experienced* is not the same as *I am sorry for the pain I caused*,' she will say.

'She's not sorry,' Sarah will say. 'She'll never be sorry.'

Back in courtroom 318, it is time for the judge to make her sentencing remarks.

She does not hold back.

'Ghislaine Maxwell is not being punished as a proxy, but for the role that *she played* in the scheme.' Judge Nathan pauses after the words 'she played' and lets them hang in the room.

'The evidence showed that Ms Maxwell was instrumental in the abuse of underage girls and that at times she participated in that abuse ... Ms Maxwell's conduct was heinous and predatory. She worked with Jeffrey Epstein to select young victims who were vulnerable.

'The harm caused by the defendant is incalculable,' she says. 'The victims bravely came here and testified before this court about what happened to them. My sentence today must reflect the significant and lasting harm that Ghislaine Maxwell has caused with her crimes ... Just punishment demands a substantial sentence in this case,' she says.

There is passion building in her voice now.

'The rule of law demands that, rich or poor, nobody is above the law ... The defendant has not expressed remorse or accepted responsibility for her actions. When she spoke to this court today she did, to some extent, acknowledge the pain that had been caused. What she didn't do, however, is accept responsibility for her role in causing that pain.'

How interesting, I think to myself, *that Ghislaine's apology, which rang so false to the victims and, it seems, to Judge Nathan, is ending up counting against her rather than in her favour.*

She's not sorry. She'll never be sorry.

'This court's sentence must strongly and unequivocally condemn her actions.'

With that, Judge Nathan imposes an above-guidelines sentence of 20 years in federal prison.

The court rises and as Ghislaine Maxwell shuffles out in her shackles, I take in her presence for the last time.

PART FIVE

A Never-ending Story

CHAPTER 32

New York City, 2022

Months later, I am on a call with two unnamed sources, and they bring up an article about the renowned lawyer David Boies, chairman of the law firm Boies Schiller Flexner LLP, one that I hadn't come across before.

The article tells the story of a whistle-blower named Patrick Kessler (a pseudonym), who approached David Boies after Jeffrey Epstein's death in prison in 2019, shortly after he was re-arrested in the summer of that year. Kessler claimed he was an IT specialist who was hired by Epstein to manage all of the closed-circuit television networks for all of his mansions and properties.

That night, I have a conversation with another source about Patrick Kessler – someone who would not like to be named. Someone who met Patrick in person.

By this time, I have spent enough hours and weeks around Epstein's victims to know that they all say that Jeffrey had cameras in all the bedrooms for the purpose of blackmailing the men that he trafficked girls to. The victims all knew about the cameras, knew where they were in each room, and had told me about them.

Kessler was claiming to be the person who had set up that whole internal network of cameras. And he had a conscience that had caught up with him. So when Epstein died and escaped justice, he sought out David Boies. He told him that he had *all* of the footage from all of those cameras – that he had photos and videos of very powerful men to whom Epstein trafficked underage girls. He wanted the truth to come out, he said. He wanted the men in that footage to be held accountable, because Epstein never was.

According to the reporting in the *New York Times*, David Boies had a very unusual response to this. Kessler wanted to make the footage public – to out these men. He was trying to be a whistle-blower; he wanted justice. But instead, Boies suggested that the best approach would be to keep the footage secret and use it as a threat against the men in order to elicit huge civil payouts from them. The logic, Boies explained, is that if they show these men that they have a smoking gun against them, but say they'll keep it quiet if the men pay up, then the settlements will be enormous – given the net worth of the men we are talking about.

But it didn't stop there. Boies had a second plan – he said that they should also consider approaching the men themselves, explaining that they had proof of them sexually abusing under-age girls, and using that to get the men to hire Boies' firm to represent them, thereby eliciting exorbitant legal fees, and the legal and commercial business of the men's companies, for life.

If what is reported in the *New York Times* is true – and I have to stress, this is not my reporting and so I cannot verify it first-hand – then what Boies was suggesting was not only extortion through the guise of legal representation, but, much more importantly, an attempt to keep secret some vital evidence of just how widespread the Epstein sexual abuse ring was.

The conclusion of the *New York Times* piece about Kessler was that he was a fraud – that he never knew Epstein, never had any footage. So that was that; the story vanished.

A few days later, I have been digging around this story, and I am on Zoom with a source who wishes not to be identified, but they are someone who met Patrick Kessler, and who saw his footage.

'I spent hours with the guy,' the person tells me. 'He showed me the footage … I'm pretty good with IT, and he explained to me how he captured everything and exported it after Epstein died … Lucia,' he says, almost trailing off, 'I think he was for real.'

'What do you mean?' I say.

'Well, the *Times* concluded that he was a fraud, but I don't know why, and they never explained it. My honest interpretation was that Kessler was legitimate – that he was there, that the footage was real. I saw it with my own eyes. I recognised those men in it … I think you should try and find him,' my source says. 'He's still out there, and I think he's got a mountain of evidence.'

Kessler went into hiding after the *New York Times* story, and no one has heard from him since. But hearing the sincerity in this person's voice – hearing how much they really believed Kessler when they met him, how much they want the true extent of the Epstein story exposed – it's hard not to question whether it's possible that Kessler really was who he said he was. I promise the source that I will do what I can to find Kessler.

In the summer of 2022, Sarah Ransome gave me an exclusive interview about the fact that she was filing a formal complaint against David Boies for taking advantage of her as a vulnerable client.

Sarah Ransome filed a grievance against her former lawyer David Boies, alleging he 'mistreated' her while representing her in a civil case against Epstein, Ghislaine Maxwell and three of their alleged co-conspirators.

Ransome told me in an exclusive Law360 interview before the 19 August filing that she felt betrayed by Boies. Her complaint, filed with New York's Attorney Grievance Committee, covers conduct by Boies and other members of the legal team he led while representing her from 2016 to 2020.

Among the allegations, she claimed Boies and his legal team pressured her into giving a deposition to help Virginia Giuffre's case against Maxwell and did not properly represent Ransome's interests in her own case, which the Boies Schiller team guided to settlement.

'Boies mistreated me and I feel completely betrayed by him,' Ransome said.

Ransome's current lawyer, James Marsh of Marsh Law Firm PLLC, advised Ransome on how to start the formal complaint to the Attorney Grievance Committee detailing Boies' alleged misconduct. Marsh reviewed the complaint after it was filed and believes Ransome did a good job expressing her concerns about her prior representation.

'Sarah has always been her own best advocate and she has always been incredible at fighting for justice,' Marsh told me.

Ransome had little personal contact with Boies and interacted mostly with other attorneys at Boies Schiller. She spoke to him once over the phone and met him in person when she addressed the court in relation to Jeffrey Epstein's death in 2019. Despite the limited interactions, she holds him responsible for the alleged misconduct.

'We are surprised and disappointed if the statements attributed to Ms. Ransome accurately reflect what she has said,' a Boies Schiller spokesperson said. 'Those statements are not accurate and are inconsistent with the record, including what she has publicly said and written in the past. We have great sympathy for what Ms. Ransome has endured, and we wish her well.'

'Boies Schiller's dedication to helping shut down Jeffrey Epstein's sex trafficking ring and to finding justice for survivors has involved a battle spanning nearly a decade and an incredible resource commitment by the firm that includes thousands of pro bono hours by our attorneys and staff,' the spokesperson continued.

The firm said it has not been given a copy of the grievance and has not been able to review it.

'Legally under New York State's ethical rules, we are prevented from responding to many details in this article. We asked Ms. Ransome's counsel for permission to do so in order to correct factual inaccuracies, and they have not responded,' the spokesperson said.

Ransome told me that when she first engaged Boies and his firm, Boies instructed her that they would only represent her in her civil case against Epstein, Maxwell, and alleged co-conspirators Lesley Groff, Sarah Kellen and Natalya Malyshev if she agreed to give a detailed deposition in Giuffre's civil case against Maxwell.

Groff, Kellen and Malyshev all worked for Epstein and have been accused, including in Ransome's lawsuit, of enabling his sex trafficking scheme, though Groff, Kellen and Malyshev have never been charged with or convicted of any criminal offences.

'I did not want to give that deposition, but I was told I had to or they wouldn't represent me,' Ransome said. She believes the law firm did this to boost settlement chances for their other client, Giuffre.

'That's a clear conflict of interest,' Ransome said.

Ransome's grievance also brings up threats to the privacy of her 2017 deposition as part of another case the firm brought on behalf of Giuffre, this time against Harvard professor Alan Dershowitz.

Giuffre has accused Dershowitz of sexually abusing her while she was being trafficked by Epstein and has sued him for defamation after he responded to these allegations by calling her a 'certified, complete, total liar'.

While Ransome's grievance says Boies Schiller 'asked the court' to unseal the deposition, court records indicate it was Dershowitz in 2020 who pressed the court to unseal all the confidential evidence produced in Giuffre v. Maxwell.

At that time, Boies Schiller had already been disqualified from representing Giuffre in the Dershowitz case, since its attorneys could be called to testify as part of the underlying allegations in the case, according to a court order.

Other attorneys for Giuffre were on board with at least disclosing records that directly concerned Dershowitz. However, before making its decision on the bid to unseal records, the court asked the Jane Does, which include Ransome, to register any objection.

Ransome added that Boies Schiller, who were her attorneys at the time, did not inform her about the unsealing attempt, nor that she would have to file an objection to protect her deposition. Ransome was informed by another Epstein victim, Maria Farmer, and had to approach Boies Schiller to ask what was going on and how they could help her file an objection, according to emails seen by me.

It is at this point that Boies Schiller informed Ransome that she would need to hire new lawyers to lodge her objection to the motion to unseal, according to emails seen by me.

'They let me down greatly by saying they couldn't represent me in my objection to the unsealing,' Ransome told me. 'They never informed me until literally right at the last moment when it was highly unlikely I could find legal representation and file a motion in time.'

The court did end up granting an extension to the Jane Does, which gave Ransome time to secure new representation. In a letter from 25 August 2020, Ransome's current lawyers, Robert Lewis and Marsh, urged the court 'not to grant disclosure of the materials' and that Ransome 'should not now be forced to endure further emotional turmoil by being pulled (unwillingly) into another round of heated litigation, with its attendant public feeding frenzy'.

'It was 100% my understanding that my deposition would be kept confidential. They promised me it would be hidden,' Ransome told me. 'They knew that deposition had sensitive material about my private life and family, which I was incredibly embarrassed about.'

In September 2020, U.S. District Judge Loretta Preska ultimately granted Dershowitz's request to access sealed materials in the Maxwell case that referenced Dershowitz, which could be made public if the case heads to trial.

Ransome takes issue with actions beyond the deposition and the disclosure controversy. Among her chief concerns, she argues that she is disturbed by a photo of Boies at a dinner with Bill and Hillary Clinton. The photo was originally circulated in 2018, after Ransome had agreed to be represented by Boies Schiller. Ransome says that she considers the personal relationship a conflict of interest because Epstein allegedly used his friendship with Bill Clinton to encourage girls to join his circle.

Juliette Bryant, another victim of Epstein's sex trafficking ring, told me that she 'met Epstein when he was in Cape Town with Bill Clinton. This gave him credibility.'

Ransome says that, despite Boies' well-known work on behalf of the Clinton administration in suing Microsoft and representing former Vice President Al Gore in the fallout over the 2000 presidential election, the connection never occurred to her.

Ransome also alleges she was asked to put her name to an op-ed, written by another attorney, John Stanley Pottinger, who works closely with Boies, titled 'How David Boies Saved Me'. Pottinger, also a high-profile attorney, served as assistant attorney general for civil rights during the Nixon and Ford administrations.

Ransome agreed to say she had written the piece, but said she felt as though she couldn't say no, according to the grievance. Pottinger did not respond to a request for confirmation or comment.

The piece was published under Ransome's name in the *New York Times* on 15 November 2017.

'I feel that they used me,' Ransome told me.

Ransome's claim is not the first time Boies has been accused of crossing ethical lines. Actress Rose McGowan claimed he helped former client Harvey Weinstein cover up sexual misconduct allegations by hiring an intelligence firm to collect information on her, and he has also been separately accused of hiring that firm to suppress a *New York Times* story on Weinstein.

Under the terms of the settlement that Boies Schiller secured for her, Ransome is not allowed to disclose how much she received, but she told me she is not happy with the outcome and felt pressured to accept the settlement in the wake of an attempted suicide.

'I was in no fit state to make a decision like that, and I would not have accepted that settlement if I had understood that I wasn't being properly represented.'

Emails seen by me also show that lawyers at Boies Schiller helped Ransome delay a deposition in the wake of her suicide attempt and injuries because she was not in a fit state to give evidence. However, she was also asked to accept the settlement in that state, according to photos and emails seen by me.

Pottinger advised Ransome to settle the case at an early stage to keep costs down, according to an email seen by me.

'We are just on the verge of racking up larger costs as the case comes closer to trial and there will be more depositions, more travel, the retention of expert witnesses, and the like,' Pottinger wrote. 'But right now, neither side has accumulated big costs. Which suggests this is a time to settle if settlement is a possibility.'

Ransome now believes that Boies and his firm did not have her best interests in mind when running her civil litigation.

In 2020, Ransome expressed this view to Brad Edwards, an attorney who was working alongside Boies Schiller on her case, in an email seen by me. 'I no longer want to be represented by Boies Schiller,' Ransome wrote. 'I understand this is complex but I don't feel they have worked in my interest or the other victims.'

In his reply to that email, Edwards declined to take over her representation but encouraged Ransome to voice her concerns to Boies Schiller.

It staggers me, even after years and years of reporting on these kinds of crimes, even after all of my own issues with trust in the wake of my abuse, that it could be the case that a victim might not even be able to trust their own lawyers. Until he switched sides and became an advocate for survivors, David Boies spent many years representing Harvey Weinstein, and it has been widely reported that he helped silence the Weinstein victims when they came forward. When I met Rowena Chiu, the Harvey Weinstein victim you will be very familiar with if you have seen or read 'She Said', the *New York Times*' reporters accounts of how they finally got the Weinstein story over the line, she confirmed to me that it was widely known that it was Boies' job to find and silence women who might report his abuse.

CHAPTER 33

Oxfordshire, 2023

My 'pod' at Khiron House clinic is bare but welcoming: a single bed with an azure blanket and pillow. On a desk sits a deep-navy-coloured journal for me to write in, underneath a copy of *The Invisible Lion*, a book about trauma treatment written by the doctor who runs the space, Benjamin Fry. Its cover is bright, bright blue. (The only thing I write in the notebook on that first day is: 'February 8, 2023. Day 1 of 30. Everything is blue.')

By the time I arrive at this imposing Victorian building in Oxfordshire, home of one of the world's leading residential trauma-treatment centres, I have already had a number of examinations at the clinic's outpatient centre in London, but I do not remember any of them. I only remember snippets of the drive. I remember heaving sobs and shallow breaths. A kind-looking woman greets me: 'Lucia, it's so nice to see you again.' I have never seen her before in my life. Or rather, I have, but I do not remember it.

I'm here because I have post-traumatic stress disorder (PTSD) so severe that my brain has gone into collapse mode to protect itself: what the experts refer to as structural dissociation. I am having memory blackouts. It's been triggered, in part, by this book. For over a year, I have been interviewing survivors almost every day, hearing details of abuse that you would not believe. This is my choice. I am lucky to have the job I have always dreamed of. But vicarious trauma, suffered through interviewing people about their darkest moments, can be more potent than you might imagine. Especially when you know exactly how they feel.

As you know, like many of Epstein's victims, I was groomed and sexually abused by an attachment figure. My abuse started at the age of nine. At 15, I was violently raped by a stranger. I foolishly thought myself immune to the memories the victims' stories would bring up for me. For months I have been cognitively convinced that I'm coping, but I am not. I am becoming very sick and losing weight, and have been diagnosed with pancreatic insufficiency – which doctors say can have many causes, including 'severe emotional distress'.

So here I am, at Khiron House, a centre that focuses on what is known as 'polyvagal theory', one of the most cutting-edge, science-based trauma treatments in the world. It's known to work on people, like me, who have tried everything else – cognitive behavioural therapy, dialectical behaviour therapy, psychoanalysis, hypnosis, ayahuasca, eye movement desensitisation and reprocessing – but have not been able to recover.

A support worker takes away my laptop, my headphones, my phone, my Kindle. I knew this would happen; in all rehab centres, but especially trauma clinics, you are asked to commit to not engaging in any relationships with the outside world during treatment. As the support worker takes my laptop charger I hear myself saying: 'What's the harm in me having it? I can't charge anything …' before I realise that she's also packing away the fluffy rope that ties around the middle of my bathrobe.

And with that my new, bubbled life begins: 30 days of the most intense therapy I've ever experienced. I am staying in the highest level of the clinic, with 24-hour mental health support workers.

The treatment given on my ward is an exhaustive eight-hours-a-day programme, sometimes solo, sometimes with other patients. It's based on the theory that trauma, and the enduring sense of danger that the patient is left with, causes our vagus nerve (a vital cranial nerve that controls numerous bodily functions) to malfunction. When this happens, our survival states can be triggered by memories, rather than the present moment. Yet the brain experiences them as though they are still happening, and the vagus nerve responds accordingly: *fight, flight or freeze*. I'll soon learn that I have been living in this mode for years.

Each day in the clinic is very similar. A strict routine can calm the nervous system, so I stick to a morning shower-coffee-apple combo like it's gospel. On the days when I have individual therapy sessions, my therapist collects me from the group room at 8am.

During the first session, I try to tell her my story, but she keeps stopping me to say: 'Pause. Breathe. Tell me how your body feels.' I soon learn I won't ever finish telling my story to her. Instead, we'll spend hours pausing after each sentence as she asks me what my body is doing. At first, I am so unused to this that I just blankly say, 'I don't know.'

'Well,' she says, on day one, 'your right foot is twitching, sometimes even tapping the floor. Have you noticed that?' I had not. 'That's a flight response,' she explains. 'In recounting this memory, your body – through your leg muscles – is trying to tell you to run away.'

It's in the group therapy room, adorned with bright posters describing ways to be present, that I meet the five other patients on my ward at the clinic for the first time. I cannot tell you anything about the trauma experienced by them, except that it was extreme. They are people who have lived through horrendous violence and abuse, again and again, throughout their lives.

There are four group therapy sessions each day: at 10am, 12pm, 2pm and 4pm. Each is different and designed to calm down our traumatised nervous systems in different ways. The most unique to this clinic is the polyvagal theory therapy.

In these sessions, we are taught how to identify when the body has entered different survival states, through biofeedback. We monitor our heart rates and look out for the kinds of involuntary leg movements I mentioned earlier and notice when we cannot sustain eye contact. On the first day, though, I just stand there, staring. Everything terrifies me. I feel like I can trust no one.

'I recognise that blank look,' a fellow resident says. I will soon come to know that she shares many of the same PTSD triggers as me – a loud noise or a certain smell can cause us to experience the worst moments of our lives all over again. It's a sensation of the past and present merging; a memory becoming more powerful than anything your senses are picking up in the real world. In my case, when it happens, I feel as though I am literally 15 years old again, being sexually assaulted with a knife to my throat.

The resident introduces herself, then says: 'But don't worry, you probably won't remember any of what's happening right now. You can ask us again tomorrow.'

Coming out of a state of dissociation is very painful. It feels frightening and shameful to realise you have lost whole hours or days that you cannot retrieve, and it is tough to constantly assess your nervous system and emotional state. There are days when I can't imagine lasting the whole month.

Each night I write in my diary. At the top of the page, I write the date, followed by, 'Day 1 of 30, day 2 of 30, day 3 of 30, day 4 of 30.'

One day I just write: 'Today was the hardest yet. I don't think I can do this.'

That day I have an individual session, during which I have to confront some terrifying memories, the kinds of which I have long tried to bury, and spend the rest of the day trying to regulate my nervous system, in all the ways I am being taught in the clinic. But despite focusing on my breathing, feeling my feet on the floor and repeating to myself, 'It's February 2023. I am 31 years old. I am not a child anymore,' I still feel lost and completely alone. I'm afraid that even this, the best centre in the world, cannot help me; I'm too damaged. I worry my life will never be anything other than what it's been since my abuse – a constant cycle of fear, survival responses and self-destructive numbing behaviours.

But then the treatment starts working. In my solo therapy I get better at listening to my body when involuntary movements tell me I'm diving too far into a memory. I notice when I cross my legs and arms across my body (usually a 'freeze' response) or feel pulsating energy in my arms and shoulders (a 'fight' response – the body telling me to prepare to take a swing at the ghost of a man in the memory).

The thirteenth day is the last time I note down how many days have passed. On the fifteenth day I realise that the chronic abdominal pain I've had for 13 years as a result of internal injuries from my rape as well as endometriosis has largely gone away as my nervous system has regulated.

I start to have moments of joy. One time, the resident cat, Missy, follows me all the way to the therapy room for my individual session and sits there as we speak. Another time, I am rushing back to my pod after a session because I know I am about to cry, and another patient stops me. 'Are you okay?' he asks.

I say: 'I can't talk because I'll cry, and people get angry at me when I cry.'

'Not all people,' he says. 'This is what we're learning here – once we can look after ourselves, we can also tolerate the pain of others.' And he moves me towards a bench and I cry and cry, for hours, and he listens and he hugs me.

Later that day, in 'creative expressions' therapy, I am asked to draw a moment of happiness. I draw him and I on the bench, with the words 'Not all people' written underneath.

I begin to bond with the group. We cook dinner together every night and make dark jokes about the fact that we have to ask mental health support workers to unlock the 'sharps' cupboard every time we want to chop vegetables. We watch *Friends* on repeat in the evenings. We have pillow fights. We kick a football around the group therapy room. We make up code names for each other. Mine is 'Missy' – after the cat.

It's these connections with other residents that push me to become well again. And as we learn different techniques to bring ourselves out of a survival state – things you will have heard of, such as mindfulness, but tailored specifically to our triggers and our memories; for example, sexual assault survivors may find it easier to ground themselves with legs crossed, despite the accepted wisdom that being grounded means having both feet on the floor – we are able to help others when they're struggling, using these tools as we repeat to each other: 'Do you hear my voice? It's 16 February 2023. You are an adult who can protect herself. You are in the group therapy room. Nothing can hurt you. Your body is responding to a memory. The present moment is perfectly safe.'

On my last day, I remember driving to be admitted to the clinic. I'd never felt so overwhelmed by my PTSD symptoms and the fear and self-loathing they leave me with. Now I feel like, one day, I might find some peace. I'm sure it will be harder work even than I imagine, despite having written two books on the subject. But I feel like it is really, truly possible for me.

My therapist warns me that my chronic pain will come back, out in the real world, when I'm not so focused on regulating my nervous system, so I am not surprised when it does. I'm also not surprised when painful memories seek to pull me under again. Now, though, I know exactly what to do in order to stay in the present: I stop, take five minutes to scan my nervous system and re-regulate.

I check my pulse, my breathing; I check for sensations in my body. Then I do an alternate-nostril breathing exercise – taking one deep breath in and out through one nostril with the other closed, and then the reverse.

Healing from trauma is a slow and difficult process, and for some it is a life-long quest. There is no finish line. I still have bad days, because I can't change what happened to me. But what I can do is learn to live with it, and build a life around it – and suddenly, after just 30 days of intensive treatment, that feels possible to me. I am back to working on my book again, but with a completely new perspective, both on the sections of the book about my own PTSD and the sections about the survivors I interviewed. I set out to give a voice to the stories of other survivors, but I ended up learning a lot about my own survival needs along the way – both from the Epstein victims (now my friends) and from rehab.

CHAPTER 34

London, 2023

In early 2023, I spend hours on FaceTime with Liz Stein. She's just started working (it's the first time she's been well enough to work full time since she was hospitalised when she finally escaped Jeffrey Epstein and Ghislaine Maxwell) at an organisation that supports victims of sex trafficking. Each day she acts as a case worker and support worker for girls as young as 13 who have just escaped their abusers. I feel so grateful that those girls have Liz now; there's no one I'd trust more with my 13-year-old, traumatised, abused heart.

Liz is happy. She enjoys working and she and her partner are building a home together. She is still chronically ill – she always will be – but she is more mobile than she's been in years and she spends longer and longer stretches out of the hospital.

Every time I'm in pain, I call Liz and her wisdom brings me back to the surface. My life is so much better for her constant, reliable, kind, brilliant presence. Seeing her happy makes my heart so full of love for her that it overflows and tears fall down my cheeks.

Liz sends me a picture of her desk at work. She is so proud to have a desk, to be well enough to qualify for one. In the picture, I can see her desktop and her mousepad, and next to it a pile of books. In the pile are my two books and Sarah's books. Sarah published a memoir about her abuse at the hands of Epstein and Maxwell entitled *Silenced No More: Surviving My Journey to Hell and Back*, in 2021.

Alongside the picture, Liz's message says: 'I keep a small stack of books on my desk. One of the social workers walked past and said, "I loved *My Body Keeps Your Secrets*! The author has such an amazing perspective on trauma." I smiled and said, "She absolutely does. And I'm lucky to have her as a friend."'

And again, I think about how something so beautiful can come from something so ugly.

Carolyn, too, sounds better than she's ever been, every time we speak – which is nearly every day. It's been months since I spent time with her in West Palm Beach, but we speak on the phone or over FaceTime almost daily. I regularly wake up to messages from her that just say: 'I just wanted to be the first person to tell you today that I love you and you are worth it.' As I'm writing this, I am going through our thousands of words of WhatsApp history, and I reflect on just how much her love has kept me afloat.

Recently, I was going through a terrible personal experience with a friend who was being abusive to me while drunk. It was deeply upsetting me, the things she was saying, and then she'd always call and apologise the next morning, saying she was lashing out because she knows I'm a safe person to take things out on and that she was ashamed of herself for relapsing on drink. But I cried and cried about it on the phone with Carolyn, because her words had been so hurtful, so close to home. Some of them had directly triggered my own memories of abuse, as though she knew exactly what to say to hurt me the most.

On FaceTime, I ask Carolyn: 'What if she's right? What if I really am worthless and full of something evil and toxic, just like my gym mentor and my rapist and my abusive partner made me believe? Could all these people be wrong?'

'Lucia,' Carolyn says slowly. 'I need you to listen to me very, very closely. I have been clean for a long time, but I know what it's like to be an addict. I know what it's like to take out your pain on those closest to you.

'These things she is saying are not true. She knows that they are not true. She is saying them *because* she knows they are not true and because she knows you well enough to know that these words from your abusers are the things you are most afraid of becoming.

'Her aim right now has nothing to do with the truth, and nothing to do with you. She is trying to hurt you because she's hurting.'

Carolyn pauses for a long time, and then asks me to get a piece of paper and pen to write something down. Through my tears, I oblige.

'I'm ready,' I say.

She says, 'I want you to always remember these words: *hurt people hurt people.*'

She watched me write it down.

'Now say it to yourself every time this friend is vicious or any time you need it. *Hurt people hurt people. Hurt people hurt people.* Just keep saying it. It's the truth.'

I still have that piece of paper; I carry it with me everywhere.

Carolyn gives me some of the best advice I've received in my life. Just like Liz's and Sarah's, Carolyn's wisdom is impossibly hard-won. And I'm so grateful for this gift; the fact that they kicked and screamed their way through hell and back and came out the other side with so much to teach the people they love. I am so grateful that one of the people they love is me.

And again, I think about how something so beautiful can come from something so ugly.

A few weeks later, Carolyn tells me she is selling her house and moving to North Carolina. She is so sick of her family being hounded by private investigators, of men in black cars taking pictures of her children while they play outside. You'll remember from the prologue of this book that Carolyn and I were both followed around Palm Beach and threatened just because someone, somehow, knew that I was coming to interview her for my book.

'I want to move on,' she says. 'It's over now. I'm ready.'

The move is a nightmare, as all interstate moves are, but she calls me when the family are settled in. She loves the new North Carolina house. She loves being away from Florida. She tells me she feels free.

On that phone call, she sounds the best I've ever heard her. I can hear the smile in her voice. I can tell she has finally found some peace. Like Liz, like Sarah, like Juliette, like Jessica, she is one of the strongest and kindest people I have ever met. She has survived so much and still has so much to give. She deserves the world.

CHAPTER 35

London, 2023

The reason I decided to get up in the middle of the night every night for several weeks to cover this trial is because I believed it would shed light on some of the concepts that we, as a society, still deeply struggle to understand: grooming, child sexual abuse, delayed disclosure and traumatic memory. And I was right. In many ways, this trial – and I hope, if I've done my job, this book – will help contribute to a better, truer and more scientific understanding of how grooming, abuse, disclosure and memory work, and importantly, the lasting harm caused to victims of abuse – not only the harm caused by their abusers, but also by the way they are treated by society in its aftermath. This is true for all traumatic memories but particularly for those of us who have endured organised child abuse. This is the term used to describe the experience of becoming trapped in the grips of a manipulative predator who has a 'playbook' ('playbook' here meaning a carefully-devised strategy that is repeated and known to work on selected victims), access to children and who enacts a repeated pattern of abuse on a number of victims.

Although I have never reported my abuse to authorities and never endured a trial, I have had my story questioned and torn apart again and again and again by strangers, readers and even friends. It will happen again when I publish this book. It's hard to describe the impact of this, because it is so cruelly linked to how abuse itself makes us feel: being abused by someone we trust, someone who is meant to protect us, leaves us feeling unable to trust our own perceptions of the world. It leads us to question everything – most of all our own value. We learn to trust other people's interpretations above our own because our abusers convince us that our own perspectives are damaged and worthless. So when this doubt and gaslighting, already deeply rooted in our own psyches since childhood, is hurled at us by others, it feels like confirmation. That we, those of us who are trauma survivors, and, more specifically, survivors of organised child abuse, are inherently untrustworthy, unloveable and worthless. That is certainly how it has felt for me each and every time someone questions my memories, my timeline or my symptoms. It is inherently retraumatising because it came first from the mouths of our abusers, and the shame and fear and confusion hits us like a bullet to the chest all over again. How do you navigate the world with a broken compass?

We are disbelieved, cross-examined and expected to remember every detail of a pattern of abuse. Annie, Jane, Kate and Carolyn, me: all of us are called liars if we do not measure up to these impossible standards. This lack of understanding, and the way it causes society to question us with no knowledge of how disclosure and traumatic memory actually work, retraumatises us again and again. We experience it from the public, of course. But we also experience it from friends, colleagues and our communities every time we speak up. I want that to change.

I can't solve everything – in fact, I can't solve anything, I'm just a journalist – but I can tell you what I've learned from this trial and how I think we can do better. Firstly, the science of traumatic memory must be included, and adduced as evidence through an unbiased, qualified expertise witness, in every trial of this nature. The truth is that those who live without trauma have absolutely no concept of what it is like to have a memory that gets frozen in the amygdala; to live in a chronic state of fight-or-flight, to have memories that cannot form narratives but which only appear to us as flashes of images, smells, sounds, tastes. Annie remembers the moment she realised that Jeffrey might be able to see her exposed breasts being massaged by Ghislaine. Jane remembers hearing the expression 'grandfathered' for the first time. Each victim could describe certain things about the walls of Epstein's homes, the colour of sofas, the smell of massage oil. I have learned through my study of trauma that this simple phrase sums it up best: traumatic memories are not about what happens *to* us, but what happens *inside* of us. We will register, as fragments, the moments that our nervous systems sense that we are in danger. It is the effect of certain moments on our sense of danger and safety, controlled by the amygdala, that is remembered.

Dr Rocchio touched on this, but she spent most of her testimony on delayed disclosure. This trial would have been more powerful if the prosecution had called an expert witness to speak specifically about traumatic memory. Because here's what the current neuroscience, neurochemistry and neurobiology says: when a traumatic event occurs, the body's fight-or-flight mode means the pre-frontal cortex and all parts of the brain, including the brain stem, that are responsible for narrative memory get shut off. That's because the body shuts down every single function that is not needed to either fight, flee or freeze. With regular memories, when an event occurs, it is placed into a narrative and stored in the brain stem. But traumatic memories are never able to be processed in this way – they live forever in the amygdala, and as I mentioned, they live as flashes of emotion triggered by sounds, smells, sensations. Because we cannot store them as long-term, narrativised memories, without professional help (seven years in my case), it is simply not possible for the brain to remember them consistently. This is a survival mechanism – it certainly helped me escape from the man in the abandoned bathroom. But years later, if we want justice in a society that does not understand this basic science –

we will be punished for the precise elements of a memory that *prove* that it is traumatic.

As I wrote when I was working on my first memoir of abuse, and struggled with a copyeditor who demanded that I remember exactly how many flights of stairs I ran down:

> When we ask abuse victims for the details of their stories, we set them up to fail. We want them to make mistakes. That way, we won't have to struggle with the idea that their stories might be true. We find what's missing and we yell you're lying and we excuse ourselves. But here's the real, tragic fact of it: the fragmentation of our memories of abuse are the strongest evidence that they are true. If the experience was traumatic, it will not be able to be accurately recalled. If we are telling the truth, our story will be fragmented.

In accusing us of lying – in cross-examining us in the way that the Epstein victims were cross-examined – society is trying to bait us into destroying the *truest* part of this story. The part that's missing. The parts we don't remember, can't remember, can't place in an exact day or month or year, will never remember, never even knew, cannot know, will never know: the part that is lost, not in spite of the story's truthfulness, but because of it.

Those lucky enough not to live with those fragments need to understand this concept, because you might find yourself on a jury one day, and you might believe that an inconsistency in someone's memory of traumatic events renders them less credible. In fact, it renders them more credible.

The second crucial concept here is grooming, and it's one I faced questions about in the press gallery almost every day of the trial. None of the other journalists understood why you would stay in touch with someone who was abusing you, and in many cases it made them doubt the victims' stories. But I know why because I've lived it and because I've been researching it for ten years.

The very purpose of grooming is to create confusion and distrust of oneself (remember Jessica's words: *I. Will. Never. Trust. Myself. Again*) in order to begin the abuse. What that means is that the perpetrator first builds trust with the victim, often choosing their marks based on a need that is not being met – in Epstein's victims' cases, often money or parental attention – and exploit that to make the child feel seen and heard, often for the first time in their lives. That trust involves compliments, gift-giving, and expressions of love – things many of us grooming victims had not experienced before. This creates a sense of love and loyalty in the victim that becomes very, very hard to shake in a young mind. This trust was built in the moment Annie felt like she deserved expensive boots. In was the moment Ghislaine asked Kate about her career ambitions. In the moment Jeffrey handed Jane money and said he knew her mother was struggling with rent.

Once that love and loyalty is secured, the abuse begins. Now, what most of you, those who didn't experience child abuse, don't understand is that it is incredibly confusing when someone who promised to help you, to save you – and more than that, some-one who promised to look after you when your own parents wouldn't or couldn't – starts to hurt you.

The child mind is reliant on adult care, and so it is hard-wired to believe that adults are competent and responsible. So when those we love and those who promised to care for us when no one else would begin to hurt us, we find it difficult to fathom that the adult is at fault. And so we blame ourselves, and we continue to try to please the perpetrator in the mistaken belief that if *we* become better, the abuse will stop and we will be able to rewind to the time when the perpetrator was loving and kind.

We don't believe they are hurting us on purpose, we make excuses for them, we often don't want to get them in trouble because they have set themselves up as our only protectors. If we lose them, we will be alone. And as a child, to be alone in the world is a threat to survival.

So yes, some of the victims stayed in touch with Jeffrey after they escaped the abuse. Yes, I stayed in touch with my gymnastics mentor long after I got away from him. Because we need to know that the good parts were real. We need to know we are not crazy or inherently bad; that the love that we felt was justified and valid. And that's also why we keep going back to perpetrators even after the abuse starts – because we want a different ending; we've been shown the good parts and we want them back. We think we can find a way to get back there. As Dr Rocchio said: *we keep the hope alive.*

Going back, or staying in touch with, perpetrators is not a sign of a lack of credibility of the victims; it's a sign of the masterfulness of the abuser. It means their manipulation has worked. Again, it's not proof that the abuse didn't happen. If anything, it's proof that it did.

And, of course, delayed disclosure. We need to understand everything you heard from Dr Rocchio: children and teenagers will *almost never* disclose their abuse in full during or immediately afterwards. This is connected to the grooming, the manipulation, the not wanting to betray the perpetrator, the wish to keep the hope alive. We need to understand that scientifically – not just anecdotally – disclosure is vague, fragmented and occurs over a long period of time, and is usually made first to a trusted peer or first intimate partner rather than police, parents or teachers. This is the reason that many victims were not named in the 2007 indictment: because, even though they had, by 2007, whispered fragments of stories to romantic partners, blurted out *that money wasn't fucking free* in the midst of a heated argument with a single parent, nodded silently when someone asked *did something bad happen to you?* it would be years before they would feel able to make full disclosures to authorities, whom they knew would be prone to disbelieving them and would dig for proof that the world does not contain this kind of debasement.

The defence tried to confuse each testifying victim with statements from different interviews over many years, hoping the jury would not understand that a story of abuse never appears fully formed, but has to be slowly handed out to those we trust until it becomes whole again. I like to explain this best to those who are lucky enough to not be hounded by fragments of traumatic memories by using the etymology of the word 'remember'. It is, originally, the opposite of 'dismember', which means to take apart. 'Re-member', therefore, actually means 'to put back together'. We know this is especially true of traumatic memories.

These memories are, by their very definition, slippery and hard to pin down, like a dream that evaporates as you try and remember it. So recounting them is a terrifying endeavour, and one that takes a lot of practice, trust and guidance.

Bri Lee makes the suggestion in her book *Eggshell Skull* that judges should be able to give jurors instructions about sexual offences based on clear scientific data about disclosure and memory: 'Bear in mind this warning: There is a strong statistical probability that you will presume this woman is a liar.'

So, what can this mean in terms of the law? First, statutes of limitations should be removed from historic sex offences and any offences involving traumatic memories. The most common timeframe – six years – is simply never going to give an abuse victim enough time to come forward. If we take my case as an example, given that the abuse started when I was nine, I would have had to come forward by 15, at which time I was still being abused and still very deeply attached to my perpetrator, even though I knew he was hurting me.

New York State has recently taken a major step forward in this regard. The Adult Survivors Act, signed into law in November

2022, removed the statute of limitations for all child sex offences so that victims who disclosed more than six years after the abuse – ten years, twenty years – could sue their perpetrators in civil court. However, the Act has what is known to us lawyers as a 'sunset clause' – it only operates for one year. It expired in November 2023, and the statute of limitations was re-instated. I was very close to many Epstein victims who had to use this short window – 12 months is not a long time in the law – to get their cases filed, and it was incredibly stressful and retraumatising to have that time limit. Still, those women have now filed suits against Maxwell that they otherwise would never have been able to file, which is an incredibly good thing. But we can do better: removing statutes of limitations should not need sunset clauses that place immense time pressure on victims.

Another solution that could be easily implemented to manage the retraumatisation of victims by the justice system is a simple one: judges should have the authority to disallow lines of questioning about, for example, grooming or traumatic memory that are unscientific. Just think about the amount of suffering each testifying witness could have been spared if Judge Nathan could have been given the power to sustain an objection to questions about inconsistent memories, or about why they kept going back, purely on the basis that those attacks fly in the face of very conclusive neuroscientific evidence about abuse.

I've realised while writing this book that we also need to make significant changes in the way our defamation laws currently prevent victims and journalists from speaking up about abuse. There is so much that I know about what Jeffrey Epstein, Ghislaine Maxwell and many other perpetrators who have not ever been named before did to their victims. I have investigated this case for almost four years and what is included in this book is only a fraction of what I know. That's because the major jurisdictions that this will be published in – the UK, the US and Australia – are all showing trends in which the courts are becoming more and more hostile to investigative journalism, and defamation cases are being weaponised by alleged abusers to silence both journalists and victims. My publishers would not let me publish swathes of never-before-reported information about the Epstein sex trafficking ring because they are afraid of being sued. Again, I spoke to Jennifer Robinson about this.

Here in the UK, where I am based, I work as a court reporter and I cover trials day in, day out. I have covered more and more defamation cases that show that the courts are increasingly siding with the wealthy and powerful over alleged victims and journalists. I've spoken to many women who have been advised by lawyers not to speak out in the current climate because their perpetrators will likely bring defamation claims and will likely win. The high-profile case of Carole Cadwalladr is a prime example: Cadwalladr, an investigative journalist at the *Guardian*, originally defeated a defamation case brought against her by Arron Banks, a Leave.EU campaigner who she investigated, only to find it a pyrrhic victory when the Court of Appeal ruled against her and ordered her to pay hundreds of thousands of pounds in legal costs.

In another prime example, activist Nina Cresswell reported her sexual assault to the police in 2010. They did nothing. However, her perpetrator found out about the police report and sued her for libel – another example of these laws being used as weapons to silence victims. But, because of the uptick in these defamation and libel cases being brought by alleged abusers, the Good Law Project stepped in. The organisation, which funds public interest litigation, defended Cresswell against her alleged abuser – and won. They won both on what is known as the truth defence – a statement cannot be libellous if it is true – but it also helped establish, at least in England and Wales, what is known as a public interest defence. This means that the courts should be aware of the public interest in either victims or journalists reporting on accusations, and that this should be considered when alleged abusers sue their alleged victims for defamation over sexual abuse allegations.

Judge Heather Williams, in her judgement handing the win to Cresswell, said, 'I am satisfied that the defendant has shown that her belief in relation to each of her statements that it was on a matter of public interest was a reasonable belief in all the circumstances.' This judgement was a huge step forward in terms of fixing a broken justice system that continues to fail survivors – and we must keep pushing for a strong public interest defence in defamation cases.

Right now, I am working with a woman whose alleged abuser confessed to sexual assault, in addition to the mountains of other evidence of his crimes against her, and yet the police have done nothing. I am currently trying to report this, as it shows just how hard it is to get a sexual abuse complaint taken seriously by the police. But unfortunately, every single outlet I've approached has said that while it's an important story, they will not publish it for fear of her alleged abuser suing the newspaper for defamation.

Switching jurisdictions for a moment, most Australians know the story of Brittany Higgins and her allegations against Bruce Lehrmann. That Higgins, a political staffer, alleged that Lehrmann, her colleague, raped her in Parliament House. That he faced a criminal trial. That this criminal trial was aborted because it was revealed that a juror had brought outside research into the jury room and that ultimately the Crown Prosecutors decided not to re-prosecute. Lehrmann then sued Channel 10 and former host of *The Project* Lisa Wilkinson for defamation and so the legal proceedings as to the truth of these allegations continue.

'I'm seeing the same thing all throughout my legal practice,' says Robinson, who is from Australia but currently works in London. 'More and more women are afraid to speak out because of legal threats in defamation, privacy, breach of confidence or contempt.

'What we're seeing is an incredible amount of self-censorship, where survivors will choose to stay silent – or choose not to report to police – once they understand how the law would treat them.'

To be clear, this isn't just an issue that impacts the case of Lehrmann and Higgins – nor is it an issue that only affects victim-survivors and alleged victim-survivors. It's an issue that affects everybody – people of all genders – because, at its core, it's a question of free speech. It also affects the rights of victim-survivors and their families and friends and impacts the ability of those accused to defend themselves and be heard. That is why it's important to write this story – because free speech affects us all, and it is under threat.

Robinson has co-written a book on this issue, titled *How Many More Women?*, with author and fellow human rights barrister Keina Yoshida. When we meet, I ask her to explain the impetus for putting in print the issue of the silencing of women by the law.

'So much of what we advise on never becomes public – and we wanted the public to know what's happening in the law and how much about violence against women is being censored,' she explains of her line of work. 'We advise survivors, friends and families of survivors, rape crisis centres and women's rights groups about the risks of defamation and the rise and rise of non-disclosure agreements.'

Increasingly, what we're seeing is a war of opposing forces. There is a huge gulf between the cultural progress we have made in terms of having an open public debate about gender-based violence and the largely hidden but very effective legal backlash against that cultural change. Legal mechanisms – like the threat of being sued for defamation – are imposing a chilling effect on the ability to speak openly about violence; a semblance of free speech that we finally arrived at, after centuries of silence, with the #MeToo movement in 2017.

As the journalist and social justice advocate Tracey Spicer has commented, they have some of the 'toughest defamation laws in the world'. But it's more than that. Unlike in the US, Australia's defamation laws place the onus on the person making the allegation to prove its truth. Conversely, for example, in the Johnny Depp vs Amber Heard case, the burden was on Depp to prove that the allegations were false and made with malice. In Australia, a victim is *presumed* to have defamed the alleged perpetrator unless they can prove that what they said was true or in the public interest.

'So many people come to us thinking it's safe to speak out in the post-#MeToo era and we have to keep advising them that it's not,' says Robinson. 'We have to get them to understand that the legal threats are real and that's why we need to change the system. We need a way for women to speak out in the public interest without disproportionate legal threats.'

But Robinson tells me it's not even that straightforward – the legal mechanisms being used in Australian courts and around the world to silence those engaged in the legal process haven't just sprung up in the wake of #MeToo. 'These laws have always been there, but as victims have broken the cultural silence about violence, these laws are being increasingly weaponised against those who speak out,' she tells me. 'The law is being used to silence those who dared to break that cultural silence – and it's happening everywhere.'

Because we are seeing an increase in defamation suits being filed by alleged perpetrators, however, there are some changes that need to be made to legal proceedings to protect the mental health and safety of those accused of defamation when making allegations of violence. None of this is a criticism of the use of defamation proceedings to defend one's truth – the question here is about the way the law needs to change so that it can only be used for this legitimate purpose and not to threaten or silence alleged victims who want, and have the right to, pursue credible allegations.

For example, Robinson explains, 'the criminal law system has a number of protections in place for alleged victims.' In theory at least, 'alleged victims of sexual violence are supposed to be given protection in the criminal courts to help them through what is inherently a retraumatising process – like special measures while giving evidence, and jury directions from judges reminding juries to ignore the stereotypes and tropes about sexual violence when they are considering the evidence,' Robinson says.

But in defamation proceedings, which take place in civil rather than criminal courts, alleged victims do not have these protections, despite the fact these proceedings are equally retraumatising. If anything, defamation proceedings are more retraumatising, because victims are made the defendant, rather than the complainant; they are being sued in civil proceedings and required to get up on the stand and be cross-examined on their allegations. There are no support workers, no helplines, no legal aid or funding support to defend the case – or defend their truth.

'In the civil courts, counsel and judges aren't trained in how to protect alleged victims from retraumatisation in the way they are in criminal proceedings,' Robinson says. 'We need more trauma-informed training.'

To bring this point home, Robinson notes that the reason prosecutors cited for not re-trying the criminal rape case against Lehrmann was to protect Higgins's mental health – and yet now that he is bringing defamation proceedings, those same risks to her mental health are present, only with fewer protections for her. (Higgins could be subpoenaed to give evidence, but has volunteered to do so in the defamation proceedings, where she will be cross-examined about the facts – just in the civil court, rather than a criminal court – to defend her truth.)

The other key way we could reform defamation law to ensure it is used to legitimately protect reputations and not as a weapon of silence, is something that could be easily and reasonably changed: and that relates to costs.

'It is extremely expensive to find yourself having to defend a defamation lawsuit – and many alleged victims simply cannot afford to do so. The decision not to defend their truth – even if only based on the fact that only the middle class and wealthy have access to lawyers – can be taken by the public as an admission that the alleged victim has lied,' says Robinson

'Too often women are silenced because they cannot afford to defend their free speech – there is no legal aid for defamation. And what does free speech even mean if we cannot afford to assert our right to it?'

Another reform suggested by Robinson to ensure that defamation threats are not being made purely to silence meritorious claims is to 'increase the cost risk to the person bringing the suit'; that is, to include in our law some kind of barrier for bringing a defamation claim, so that it is no longer the case that anyone wealthy enough to pay a lawyer can bring a defamation suit and retraumatise an alleged victim without sufficient evidence.

Another way to ensure the law isn't being abused is to strengthen what is known as the public interest defence. Most people are familiar with the truth defence to defamation. Under Australia's defamation laws, it is not possible to damage someone's reputation if what you are alleging about them is true. Therefore, we have a 'truth defence' – if the defendant can prove that their allegations are true, there can be no defamation, because the damage to reputation will have been caused by the person's own actions, not the allegations. Alleged victims also have some access to a defence if they can prove that their free speech is in the public interest. But Robinson believes this isn't enough.

'We need the courts to make clear that these cases will be treated as cases that are in the public interest – we can't tackle violence against women in our society if we cannot talk about it,' Robinson says. 'If we had clearer public interest defences for alleged victims, this would also act as a disincentive for anyone bringing a defamation suit.'

Lawmakers have proposed remedying some of these problems with the legal #MeToo backlash with what is called anti-SLAPP legislation – short for 'strategic lawsuit against public participation'. This is referring specifically to defamation suits brought by powerful individuals against journalists or accusers in order to threaten or silence, rather than based on a genuine belief that the allegations made are false.

'Anti-SLAPP legislation would strengthen an alleged victim's ability to claim that reporting violence is in the public interest, and would also make it easier for judges to strike out unmeritorious claims at an earlier stage, with lower costs for the alleged victim/defendant and less emotional distress,' says Robinson.

'We do need these laws, but they won't be a silver bullet,' she adds. 'But fighting for these laws should certainly be on the radar of free speech advocates in Australia. Many women experience defamation claims as a continuation of abuse long after they have left their alleged abuser,' continues Robinson. 'For example, if an alleged perpetrator brings a defamation claim, they can get access to the alleged victim's medical records and text messages. Such claims also require alleged victims to be in court, threatening their mental wellbeing and financial security because of the cost and stress of the proceedings, which can also be a form of abuse.'

To be clear, once again, Robinson is not speaking here about Lehrmann's case. She is speaking specifically about other cases in which perpetrators know the claims are true but use defamation lawsuits to avoid the consequences of their actions. This is becoming increasingly common, as high-profile defamation cases – a number of recent and widely-publicised cases involving international celebrities spring to mind – illustrate that for alleged perpetrators, this use (and potential weaponisation) of defamation lawsuits can work.

And here's the rub: the cultural moment we are in would have us believe that we are starting to take gender-based violence seriously. Like most avenues of life in the flush of social change, we're much better at talking about the progress we've made than actually turning the conversation into action. But action cannot happen without the support of the legal system behind it. Nor, says Robinson, if we don't know the extent of the problem.

'The government is always asking: what do we do to fix the problem?' she says. 'Our point is that you can't fix the problem if you don't understand the scope of it – and as these legal threats cause more and more women to self-censor, we will have less of a picture of just how ubiquitous this problem is. That's why we need stronger public interest laws and defences – it is squarely in the public interest for women to feel safe and encouraged to speak about their experiences and for us to be able to meaningfully quantify gender-based violence.'

The judge in the Lehrmann case made a sweeping order demanding that journalists not report on allegations or the surrounding issues to ensure a fair trial for Lehrmann. Now, as a court reporter, I see these orders all the time and they are valid – the right to a fair trial is paramount for all. But this order was much more extensive than the ones we court-watchers usually see and could set a dangerous precedent.

Robinson described the judgement as being unique, even for Australia. For example, the judgement said that journalists could not even describe Higgins as 'brave' or 'courageous' ahead of the trial and warned they had to be careful about having discussions concerning sexual harassment in the workplace. The effect of the judgement was that all authors and publishers – including Robinson and Yoshida – were told they had to remove all references to the Lehrmann case and Higgins's story.

'Contempt laws exist to prevent the press from reporting that someone is guilty and thereby prejudicing a jury and undermining the defendant's right to be presumed innocent,' Robinson says. 'They are not supposed to stop journalists and publishers from discussing the case *at all*.'

As Robinson and I speak about this, I recount to her my own shock at the order and, in particular, at how journalists were responding to it on Twitter. I remember seeing so many journalists warning others not to say *anything* about the case and thinking to myself: *hang on, this is a freedom of the press issue. Why aren't we talking about that?*

Robinson explains that the judgement had a muting effect: it wasn't clear to journalists and publishers what they could safely say, which limited public conversation about the case, including whether this was a legitimate restriction on free speech, the free press and the principle of open justice.

Robinson also explains to me that when she was writing her book – before the contempt judgement in the Lehrmann trial occurred – she put together a document of all the media articles and public comments being made about the case to eventually cite when she sat down to write. But by the time the book was being fact-checked, when she searched for the tweets, comments and articles that she had cited in the book, a not insubstantial number of them were gone.

'The internet had been scrubbed of important information about this case,' she says.

Robinson and Yoshida – and their publisher – refused to remove all references to Higgins's story and instead decided to redact the book: blocking out what they had intended to say until after Lehrmann faced trial to comply with the contempt judgement, while demonstrating to readers how the law operates to censor women from speaking about their experience of violence and the media and publishers from reporting on it. They plan to release an unredacted and updated version of the book when the trial concludes.

As I've said – as a trained lawyer and legal reporter myself – I believe wholly and deeply that everyone accused of a crime should have the right to defend themselves. But I also believe wholly and deeply in the alleged victims' right to be heard – and right now, the law is restricting their ability to be heard. And from what I can see in my own decade of reporting, plus from what I've heard from Robinson, is that it's only getting worse.

Robinson says we need to improve how women making allegations of gender-based violence are treated, not just in the criminal courts, but also in the civil courts. 'I've had other lawyers tell me their clients have decided not to report because of what happened to Brittany, to Amber,' Robinson says, acknowledging the barriers alleged victims face not only when they come up against the criminal justice system, but also the silencing that occurs in media law. 'I have a friend, who is comfortable with me sharing this. Immediately after seeing the news about the Lehrmann prosecution falling apart, and what Brittany went through, she said to me: "this is exactly why I never reported my rape".'

It would be easy to dismiss this story as a matter for the judicial system: *let's leave it to the judges and politicians to work out.* But as Robinson explains, its implications are far reaching and extend beyond the courts and into our everyday lives, impacting relationships with friends and family in ways we often don't consider. Just look at the Johnny Depp v Amber Heard case in the US.

Robinson represented Heard in the UK defamation proceedings that Depp brought against *The Sun* newspaper, the case which Depp lost because the judge accepted Heard's evidence was true. Depp later went on to sue Heard for defamation in America, and won before a jury in Virginia. Robinson says she has repeatedly seen the effect of the US case outcome on clients who come to her for support with rape and domestic abuse claims.

'The way Heard was attacked, ridiculed and demeaned online was appalling,' Robinson says. 'The thing I kept telling people was this: if someone in your life is a survivor of sexual or domestic violence and they see you sharing something mocking Amber Heard, they will never feel safe coming forward to you.'

I felt this myself during that trial. I tweeted that 'Johnny Depp won't see your posts turning Amber Heard's graphic rape allegations into a humiliating meme, but your friends who have survived sexual violence will'. It quickly received 11,000 likes and I have had people come up to me at parties, in tears, telling me that this tweet expressed their exact feeling – that now they will never be able to speak about their experiences to family and friends who engaged in the mocking of Heard.

And so, Robinson says, we need to think about just how extreme and far-reaching the impact of cases such as Depp v Heard is – it's not just survivors not coming forward to Robinson, for example, for legal advice, or the police, or a doctor; it's also stopping people making disclosures to their own friends and family.

All of this chimes loudly with me. Like Robinson's friend, I never considered reporting my own experiences of abuse to police, because I knew how I would be treated. That was back in 2007 and from what I'm seeing in my day-to-day work as a legal journalist and hearing from world-leading experts like Robinson, it could be even worse now than it would have been if I had reported it 16 years ago.

And here's more, if you still need convincing: in addition to the way our defamation laws are protecting alleged abusers, the ability of our criminal justice system to deal with rape complaints is worsening. In 2021, 1.5 per cent of rape complaints in Australia resulted in a conviction. In 2005, it was 12.5 per cent. In 1989, that same figure was 17 per cent. Many see our cultural conversation and believe that our legal system is getting better at delivering justice. But it's getting worse, both in the criminal and the civil courts. And that's something that should concern every one of us.

CHAPTER 36

London, 2023

Carolyn is dead. The words echo in my mind again and again and again and again and again and again until maybe I'll believe them. Until maybe they'll make sense. Carolyn is dead. Carolyn is dead. Carolyn is dead.

I am at work on Friday, 26 May, and I'm on a call so I can't answer when Carolyn's husband, John, calls me. This is not unusual; John calls me often; we have become close since my visit to Palm Beach. I assume he just wants to chat, to vent about the stress of the move to North Carolina, to tell me, as he does so often, just how much he loves his beautiful, incomparable wife.

But he isn't calling to tell me any of that.

After the missed call, I get a message from him that says only this: 'please call me when you get this she really loved you.'

Of course, the words themselves aren't in that message. But I know. Time stops. And all my edges blur. The office, my desk, my computer, begin moving. I am a spinning top inside a world with edges that are closing in on me. Carolyn is dead.

I call John back and he is in pieces. I can tell you I've never witnessed a love like theirs – a love so totally devoted; two people who found love in the darkest place – a rehab facility in Florida over a decade ago – and from that moment on promised to look after themselves so they could look after each other. Promised to love and care and listen and to support each other no matter what. For years now, their relationship has been an inspiration to me.

They'd had to come back to Palm Beach for three nights after the big move to North Carolina to sort out some of Carolyn's affairs. After that first night back in Palm Beach, she didn't wake up.

'I don't know how to live without her,' he says. 'But I have to – for the kids.' And I know he will. He would do anything for those kids, even staying alive when it would be easier not to.

As I write this, we don't know how Carolyn died. Her husband has told me that the night before, they'd made a Caesar salad – Carolyn's all-time favourite meal. They put the kids to bed and both went to bed happy.

'She was happier than I've seen her in years these last three weeks,' he tells me, echoing my own thoughts about the last few weeks of Carolyn's life.

'I kissed her goodnight, and she was happy and at peace,' he tells me. 'And then she woke up dead.'

A police investigation and an autopsy are ongoing. The medical examiner said there was no obvious medical reason for her death, but I know she was scared her whole life that Epstein, or the men he trafficked her to, would silence her somehow. I'm not saying I believe there was foul play involved – although that is something the police are investigating – but what I do believe is this: whether her death was orchestrated directly by one of Epstein's circle or not, they killed her. They put her through abuse and its aftermath – addiction, mental illness, terror – which are, in some cases, simply not survivable. She was 36 and she did everything she could to survive; she fought harder than anyone I've ever met. But some things are too terrible, too evil, to sustain a life. And I am so angry, because if there was any life on this earth that deserved to be saved – with all the wisdom she had to share, with all her caring, with all the love she had to give – it was Carolyn's.

I won't stop investigating Jeffrey Epstein and his associates until I'm satisfied that every name has been named, until every perpetrator has been held accountable. I know it's what she would have wanted me to do.

CHAPTER 37

Oxfordshire, 2023

As I write this, I have been re-admitted to Khiron House for further inpatient trauma treatment because of the impact of Carolyn's death and the stress of trying to tell these stories right. I want to offer some more solutions. I really do. But I don't have all the answers. Right now, I feel like I have no answers at all. I feel empty and bereft. I feel hopeless. I feel like any legal reforms to support childhood sexual abuse victims that I could offer right now would mean nothing, because none of them will bring my friend back.

But again, I will try my best to sum them up.

As I mentioned, the way that Carolyn, and Annie, and Jane, and Kate were cross-examined in the Maxwell trial should not be permitted by law. Questions such as those we saw in this trial – questions suggesting to victims that they are making up a story for a payday, questions suggesting to victims that they are not credible because they are actors and therefore likely to be performing a fictional role on the stand, questions suggesting victims' decision to wear boots given to them by perpetrators undermines their believability – should not be allowed.

It would be easy to outlaw these questions, particularly in cases where they relate to the *very reason* these victims were chosen for abuse. Jeffrey Epstein chose these girls because their families had no money, so to accuse them now of 'making up stories' in order to get a quick payday is obviously going to be particularly traumatic for them. Similarly, with the second example – Epstein chose Jane because she wanted to be an actor or a singer. That's how he groomed her and her mother: by promising to pay for her education at drama school and linking her up with his connections in Hollywood. So using the fact that she made good on that dream, not because of Epstein, but in spite of him, against her, to discredit her and call her a liar, is despicable. It should not be allowed in any courtroom.

The fact that hours of humiliating cross-examination were taken up by the fact that *Annie wore the boots Maxwell bought her and no reasonable person would wear a gift given by an abuser* feels almost criminal to me and should not have been allowed. Anyone who understands grooming – like myself, from my own experience – understands how absurd this is. Again, Annie was chosen because she came from a poor family and had never seen a $100 pair of boots in her life, let alone owned some. A key element of grooming is meeting a need of the child's that is not being met at home. *Of course* Annie wore the boots. She was 16 years old and couldn't afford the clothes she wanted. The boots were part of the grooming. I treasured gifts that my gym mentor gave me – not because he was sexually abusing me, but because he was giving me attention that my parents couldn't give me at that time, through no fault of their own – and, master manipulator that he is, he saw that in me the second he met me.

It would be so easy to outlaw cross-examining attorneys from bringing up a victim's sexual history, their history of drug and alcohol abuse (which, as I've said before, corroborates their abuse testimony more than it discredits it, if you look at the statistics).

Second, again as I mentioned earlier – statutes of limitations. Statutes of limitations can be waived in exceptional cases, such as this one. But we know from the science, we know from Dr Rocchio, that child abuse victims are not able to come forward within five years. It took me 14 years to acknowledge that I had been abused by my gym mentor beginning at nine years old; by a person who I loved and trusted and who I believed would make my dreams come true.

Statutes of limitations should never apply to grooming or sexual abuse offences. It goes against all the trauma science we now know, and it denies victims justice again and again and again.

Third, we need expert witnesses of grooming in every single child sexual abuse trial. We need Dr Rocchio, but we also need more. We need expert psychiatrists who can explain to juries why memories of childhood abuse are difficult to narrativise, to put in an order. We need a commitment to actually understanding how grooming and the consequent abuse works – both inside and outside the courtroom.

I'm not a practising criminal lawyer, I'm merely a court correspondent and a survivor of grooming and child sexual abuse. I won't pretend to be able to offer any expertise other than what I've learned from the Epstein victims, what I know from my own life and what I know from my limited legal training. So I don't have an answer. I just have anger, and sadness, and a raging sense of injustice that will keep me working on this story until every single grown man who sexually abused my friends has been named and held to account.

There is so much more that I know, that I wish I could print in this book, about Carolyn, about every Epstein victim, about Epstein himself, about how the victims were failed by law enforcement and even their own lawyers. About how sometimes, the call is coming from inside the house. About the lasting harm that causes.

I cannot tell you those things now, but I can promise you that I tried. I did everything I could. I hope that one day the courts and lawyers and newspapers and publishers will be brave enough to print what I know.

Until that happens, all I can do is leave you with this: Goodnight, Carolyn. I will miss you forever.